EXPLOSION GREEN

PRAISE FOR DAVID GOTTFRIED AND *EXPLOSION GREEN*

"Our future depends on integrating sustainability into all that we do. David Gottfried's pioneering work is proof that we can do it, and *Explosion Green* tells us how to do it, and why it's the best way out of our economic doldrums and back into the future business."

— PRESIDENT BILL CLINTON

"David Gottfried is the father of the green movement. This book is a must read for any serious student of how to design new systems and green building."

— ART GENSLER

"David Gottfried set a world of improvement in motion. The global built environment is now incorporating sustainability as standard practice and as a result is making better buildings that are profitable for the bottom line, the planet and its people."

— GERALD D. HINES
Founder and Chairman, Hines

"No organization has had a bigger impact on the environment than [the USGBC]. In sharing himself and the fabric of a life well directed, we can find ourselves and know that little or nothing exceeds our grasp if we love the world as well as David has."

— PAUL HAWKEN
Author, *Ecology of Commerce*

"David Gottfried not only accelerates the cause with a contagious passion, he also provides a clear path towards delivering the transformational change the world needs."

— DOUGLAS FRYE
Global President and CEO, Colliers International

"This is a story about an idea. An idea that became an organization. An organization that anchored a movement. A movement that is changing the world. David and his relentless pursuit of the possible helped invent the spark and carry the torch for this revolutionary idea that led us to start the USGBC and later the WorldGBC."

—RICK FEDRIZZI
President, CEO and Founding Chair, U.S. Green Building Council

"This book is inspiring and also a great story of how one man can change the world. David Gottfried and I worked closely to build the China Green Building Council."

—QIU BAOXING 仇保兴
Executive Vice Minister, Ministry of Housing and Urban-Rural Development, People's Republic of China

"A remarkable story of a remarkable transformation. David Gottfried's efforts transformed the building industry and himself. This beautiful memoir illuminates the challenges of change."

—AMORY LOVINS
Cofounder and Chief Scientist, Rocky Mountain Institute: Author, *Reinventing Fire*

"David's inability to accept the imperfect nature of systems and institutionalized practices have required him to move forward without a map. He has shown us that we each have the potential to reshape our personal behaviors and recalibrate the value systems for entire global markets."

—CHE WALL
Cofounder, Green Building Council of Australia

"I've known David for over a decade and been hugely inspired by his work in founding and growing the global Green Building Council movement. This book can change your life and help inspire you to not only dream big, but put it into action."

—JIM ALLEN
President & CEO, Sloan

"David Gottfried's work has been instrumental in connecting the marketplace to game-changing products. Read about it and get in the game."

—RAO MULPURI, PhD
CEO, View, Inc.

"Transformation of the most important sector in the nation's energy economy resulted from David Gottfried's pioneering work. Students and professionals will be inspired by this book as it describes the pathway that led to such monumental results."

—GIL MASTERS
Professor Emeritus of Civil and Environmental Engineering, Stanford University

"*Explosion Green* shows us how our passions can accelerate sustainable business and change the world. I've been privileged to participate in David Gottfried's story describing the world's most incredible transformation of its largest industry."

—KEVIN HYDES
CEO and Founder, Integral Group, Former Chair, U.S. and World Green Building Councils, Founder, Canada Green Building Council

"David inspires us to believe we have the ability to envision a future that we might create. He has lived it firsthand and generously shares his learning with us."

— MARIA ATKINSON AM
Cofounder, Green Building Council of Australia

"A refreshing, delightful and candid memoir of how a young, bright 'Type A' developer created a revolution in how buildings are designed and built, and finds his higher self in the process."

— SIM VAN DER RYN
Professor Emeritus of Architecture, UC Berkeley, Author, *Design for an Empathic World, Ecological Design* and *Sustainable Communities*

"*Explosion Green* will not only inspire you, but change your life. This beautifully written book portrays the creation of the global green building movement, while catalyzing each of us to proactively foment the change we hope for the world."

— L. HUNTER LOVINS
President and founder, Natural Capitalism Solutions
Coauthor, *Natural Capitalism*

"There are serial entrepreneurs, who have founded multiple, successful companies, and serial change agents, who have guided change in multiple institutions, but David Gottfried is the exceptionally rare individual who is a serial founder of change movements. Embedded in the stories he tells in *Explosion Green* is David's secret formula for success."

— DAN SLONE
Partner, McGuireWoods, USGBC & WorldGBC General Counsel

Also By David Gottfried

Greed to Green
Greening My Life

Offerings By David Gottfried

Regenerative Ventures: www.regenv.com
Regenerative Network (Green product consortium): www.regen-net.com
Green Building Online Video Offerings: www.regenbuild.com
Regen360 (Green Life Academy): www.regen360.net

Meet David online and receive a free digital copy of
Greening My Life at www.dgottfried.com.

EXPLOSION
GREEN

ONE MAN'S JOURNEY TO GREEN
THE WORLD'S LARGEST INDUSTRY

DAVID GOTTFRIED

New York

Published in New York, New York, by Morgan James Publishing. Morgan James and The Entrepreneurial Publisher are trademarks of Morgan James, LLC. www.MorganJamesPublishing.com.

The Morgan James Speakers Group can bring authors to your live event.
For more information or to book an event visit The Morgan James Speakers Group at www.TheMorganJamesSpeakersGroup.com.

BitLit
FOR ALL THE BOOKS YOU OWN

FREE eBook edition for your existing eReader with purchase

PRINT NAME ABOVE

For more information, instructions, restrictions, and to register your copy, go to **www.bitlit.ca/readers/register** or use your QR Reader to scan the barcode:

ISBN 9781630470227 (paperback)
ISBN 9781630470241 (hardcover)
ISBN 9781630470234 (eBook)
Library of Congress Control Number: 2013916760

COVER & INTERIOR DESIGN:
Jean Orlebeke, www.obekdesign.com

In an effort to support local communities, raise awareness and funds, Morgan James Publishing donates a percentage of all book sales for the life of each book to Habitat for Humanity Peninsula and Greater Williamsburg.

Get involved today, visit
www. MorganJamesBuilds.com

Habitat
for Humanity®
Peninsula and
Greater Williamsburg
Building Partner

To my global green building colleagues
who have kindled the flame of green building into
a massive renewable force of transformation.
May we each learn from each other
and push up the mountain to new heights,
striving towards regeneration.

CONTENTS

FOREWORD: BLESSED UNREST   xiii

INTRODUCTION   xv

PART ONE: BEGINNINGS

1   China Green   2

2   Makeover   6

3   Learning the Game   11

4   First Sighting of Green Building   21

5   Green Doesn't Pay the Bills   32

PART TWO: GREEN BUILDING

6   Jobless in San Francisco   50

7   Cold Calling   61

8   The Start of a Movement   70

9   Building the USGBC   84

10   What Now?   101

11   USGBC CPR   123

12   LEED Rolls Out   127

13   Growing Up   134

14 Pushing Limits   139

15 GBC Goes Global   153

16 The First Greenbuild   167

17 The Greenest Little Home in America   179

18 Regenerative Ventures   212

19 Shades of Green   223

PART THREE: REFLECTIONS

20 The GBC Movement at Twenty   230

21 What's Next?   253

EPILOGUE   272

AFTERWORD: THE ART OF BEING
A SERIAL FOUNDER   279

THE EARTH COMMANDMENTS   282

BOOK SPONSORS   283

ACKNOWLEDGMENTS   285

ABOUT THE AUTHOR   287

A NOTE TO YOU, THE READER

Some of the material in Part One and Part Two of this book has been adapted from David Gottfried's earlier two books, *Greed to Green* and *Greening My Life*. Part Three is brand new. Many of the scenes in the book are snapshots or syntheses of my experiences and interactions with Green Building Council participants, clients, friends, and family members. As a memoir, the scenes and stories have been recreated from memory and impression. In some cases, I dramatized the facts to make a point, but have done my best to convey the essential elements. I have also taken the liberty of changing some details, names, and locations to protect the privacy of others.

FOREWORD: BLESSED UNREST

By Paul Hawken
Author: *Ecology of Commerce, Blessed Unrest,*
Coauthor: *Natural Capitalism*

Martha Graham, the great dancer and choreographer, once described the creative process as "blessed unrest." The same could be said of David Gottfried. Despite his good fortune in the conventional world of real estate development, he was blessed with unrest, his unceasing curiosity and concern. Anyone who knows or has met David can feel the energy. It is a toe-tapping, eye-flashing kinetic that takes on any challenge. What he took on was the building and construction industry and its relationship to living systems. He took on the biggest industry in the world. Like I said, blessed unrest.

Sustainability is about the relationship between the two most complex systems on earth—human and living. The interrelationship between these two systems marks every person's existence and underlines the rise and fall of every civilization. While the word *sustainability* is relatively new, every culture has confronted this relationship for better or ill. Historically, no civilization has reversed its tracks with respect to the environment but rather has declined and disappeared because it forfeited its own habitat. For the first time in history, a civilization—and its people, companies, and governments—are trying to arrest this slide and understand how to live on earth. This is a watershed in human existence.

To say this book is about the power of one person to change the world, though true, would be a cliché. This book is not about David, sustainability, or even green buildings. It is about the mystery of change. Although it is axiomatic that everything changes, it is a mystery as to *how* things change. What we have here is a first-person and animated account of how things did change. When you read it, you will draw your own conclusions. Yes, his is a story of pluck and determination, to be sure. And it is one of timing, hard work, and manufactured luck. But above all, it is a story of conviction. Not the conviction that makes others wrong, but more an affirmation: of what is right and what is possible. I have heard David speak several times, and without doubt what he shares above all is enthusiasm, a word that comes from the Greek roots "en theos," meaning within God. I have said that if this movement toward a green and just world is to succeed, it will be because we will build a more interesting sandbox for everyone to play in. That is what David did: he founded and helped build the most important green trade organization in the world. There is virtually no second place. Thousands of people and companies are playing inside it, creating the best standards in the world. Nothing compares with the growth, magnitude, and import of the U.S. Green Building Council. No one has done the metrics, but I believe it is safe to say that no organization has had a bigger impact on the environment than this one in terms of energy and materials saved, toxins eliminated, greenhouse gases avoided, and human health enhanced. And that is just the beginning.

It could be said that every person has the responsibility to live in his or her own time. This is our time: stunning in its promise, terrifying in its direction. David is living now. In this book he shares his passage into a world of care and change. He is brilliant, yes. But he is also everyman. He has weaknesses and longings and aversions, just as we all do. In seeing him sharing himself within the fabric of a life well directed, we can find ourselves and know that little exceeds our grasp if we love the Earth as well as David has.

INTRODUCTION

By S. Richard Fedrizzi
President, CEO and Founding Chair, U.S. Green Building Council
Chairman, World Green Building Council

This is a story about an idea. An idea that became an organization. An organization that anchored a movement. A movement that is changing the world.

When I first met David Gottfried in 1993, a lot was happening:

- Bill Clinton was elected president and the European Economic Community and NAFTA were born.
- It was the year that Islamists made their first attacks on the World Trade Center and that Branch Davidian made its last stand in Waco, Texas.
- Intel shipped its first P5 Pentium chip, and the World Wide Web made its debut at CERN. *Wired* magazine published its first issue and began chronicling another movement that would also change the world.

When David first found me and we started talking about how we could build better buildings, the idea that we would change the world was one of those things you scribble on a napkin at 3 a.m. after hours of brainstorming lubricated by more than a little wine. David was determined to make this idea a reality, no matter the cost, whether in money or time.

We focused on figuring out a business model for this crazy idea, like the thousands of other start-ups that were popping up everywhere during the dot-com nineties. Like any start-up, we needed an infusion of capital to realize our idea. But the infusion we needed most wasn't *financial* capital. It was *human* capital. We needed people to join us, and to start working *with* us to make the U.S. Green Building Council a reality.

David mostly dragged in what you might call our first round of investors. But they weren't investing money—they were investing themselves. They were early adopters: the architects, the builders, and the businesses who, when we asked them, "Will you become a member of USGBC," boldly answered, "YES!"

As our early *investors* joined us, we refined our product, drawing on the expertise, the experience, and the foresight of the visionary minds we had gathered into our nascent organization. And early on, the cumulative input from all these experts and stakeholders helped us to create LEED.

Today, LEED is the most widely used green building rating system on the planet. LEED is how the green building movement shares best practices and puts its stamp of approval on great buildings, a badge they wear like a badge of honor—everything from California Academy of Sciences to the Empire State Building to the Marlins Park to The Merchandise Mart—nearly two hundred thousand projects are either certified LEED or are in the pipeline to become so.

The success of LEED has been staggering. And it's a perfect metric for the success of USGBC—because when people adopt our standards and seek our certification, they're making a statement: not just that their building meets certain leadership criteria of design, and of energy and water conservation, but that they are part of a worldwide movement.

LEED's worldwide success is such that *The New York Times* recently noted that about 40 percent of the square footage currently in the LEED certification process is *outside the United States.*

When David began writing about the green revolution, he captured the zeitgeist on how an industry was changing; how the practice of architecture, building science, even real estate needed to shift, to open up to the possibility that our built environment could do everything it historically did—give us shelter, habitat, sanctuary from the elements—but it could do so in ways that saved energy, saved water, and reduced resource use and carbon emissions. He saw green as a practical, responsible approach to the built environment. And this approach would be good for everyone.

As simple an idea as that is, it was, at the time, revolutionary. After all it was the go-go nineties, when flagrant excess was a virtue and greed was the dominant operating system. The idea that you might consider using only what you needed, not all that you could, didn't compute.

But as we developed LEED, as we began to improve building controls and water fixtures, as we began to rethink building envelopes and material science, we turned on a faucet of innovation that has become one of the massively positive unintended consequence of our work. People began making money as they worked to save money. They profited from the differentiation that LEED made in their marketing.

It turned out that not only were we in the green building business, we were also in the green economy business.

And one other thing happened. We also began to understand we were in the people business, because every story about green buildings is a story about people. Despite our success ... and despite our *name* ... the real purpose of the green building movement isn't to design, build, and operate green buildings; it's to improve lives. How we design and build buildings to keep people healthy, give them a productive, pleasant environment in which to work and live, is actually an outcome of our efficient use of our natural and commercial resources.

This is what's at the heart of the movement that we started ... this crazy idea that we could change the world.

And it's happening.

I don't think it's happening because so many people are inspired by great engineering—even though they are—or by beautiful architecture—even though they are—or by amazing new energy efficiency technologies—even though they're inspired by that, too.

I think it's happening because so many people are inspired by the simple, hopeful, idea of a better world … a world that we can all build together.

A world that's built better—and is better for us, better for our kids, and better for *their* kids, too.

David and his relentless pursuit of the possible helped invent the spark and carry the torch for this revolutionary idea that led us to start the USGBC and later the World Green Building Council. His unabashed enthusiasm for this work helped USGBC become the anchor for the green building movement that's millions of people strong, on every continent across the globe. And in so many ways both profound and specific, it's because of him that twenty years later we *are* changing the world, maybe more than any other organizations on the Earth.

PART ONE: BEGINNINGS

THE FULL EQUATION ™

$$R= P- I- W$$

© David Gottfried

R: Resultant of what we're making
P: The intended Product
I: Inputs (materials, resources, capital, time, spirit)
W: Waste (pollution, landfills, social, lost creativity…)

Design Goal: Maximize R by reducing Is and Ws

1
CHINA GREEN

My alarm jolted me awake out of my jet-lag coma. I'd been dreaming of being lost at sea in a life raft, searching for land. The raft spun round and round. I was making a fishing line from the unraveling canvas and a bucket to capture rainwater. The clock was flashing 7:00, which looked more like 17:00 in my Benadryl fog. I think I'd finally fallen asleep at 3 a.m.—at least in Beijing, but more like 4 p.m. my time, the previous day in Berkeley.

I hurried to dress. The mirror shot back an image that seemed to have more gray hair, further receding of the hairline, and bags under my glassy eyes. Shenzhen was my third stop on the two-week China trip. I'd already hit Hong Kong and Beijing with Sara and then Shanghai and now Shenzhen with Nellie. Sara and I had been married ten years, and she was now a *New York Times* bestselling author of *The Hormone Cure*, with two more books on the way. Our two young kids were at our Berkeley Hills home with Sara's folks.

I grabbed my RegenChina company brochures and my business cards and stuffed them into my briefcase in the elevator. I glanced at a card, which said my name in English and Chinese and listed me as CEO and Transformation Catalyst of Regenerative Ventures. On the back it said founder: US and World Green Building Councils.

Nellie was in the dining room, wearing her "China" white pantsuit with a white silk button-down top. Her hair was wet, likely from her morning swim. She smiled, looked at her watch and said, "You ready to go?"

After I'd bolted a bowl of cereal, some watermelon, and a strong coffee with cream, we went out and hailed a cab. The start-and-stop movement and quick merging in and out of adjacent lanes all had a flow to it, even though at every moment it seemed as if we would crash into any number of other cars — all driving similarly. I shook my head, vowing never to get behind the wheel in China. What seemed like a lifetime later, we drove into a curving driveway and stopped in front of a meandering new headquarters office building. It was only a few stories high, but its mostly clean glass flowing structure of modern design reminded me of Washington Dulles International Airport's 1958 design by Eero Saarinen. It looked to be about a million square feet, circulating around a central pond and water feature.

The flowing granite steps directed us to the security desk. Both front metal doors opened and there was Alex, an energetic young Chinese architect who shook my hand so enthusiastically that his glasses almost fell off his face. He had bright sparkling eyes above a large smile. "It's an honor to meet you," he said. "My name is Alex. Welcome to our LEED Platinum building. We scored the highest points in all of China." He handed me his business card and a brochure on the building written in Chinese. The card said his title was Chief Architect. I looked quickly at the brochure's foreign text and photos, feeling a chill go through my body when I saw our USGBC logo and read the designation of "Platinum."

Nellie and I were meeting with Yu Liang, the president of China Vanke, the largest real estate enterprise in China and the largest residential real estate developer in the world. When Yu Liang entered the luxuriously appointed conference room overlooking a large fountain of gray water, he athletically extended his hand, saying "good to meet you," in almost perfect English. He was dressed casually, saying that he was leaving on holiday, but had apparently come into the office to meet me. I took a quick look over and decided he ran marathons, or was a triathlete.

I handed Yu a copy of my RegenChina brochure, presenting seven funding opportunities. I was representing some of my Regenerative Network members in their exploration to set up shop in China, beginning with a good joint venture partner. My formula for a partner included a mix of real estate and venture capital operations, as well as a great connection to the government. I learned that Yu had an economics and finance background, receiving his masters at Peking University, one of the best in China.

Vanke's founder and chairman, Wang Shi, was legendary in China and was now expanding his reach all over the world. I later learned he was one of China's foremost mountaineers and had also attended Harvard. It was clear that the firm had learned our green principles well. The building we sat in was powered by solar energy and heated and cooled by radiant energy systems, with extensive daylight penetration throughout the work spaces, uber-efficient LED lights, and even a gray-water capture and reuse system. The building also was rated Three Stars, the highest level of the China Green Building Council's rating system (inspired by LEED, BREEAM, and Green Star rating systems). I smiled when Alex informed me of this additional honor. Looking out the window at the building's fountain, spraying captured sink water into the low-water xeriscaping plants, I chuckled to myself at the memory of the years it took for me, Rick Fedrizzi, and my client, John Mandyck (with United Technologies Corporation), to plant the seed and nurture the China GBC with our good friend Qiu Baoxing, the Executive Vice Minister of the government's Ministry of Housing and Urban-Rural Development. I think it was more than a decade now since we'd all first met in Hartford, Connecticut, where he toured UTC's Research Center. It had been eight years since we autographed our books for each other in his Beijing office that was jammed tight with research papers and book stacks reaching to the ceiling at crazy angles.

"Green materials are very important," he'd said to me during that first meeting in his office, "but they must be made in China. We can use our own waste as feedstock and fuel the manufacturing with wind and solar power." After a dozen meetings with him since that first UTC visit, I'd come to think of Qiu Baoxing as the sustainability Gandhi of China and maybe even the world. Given that half of the world's building construction is in China, I believe that Minister Qiu is better placed to direct our future ecological footprint than perhaps any other person on the Earth. I hope that he has not only read, but also absorbed the trillion written words in the towering piles of knowledge in his Beijing office. Our future may depend on it.

2
MAKEOVER

I was twenty-two years old and fresh out of Stanford when my cousin Diane invited me to work for her and offered to teach me the real estate development business and take me under their wings. I said yes instantly. She and her husband, Jim, were powerful figures in the real estate world, and their business was booming. I arrived in Washington, D.C., in September of 1982.

Jim and Diane shared a vast office suite at 18th and L Streets downtown, with corner offices on opposite ends. Jim's office had a luxuriously thick tan carpet and a huge mahogany desk that made him look powerful. Diane's had bleached white oak floors, lots of light, and pleasant touches such as an antique copper umbrella stand and a glass vase with tiger lilies that matched the hues of the Borofsky portrait hanging above them.

After my first few weeks in Washington, Diane called me into her office. "Gottfried, we have to do something about your wardrobe. It's a little, uh, Reaganite."

I looked down at my clothes, an off-the-rack navy blue suit, starched white shirt, and red tie. What was wrong with my wardrobe? "It's what everyone in D.C. is wearing," the salesman at May Company in Los Angeles had assured me. But looking at Diane, dressed in a chic designer black pantsuit, framed by her

Italian glass desk and a backdrop of modern office buildings across the street, I had to admit it did feel a little stiff and cheap. Three days later, we were off to New York to go shopping.

At LaGuardia as we waited for our ride, the autumn air was crisp, hinting at winter. I pulled my worn red Stanford sweatshirt from my daypack and put it on.

Diane looked slim and elegant in a dark tailored wool skirt, an intricately woven gray sweater, and a silk scarf. The Bottega Veneta purse was new, purchased in Paris on her fortieth birthday. She glanced at her gold Cartier watch and then reapplied her lipstick, though her lips looked fine to me. Jim looked dapper: black cashmere sweater, gray slacks, and tasseled burgundy shoes. A white handkerchief peeked from the pocket of his blue blazer. His black metal-framed glasses were by Emanuel Ungaro.

Taxis honked, and you could see the drivers' faces through the windows—one hand on the wheel. Through this messy shuffle of yellows and blacks, Diane and Jim's ivory limo slid smoothly to the curb.

"Good morning, Mr. Katz. The Carlyle?" I had brought a sport coat specifically for The Carlyle, since Jim had told me they wouldn't serve you breakfast without one.

"Take us to Barneys first, George," Jim told the driver.

I'd heard of Barneys. Expensive. I had no savings, and my $2,500 paycheck was gone by the end of the month. How could I afford to shop at Barneys?

My worries ballooned when the driver pulled up in front of the impressive seven-story building. Everything about the store seemed designed to intimidate me: its hulking size, the window displays of leather purses for men slung over the shoulders of haughty-looking mannequins. Even the thin-faced door attendant, who stood staring blankly over our heads, made me feel inadequate.

On the way in, I caught sight of the price tag on a black silk bathrobe: $1,550.

Once we'd entered, as I stood staring about me, a salesman appeared. He was groomed to the point of grotesqueness, his head and face shaved to the bone, save for an arrow-shaped patch below his bottom lip; he wore a black suit, black shirt, and a knife blade of a tie. Is that what he would make me look like?

"Your job is to deliver this California boy into vogue," Diane told him. "Let's start with suits." We went upstairs, with me trailing behind. I felt overwhelmed. The men's clothing, arrayed in Italian designer galleries, featured styles for all occasions. I imagined I'd need an Italian-English dictionary just to read the fabric care tags.

"How about Armani, or Hugo Boss?" the salesman asked. He seemed to be affecting an Italian accent, which, mixed with what sounded like Midwestern inflection, sounded strange, like the speech of an actor who couldn't quite get the accent down.

"No, that's not the right look for him," Diane said. The salesman shut his mouth, cowed, no doubt, by her Chanel outfit and Bulgari gold necklace. She was so different from my mom, who still shopped at Loehmann's and sometimes wore Israeli beaded necklaces bought at the Temple's gift show. Yet they were first cousins, ten years apart in age, with the same roots in a small town in eastern Poland. "I used to change her diapers," my mother liked to say.

"What do you think about Versace," the salesman asked. Diane nodded affirmatively. Nobody asked me anything. I stood by a cascade of purple-hued shirts, feeling forgotten. The last time I'd felt like this was on a shopping expedition with my mother — buying my Bar Mitzvah suit at Rudnick's in Beverly Hills.

The suits at the next boutique were strangely angular and V-shaped, with stiff shoulder pads. "Don't you think the shoulders are kinda puffy?" I asked, crushing the wedge of fabric between my fingers. Falsies for men? Football pads?

"You'll get used to them," Diane said. Jim was thumbing through stacks of shirts. As they flipped through assorted international silks in somber hues of black and gray, I retreated toward a rack of pants. Could I get out of this? No. I couldn't disappoint them. I wanted what they had.

"How about this?" Diane held up a dark blue- and gray-patterned suit.

"That's gorgeous," the salesman said as he helped me try on the jacket. "It complements his dark coloring."

"That looks great. Try on the pants." Jim slapped me on the shoulder.

"Here, try this one, too." Diane lifted a medium-gray double-breasted suit with a thin, blue pinstripe off the rack. It only had one button. At least I wouldn't have to remember which one to button.

I went to the dressing room and put the blue suit on. The smooth, lightweight wool felt very expensive. I looked at myself in the mirror. Black curly hair covered my ears above an open baby face. I stood straight, feeling taller than my height. I caught my own eyes as you might a stranger's, and admired myself. The college kid had vanished. I imagined myself shouting orders to my own limo driver: "Take me to the Ritz."

"Gottfried, I can't believe it's you," Jim cried when I emerged from the dressing room. "You look like a different man." He punched me in the chest.

"We'll take it," Diane said. "Jim, where should we have lunch? Do you think Turveau can take us to The Plaza?"

I'd turned the coat inside out looking for a price tag, with no luck. I knew it wasn't proper to ask, but I worried it might cost as much as the used yellow VW Rabbit I'd just bought on credit, my first loan.

"We'll take both suits," Diane said. The salesman put the suits on the counter and piled shirts and ties on them—two for each new suit, Hugo Boss, Zegna, Missoni. I had never seen patterns and colors like these on clothing, so modern and bold, like Jim and Diane's painting collection.

"Now, let's get rid of those Republican shoes," Diane said. I stared at my Florsheims, wanting to hide my feet somehow.

We trooped to the shoe department. "Try this." Diane handed me a beautifully sculpted but flimsy black slip-on. It was a Ferragamo. "These are beautiful," the salesman said as he brought me a size twelve. I slipped them on with ease. They were so light and soft—more like gloves than shoes. Though they were hard to walk in, I managed a slow shuffle and looked up at Diane for a reprieve. "They look great," Diane said. I doubted they'd give any support on a construction job site, or that I'd be able to walk a mile.

A wave of heat spread across my face as I watched the total bill rise, item by item, at the cash register. The tally finished at $3,275. With each increase, it felt as if someone was incrementally shutting down my oxygen supply. I felt dizzy.

Jim glanced at my face. "Gottfried, don't worry, we're paying for the suits. You can buy the other things." He presented his Platinum card to the salesman. I took a deep breath. I couldn't afford even the extras. I paused as if I'd forgotten my wallet. But then I glanced at their faces, and suddenly I didn't care. I handed over my credit card. It would take me months to pay off, but I was financing a new life.

3
LEARNING THE GAME

I'd scored my own office just across the hall from Diane. "What title should we give you?" she had asked me my first day as we sat at the dark polished round wood table in our small conference room.

"One that gives me some authority," I answered, leaning back in my chair, hands interlaced behind my neck. Three months before, I'd been playing Ultimate Frisbee at Stanford, and now here I was in a tailored suit with my own office, choosing a title. I was twenty-two and full of beans.

"How about Assistant to the President?" Diane said.

"Great!" The title linked me to Diane, who had become a mover and shaker in D.C.

That day on my lunch hour, I went out and bought a leather briefcase. It was from Britches, a Georgetown men's clothier. The leather wasn't as fancy as Diane's jet-black eel-skin, but it was on sale, and I could always replace it in a few months' time.

Life in D.C. was starting out just as my upbringing had led me to expect it would. My father was a successful businessman, and I grew up accustomed to the associated privileges: tennis lessons and golf at Brentwood Country Club, a private plane flown by my dad, four years at Stanford, the freedom to choose what I wanted to do with my life. This background provided me with a pedigree, an intimate knowledge of the pastimes and perks of the successful. The circles my father moved in were a web of money, connections, and knowledge I could rely on when the time came. His accomplishments groomed me for my own.

After I'd been with working for Diane for a year, I became a project manager. We began to buy buildings and land that we could improve through renovation and development. Mostly we focused on urban infill: commercial office projects and rental apartments. Our real estate projects were well located, designed to meet market needs with an architectural statement, and financially well structured. However, Diane and Jim's real talent lay in cultivating relationships within the power circles of Washington and New York. Through various connections, they'd get invited to high-society parties and benefits where they met the wealthiest and most important members of the establishment. Soon enough they'd be striking deals, some worth millions, well before the properties hit the market. "It's all about contacts," my father had said when I was interviewing for Stanford. "Your grades and extracurriculars are good, but it's well-placed letters of reference that'll get you in."

Diane and Jim's friends became business partners and vice versa. There were no boundaries, and the business never stopped, even on vacations. During one Saturday brunch at their house I witnessed Diane holding her own over scrambled eggs in a discussion of foreign policy with our ambassador to the United Nations, Jean Kirkpatrick. Diane read *The Wall Street Journal, The Washington Post*, and *The New York Times* every morning, and she subscribed to at least five financial and news magazines and *The New Yorker*.

On one project, I managed the leasing and then sale of one of Diane's early buildings in Arlington, Virginia. After the settlement, they handed me a $10,000 bonus check—a huge percent of my starting salary! "Don't spend it all in one place," Diane said with a big smile. "You did a great job." They were incredibly generous to me, treating me like a member of their inner family.

After work that day I went and bought a new suit at Hugo Boss. When I got home, I called my folks with the good news, then pulled out a beer and toasted myself. I only wished I had a girlfriend to celebrate with.

As the deals closed, my net worth continued to increase. I was on my way, but with each step the triumphs needed to be bigger. I was following my father's plan, at least the one I had internalized, advancing fast, and yet the monetary buildup wasn't enough. So I channeled my energy into making more, and at a faster pace. "More is more" became my mantra.

I found out, though, that I still had an awful lot to learn.

One evening in October of that first year, Diane and I were kicking back on her couch at home. I was still living with them in their Georgetown house, sleeping in the top-floor guest room. We'd just finished dinner, pasta and a salad prepared by their maid, which we'd followed up with Ben and Jerry's ice cream, three different flavors: Cherry Garcia, Chunky Monkey, and New York Super Fudge Chunk. Diane was flipping through magazines — US News, Time, Forbes — as we watched the news, a recap of the recent Tylenol poisoning, in which seven people from the Chicago area died after taking Tylenol capsules laced with cyanide.

Jim sat next to her, looking at various construction magazines. Diane, as usual, looked elegant, even in jeans and a sweatshirt. On the wall in back of her was a large Helen Frankenthaler painting featuring masses of flowing orange and turquoise paint. I was struck by the bold interconnected flowing shapes and intricate color palette that sparked a thirst for modern art in me.

Diane looked up from her magazine and studied me for a minute. Then she said, "David, I don't like what I've been hearing about you around the office." Jim muted the television, but I kept staring at the anchorman's face. Had I heard her correctly? I'd thought everything was going well. "What do you mean?" I asked. I was panting a little.

"You've been using the computer in accounting without asking permission. And you don't address Keith Silver as 'Mister.' He's our client, and much older than you. You should show respect."

I shrank into the couch cushions. But she wasn't finished. "You question everything I tell you." She said that when I'd run some numbers on a real estate deal, I argued when she tried to tell me I'd made a mistake. "You have to learn to pay your dues. And to understand that I sign your paycheck. I am your cousin, and will always love you, but keep it up and I'll send you back to California." Her glasses reflected an image from the TV, a spaceship careening through a field of stars, out of control. It was a preview for Spielberg's new movie, *E.T.*

I stared at the ornate white ceiling trim, focusing on a particular spot but not seeing it. Who was she to scold me? Was I a child? I got up abruptly and went outside, walking past the covered pool, white lounge chairs, and a patio umbrella covered with leaves. My hands were cold in my pockets, but my face was hot. I could hear traffic on Wisconsin Avenue. The yard was deep in leaves fading from rich red and yellow to dry and brittle brown. For the first time that fall I could see my breath.

I relaxed a notch. I was Diane's young second cousin, just a kid really, and I'd been running around her company as if I were one of the owners. No one had taught me how to be a good employee—to patiently work my way up the ladder. The family-dinner "board meetings" with my dad and brothers and my Stanford case studies had taught me to understand business only from the perspective of the boss. I flinched at the image that appeared in my mind: me arriving home in disgrace, my dad waiting at the airport gate, disappointment etching his face below his Reno Air Races cap and glasses. I went back in the house. "I'm sorry," I said. "I'll do better."

The next morning, I rose at six and was the first one at the office. It was the first time I had to use my key and enter the alarm code. I later went upstairs and apologized to Mary, the person responsible for the computer, and gave her flowers. She thanked me, and soon became a friend and office ally. "Don't worry about me for dinner," I said to Diane later that day, as she and Jim headed home. "I'm going to work late." Jim nodded. Diane smiled.

I was a new man—and more important, a new employee. I tried to make myself indispensable by typing up the notes I took at the weekly management meetings that I attended with Diane, and by meticulously tracking follow-up tasks for us both. I collected and read real estate journals and market reports as if my life depended on it, and wrote up weekly status reports on my work, prioritizing the pending items. In short, I worked toward new goals: humility, conscientiousness, and adding value at each opportunity.

No sooner had I won Diane's confidence back, though, than I was faced with a new problem: trying to keep people from guessing how lost I often was. My cousins' trust frequently catapulted me into situations where I had to play catch-up—and fast. I did a lot of sweating in those days, put in a lot of late nights cramming for meetings with people who had twice my years and ten times my experience. When I found myself out of my depth, I redoubled my efforts.

Once, early on, Diane and Jim (who were off in Europe) asked me to negotiate a lease with a prospective architect tenant for a building we'd recently purchased in Georgetown, on Wisconsin Avenue. When I arrived at the meeting, I encountered ten men, most of whom had gray hair and had spent several decades working as architects and real estate brokers. It was a rainy day and dark in the conference room, which was made even gloomier by dark wood paneling. I tried to look calm despite the pangs of panic in my stomach. It was my first lease negotiation. I was twenty-four — the same age as many of these men's children, I imagined. I hoped my new suspenders and matching bow tie made me look older.

"Who represents the building owner?" asked the man from the architecture firm, Perkins + Will.

Our leasing broker, Steve Goldstein from Studley, pointed at me. I shifted in my seat. "David Gottfried," he said. I looked up as I clenched my hands into fists.

"Do you have the authority to negotiate on behalf of the building owners?" the architect asked with surprise. I realized he'd assumed I was a junior assistant to one of the other men. He gathered his papers as if he was going to leave. Everyone looked around uneasily.

For a moment I froze, feeling a dumb remark waiting to escape my mouth. I looked from face to face, my mind blank except for a humming sound. I was glad I'd worn an undershirt, because I could feel the sweat running down my back. And then, I found my voice. "Do you think I would have called this meeting if I intended to waste your time? I'm here to negotiate a deal. Shall we proceed, or should I lease the space to someone else?" (We had no other interested parties.) The room went silent.

Their broker cleared his throat. "Where should we begin?" he asked. I noticed his cuff links, brilliant white-gold squares. The lead architect picked up his copy of the lease.

Encouraged, I sat back in my chair and launched the opening salvo. "My understanding is that we don't yet have agreement on the base rental rate. What are you willing to pay?"

The principal put on his glasses and looked at his notes. "We can't pay more than $17.50 a square foot," he said.

The negotiations were in motion now—though, at first, I felt like a player in a Ping-Pong match. I was getting the ball on the table every time, but remained unsure whether I could handle the return if my opponent hit the ball with a spin. Heads in the room swiveled from me to the principal and back again. I wondered what the score was.

Then the broker entered the discussion, and I addressed his questions firmly and easily. Soon I found myself relaxing, even enjoying myself. I could do this. In the end—the negotiations went on for more than an hour—I pushed as hard as possible without killing the deal. I did make some concessions, but all at levels within my authorized parameters.

"You were fantastic." Steve, our leasing broker, patted me on the shoulder after everyone had left. "You can work with me anytime." Back on the sidewalk, I jumped up and slapped a No Parking sign. Bang! I'd nailed the deal. I was on the verge of skipping to my car when I noticed a woman looking at me and smiling invitingly, taking in the suit, the tie, and the confidence. She wasn't looking at me as a kid in a suit, but as a man, a D.C. power broker, maybe even a big shot—at least I felt like one. I returned her smile, curbing the urge to skip.

During the next year, I went on to lease all of the Georgetown building's vacant office space, plus its thirty-five apartments. I also supervised the design and build-out of the tenant improvements. Jim's firm did the construction work. I enjoyed learning how to read blueprints and walking the space as it came into being. After the project was finished, I made a long list of items that needed touch-up—called a "punch list."

Our overall leasing numbers were higher than projected, and that increased the value of the property. Falling interest rates increased our return even more. After a year, we refinanced, trading our construction loan into a larger permanent loan and pulling out the difference tax free.

I was awarded a small ownership interest in the building. When Diane later handed me my first partnership distribution, I opened the envelope to find a check for $30,000 — more money than I'd ever possessed. I hugged her. "Now you're on your way," she said.

We bought properties in D.C., Northern Virginia, and Maryland, everything from agricultural land to office buildings and large multifamily apartment communities. Diane and her new partner, Harry Gold, gave me a 2 to 3 percent ownership interest in each. "What's the value of the property?" I'd ask Diane after we closed each deal, and then I'd calculate the increase in my personal net worth. Some of the deals added over $100,000 to my paper wealth. My bank account also grew. I dreamed of hitting a million before my thirtieth birthday.

As a property owner, I also received tax-shelter benefits from property depreciation write-offs. None of us had to pay income taxes, and that made our salaries and the distributions tax free. I was surprised at how easy the game seemed. I often wondered why everyone couldn't figure this out. But I was young and later learned there was much more to the game.

Before President Reagan changed the tax laws in 1986, many developers were putting together real estate investment deals called syndications, aimed at high tax-bracket professionals. These investors were allocated a majority of a project's tax losses in return for a cash investment. Even if the development didn't make money, the investor achieved a high rate of return from the tax shelter. And the developers got the cash they needed. I took an exam in 1985 on the securities laws and broker-dealer requirements, and we formed our own real estate syndication company called D.C. Securities. My new business cards identified me as Vice President.

Harry Gold's top financial officer, Larry, was the president. His deal-structuring capabilities were impressive, and I studied every financial pro forma he prepared, even reviewing the calculation formulas on my IBM PC. He and I exchanged files through our newly purchased Hayes smart modems. Before the Internet and digital communications, the transfers seemed to take forever: I'd hit *send* and then go to lunch.

We began to buy and fix up buildings. As a project manager, I was in charge of the day-to-day work flow, helping to manage a team of outside experts: lawyers, contractors, architects, leasing agents, appraisers, vendors, and property managers. I loved being a developer. It fit me better than my old Stanford sweatshirt ever did. Taking charge seemed natural to me, especially with my father's strategic guidance and powerful voice leading me from within. It was obvious to me now that I was prewired for success.

I began to view my cousins' assets as part mine. I had my own apartment now, but it gave me great pride to let myself into their house with my own key, or borrow Diane's Mercedes convertible when they were out of town. Diane and Jim traveled extensively, so they had to delegate responsibility. Despite my youth, I became one of their most trusted associates. I attended charity functions on their behalf, and was first on the security company call list. More than once, I was awakened in the middle of the night by a false alarm and had to sprint over to their house to inspect. Having that kind of authority and responsibility at age twenty-four was amazing—and addicting.

By the time I was twenty-six and had been with the company four years, the economy was in full swing, with each of our deals adding up to an increasing personal net worth. It seemed so easy if you ran in the right circles. I never considered development to be shameful, or felt that we were compromising our integrity. After all, my cousins treated their employees and tenants well and

4
FIRST SIGHTING OF GREEN BUILDING

After eight years in development, my cousins thought it was time I learned their construction business. I still remember the heavy feeling of being a construction project manager with a beeper on my belt. It seemed that every time it vibrated, an owner was calling to tell me that a contractor didn't show or we'd painted the wrong color.

Diane and Jim could see that I had little enthusiasm for that work. "Why don't you use your business acumen to diversify the company?" Diane said to me over dinner one evening at Duke Ziebert's Restaurant on Connecticut Avenue. "The market is terrible, and we have to find other areas to leverage our core strengths."

I floundered around for a few months, unsure what direction we should take. Then one day I learned about a new project we were building out for the Washington office of the Environmental Defense Fund (EDF).

The next day I toured the space, which had been designed by a young New York architect named William McDonough. For the first time, I saw energy-efficient lighting fixtures that bounced most of the light off the white ceiling, paint that omitted toxic preservatives and didn't off-gas, natural linoleum floor tiles, bathroom ceramic tiles made from recycled glass, and toilet partitions made from recycled plastic bottles.

I was astounded. No one in our office had ever heard either of McDonough or of sustainable design. Some of the principles of energy efficiency and waste recycling were known, but the concepts of sustainable materials and indoor air quality were brand new. Focusing on energy and resource efficiency and occupant health made sense to me—but I'd never thought of it in such a holistic way before.

As a developer, I often encountered quite a different scenario. Not long before this, I'd toured a demolition site at 12th and Pennsylvania, near the Old Post Office Pavilion. Part of the structure was being saved, to be integrated into a new building that Jim's company was in charge of constructing. The rest was being junked. Overhead, a huge crane swung a massive concrete wrecking ball at the building. As the big ball bashed into the building, debris crashed down—pieces of glass, concrete, brick, steel framing, and drywall. Dust coated my shoes.

The building being torn down looked perfectly good to me, with beautiful details on the façade and hand-crafted masonry work, no doubt done by talented craftsmen in the early 1900s.

I watched with my jaw dropped, amazed the way a young boy would as trucks were loaded up with the demolition "waste" to cart it off to the local landfill where they'd pay a tipping fee charge based on tonnage. This was standard practice back then, before we took the time to adaptively reuse buildings, and if not, separate out useful materials that could be reused, recycled, and even sold.

The recycling movement nationwide was gaining momentum; people everywhere were now recycling glass, newspaper, and plastic bottles. I'd been transporting my bottles in my car's trunk to throw into a local repository, as curbside pickup didn't exist then in D.C.

I left the site and went over to an enormous, twelve-story office tower at 18th and Pennsylvania. A technology company was due to move in within two weeks, and Jim's firm was scrambling to finish the interior.

The top floor was pandemonium, with workers swarming everywhere. The walls were up and being painted. Carpet was being glued down in the hallway. The air reeked of chemicals. I sneezed repeatedly and my eyes teared as I inhaled the fumes. Looking around, I noticed the building didn't have operable windows. I wondered if they'd get the noxious smell out before the tenants moved in.

Even though daylight was streaming in on the south side of the building, the lights were on. I'd read about daylight dimmers in a newsletter from the Potomac Electric Power Company (PEPCO), the local utility, but had never seen them in the field.

They were still expensive, given the lack of demand. This would change years later, as dimmers became standard practice and even mandated by building codes.

And so it went. As landlords, we focused first on location, and then on designing attractive buildings and tenant spaces. We shopped in Italy for the marble for the façades and lobbies. Our architects worked hard to maximize the number of corner offices for big-shot lawyers, the prime tenants in our buildings. We didn't worry about energy and water efficiency because the tenants would pay the operating bills, not us. Designing to higher performance levels wasn't on the radar as an option.

With all this in my head—the waste at the construction site, the sealed windows and toxic carpets at the new offices, and the memory of what McDonough had done in the EDF space—I began studying ways to incorporate environmentally friendly elements into building and office design. This had to be our new direction.

A system rating buildings for green elements called BREEAM (Building Research Establishment Environmental Assessment Method) had been developed in England, and another one was being created in Canada. There was nothing similar in the United States. I went over to the US Department of Energy and also visited several divisions of the US Environmental Protection Agency (EPA). The focus of both these agencies was mostly on energy efficiency and waste reduction, though the EPA had recently set up an indoor air quality division in response to sick-building syndrome, which was created by the sealing up of buildings.

One day I was flipping through architectural magazines at the office, researching building materials that had low emission levels of volatile organic compounds (VOCs), when I saw an announcement for a meeting of the newly formed Committee of the Environment (known as COTE) at the American Institute of Architects' national headquarters at 17th and New York Avenue.

The next week, I went to the meeting. The AIA was lodged in a six-story semicircular concrete building; it shared a huge courtyard with the Octagon Museum, which fronted the street. I found the meeting room and took a seat in the back; as a non-member, I didn't want to draw attention to myself. The committee had formed about a year before under the leadership of an architect from Kansas City named Bob Berkebile, and he was the one who opened the lively meeting. About thirty architects then proceeded to speak over each other, interrupting and shouting things out, as they discussed a book they were producing, with funding from the EPA, called the *Environmental Resource Guide*. A chapter was being added that was concerned with the environmental impacts of aluminum from the beginning to the end of its life (known as Life Cycle Assessment). The calculation started with the extraction energy and environmental impact of the various raw materials that went into fabrication, and continued through the input of additional resource flows and ecological ramifications of the manufacturing process, construction, and ongoing use. This full-systems approach appealed to my engineering background.

The committee was sponsoring several lectures on sustainable building at the upcoming national American Institute of Architects (AIA) national convention in Boston.

The AIA was made up of a small group of committed visionaries who had begun to define green building through lectures and work on the Environmental Resource Guide, funded by the US EPA and the US Department of Energy (DOE). These visionaries included Bob Berkebile, Joel Ann Todd, Bill Browning, Randy Croxton, Gail Lindsey, Greg Franta, and Bill McDonough.

Those pioneers imbued me with a passion that I hadn't felt since my days at Stanford as a student in Gil Masters' solar classes, and before that as a camper and counselor at Camp Hess Kramer, where I learned to plant trees as part of an activity we called Avodah — literally meaning "work" in Hebrew: it implied serving God. At the time, at age twelve, I loved the work, but didn't know why. I just knew that it felt wonderful to plant a small tree, water it, and watch it grow. I still have the gold-painted hoe that came with the Avodah Golden Hoe Award I received at the end of the one-month sleep-away session.

I went to the AIA's 1992 annual conference, and those three days changed my life. "In nature there is no waste." Bill McDonough's voice boomed out to the audience of thousands in Boston's Convention Center. He wore a yellow bow tie and gray suit, and his long hair reached his shoulders. I scribbled notes in shorthand, sitting forward in my seat in an effort to capture every word, stopping now and then to shake the cramp out of my hand. McDonough said forcefully from the podium, "We must design our buildings so that they mimic natural systems." The conference had a green theme, focusing on sustainability: the preservation and conservation of resources for future generations as these apply to buildings.

At first, I felt like an intruder among all those architects. I was a real estate developer—one of the enemy. We carted buildings off to the dump and replaced them with new ones, sometimes even the same size and shape, but less aesthetically appealing. Utility bills, even if high, were passed through to tenants for payment.

I had been unable to sleep since I had arrived at the convention. My mind raced. I hadn't heard such impassioned discussion about the future of our planet since I was a sophomore taking a civil engineering solar energy class at Stanford. "We Americans like to waste," Professor Gil Masters had said at our first class meeting in 1980. "We consume about 20 percent of the world's energy, even though we comprise 5 percent of the population." I hadn't given a thought to the physical state of the Earth and how our consumption affects it since I was a boy in L.A. during the 1970s water and energy crises. At the time, my dad wouldn't let us water the lawn, flush a pee, or take long showers. A few years later the utility rates had shot up because of power shortages, and he'd yell at us if we left the lights on. Shortly thereafter, during the oil embargo, we'd wait in line for as much as an hour at the gas station.

In Professor Masters' class, students had to design and make a scale-model solar house. I spent hours on my model. It didn't look like much: fourteen inches long and ten inches wide, constructed of balsa wood and painted with two shades of brown—like a high school science project. But it was the house I dreamed of living in someday.

What you couldn't tell in a casual glance was that its design was properly oriented to the sun for passive solar heating and cooling, as well as for generating solar electricity and hot water, with the help of a roof full of south- and southwest-facing panels. There were enough solar photovoltaic panels catching rays up there for the house to generate all of its own electricity—what we now call "net-zero." Also on the roof was an organic vegetable garden—now known as a "vegetated roof." The house had four bedrooms: enough space for two kids and a guest room for my folks and future in-laws—I assumed I'd get married some day, even though I'd yet to have my first college girlfriend. The house even had a sunken basketball court with a passive heating wall (Trombe wall) that was filled with water: one of the best heat retainers. I was so pleased with how the model came out that it gained a permanent place of honor on a living room shelf, going with me every time I moved.

When I began my career as a developer, though, I lost track of my idealism; sporadic attempts to implement innovative designs sputtered out. "What about installing solar hot water in the apartments?" I asked Diane at one of our management meetings.

"That's cute," she said. "But this isn't California. People don't go for that stuff out here." I shrugged, as if to say, "Yeah, right, dumb idea."

An architect named Randy Croxton was at the podium now. "Here's a 100,000-square-foot green historic renovation I'm doing for the National Audubon Society building in New York." He pointed at a photograph of the ornate 1891 George Post building projected on a large screen. "We're designing new energy-efficient mechanical and electrical systems for this nine-story full renovation and penthouse addition. We'll use 70 percent less energy than a conventional code-compliant office building." I scribbled what he said on my pad. My pen ran out of ink midway, and I slapped my pockets for another one.

In the next slide a graph showed the green building elements Croxton planned to use: healthy paints and glues, efficient lights with occupancy sensors and daylight dimmers, four recycling chutes running the full height of the building, water-efficient urinals and faucets, and all-natural, undyed carpet made from 100 percent natural wool. They'd also installed a superefficient gas-fired absorption heater-chiller. In our developments in D.C., we met the building code requirements for water and energy efficiency and didn't think of going further. We picked building materials according to price and market trends, never giving a thought to where they came from or where they would end up. It seemed as if no one did, in those days.

The conference broke for lunch, served in an enormous adjoining room. There were a hundred tables, each seating ten or twelve people. I didn't know anyone, so I picked a table at random. We all introduced ourselves. A few of my tablemates were from Mexico; another was from Hong Kong, and the rest were from the United States. All of them were architects. As we got acquainted, the lunch facilitator's voice boomed from a loudspeaker: "Now, I want each table to work together as a team. For the next thirty minutes, your mission is to collaboratively design the world of the year 2020. How can we make it sustainable?" Each group would get thirty seconds to present its ideas to the room.

On my pad, I wrote down the key categories that came to mind: energy, water, waste, transportation, community, products, education, and work. The others at the table did the same. We then appointed Tim, one of our number, to serve as a scribe for our flip chart. He was about forty and from Vermont, and wore a black turtleneck, khaki pants, and a huge smile.

"How about energy?" Tim asked, when he'd taken his place by the oversized paper pad, felt-tip pen in hand. "What power sources and types of systems do we envision in 2020? What will our buildings and transportation systems look like?" He sketched the outline of several buildings and graphed the direction of the sun—east to west. Then he drew sun-tracking solar collectors, a large fuel cell, and several micro wind turbines.

"All power will come from the sun, from solar and hydrogen-based systems," a man from Mexico offered, looking at notes he'd written with a large antique fountain pen. He spoke excellent English, with a strong Spanish accent. His notes looked like pieces of art, with small sketches across the top and perfectly formed letters below.

"We will redesign our communities to get rid of our love affair with the car," a woman from Boston chimed in. She looked at us fiercely. "I walk to local stores to buy all my groceries. I also work at home and don't own a car, but there aren't a lot of people who are willing or able to live the way I do." As I listened, I realized with some embarrassment what little thought I gave to driving all over the place. I'd gotten my first car at sixteen. I thought of Third Street in Santa Monica, close to where I grew up, which had recently been closed to traffic. As a result it had become a place for people to dine, but also to stroll, sit on a bench, or visit with neighbors by a fountain. Soon street performers appeared and then new stores, as a higher-end pedestrian-oriented niche market began to flourish. Santa Monica had taken a busy, smog-creating thoroughfare and turned it into a prosperous, environmentally friendly promenade.

As I thought about that, a tingle ran through me — not quite an idea, but a relative of one. "We're getting too far from community," I said to the table. I thought of my chilly neighbors at my small apartment building in Dupont Circle in D.C., who pulled their Beamers and Jeeps into the garage and disappeared straight into their apartments. If I ran into them a block away, they'd walk right by me as if we'd never met.

I vowed that when I returned home, I'd break the ice by having my neighbors over for dinner.

"Sustainability starts with people," I said to my lunch group in a tumble of words. A few nodded. I was surprised at the thoughts coming to the surface, but they felt like the truth. "We harm the planet because we don't feel a connection between our actions and the environmental impact."

"What about our buildings in 2020?" Tim said. "I think they will be net generators of energy, with organic vegetable gardens on the roof and on-site water treatment." And off we went, spending thirty more invigorating minutes brainstorming our buildings of the future.

When our time was up and each table leader rose to present, I was amazed at the similarity of our visions despite our being from all over the world. We were not the only group to dream of increasing community, of rebuilding neighborhoods out of the faceless sprawl of cities and suburbs, and of designing systems that would reduce our consumption and reconnect us with the Earth.

I attended every session on sustainability I could find at the conference. I stopped at vendor booths to ask if they had any environmental products. They looked at me as if I'd been smoking dope. "All of our products are environmentally sensitive," one said to me. "We meet all of the building codes and ASTM fireproof standards." (I later learned that ASTM—the American Society of Testing and Materials—sets many of the country's product standards.) By the end, my wallet was stuffed with business cards. As I walked back to my hotel I imagined I saw a streak fly through the sky, like a bolt of lightning.

On the airplane back to D.C. from Boston I replayed in my mind all that I'd learned at the meeting. Putting my hand to my head, I could almost feel it pulsating. I felt as if I'd witnessed the start of a revolution in how we make buildings. The speakers had explained the elements of the new discipline, but it hadn't yet taken root in the industry, and the fundamentals weren't established. Even the definition of sustainable building wasn't clear. Only a handful of projects in the entire country had been designed in an ecological way. Europe was more advanced, but only by a few years. Forms of renewable energy, such as solar and fuel cells, were still in their infancy—and in that realm, the National Aeronautics and Space Administration (NASA) had done much of the pioneering work.

Back at home, something had changed in me. At midnight I pulled out World Watch Institute's *State of the World 1992*, which I'd bought in D.C. and had yet to open, and read it from cover to cover. Once a year the Institute reviewed the environmental condition of the planet: food production, water resources, energy consumption, renewable production, population growth, species destruction, deforestation, and sustainable economics. It was all related to my industry—buildings.

Buildings, I learned, consumed 40 percent of our energy, 20 percent of our water, 40 percent of our wood. They contributed 20 percent of landfill waste. Poor air in buildings made people sick. After my years as a developer, I thought I knew a lot about buildings, but this was all new to me.

Suddenly, not knowing whether I'd been dreaming or awake thinking in the dark, I sat up and switched on the light. An idea had come to me: I could make a difference in the world through sustainable buildings. Even though it was 3 a.m., I felt like getting up and devising a new game plan: tomorrow already seemed too late. I went to the bathroom to splash cold water on my face. Looking at my reflection as the water dripped down my forehead and cheeks, I felt the hugeness of the moment wash over me. *This was what I wanted to do with my life.* I made some notes on my pad, then went and stood at the window for a while, looking out at the wasteful lights of the sleeping city. When I finally climbed back under the covers, I hoped I could get some sleep and wake up with the sun. There wasn't a moment to lose.

5
GREEN DOESN'T PAY THE BILLS

I was dying to share my new vision with my cousins. The next week I dragged Diane and Jim to Manhattan to meet Bill McDonough at his office. His long hair was slicked back, and he wore the same bow tie he'd worn in Boston. He spoke with the unmistakable inflections of New England. We were looking at a photo of a high-rise that looked like a modern leaning tower of Pisa, only it wasn't leaning. "This is a building I designed for a competition in Poland," he said. "And this" — he produced another photo, of a small wood house with a sloping roof covered with solar panels — "is a solar home I built while I was an architecture student at Yale. It was my first sustainable project."

"How many of your projects actually got built, besides the solar house?" Jim asked. I tensed. Diane doodled on her pad.

"The Poland project was just a design concept. It never got built, but all of the homes did," Bill said. "I'm also currently working on a sustainable modular home concept for Russia."

Jim perked up. "We're doing some work in Russia supervising the design and construction of over a thousand homes. And Ariel Sharon has also asked us to do some work in Israel."

"That's fascinating," Bill said politely.

"Well, this has been interesting," Diane said. She looked at her watch again. "We have another appointment." The meeting was over.

My cousins weren't sure what to make of the meeting, but they were good sports. That afternoon we met with Randy Croxton, the sustainable architect for a National Audubon renovation project I'd first heard about at the AIA convention in Boston. Before starting his own firm, Croxton had worked with I.M. Pei & Partners, an internationally renowned firm. He was also the architect for the Natural Resources Defense Council's (NRDC) New York office. Completed in 1989, it was likely the first sustainably designed office space in the country, addressing light, air, energy, and occupant health and productivity.

I had visited the NRDC offices on West Twentieth Street the day before. The quality of the daylighting immediately struck me. Although it was cloudy outside, the space was bright—enough to read in comfortably. Windows lined the perimeter while skylights allowed light in from above. Croxton had also installed sensors that controlled the overhead lights with electronic ballasts; they turned on only if the daylight fell below a certain level. I'd learned that the lighting system was 75 percent more efficient than the norm. The carpet was made from recycled Coke bottles. It looked and felt like AstroTurf.

One idea in these early experiments in green building was to reduce the high amount of construction and demolition waste that was choking our landfills. During the past decade, in the 1980s, communities within the United States had established recycling programs, but the number of products—especially building products—made from recycled material was still low. The NRDC and the Audubon projects had recycled a good portion of their debris. Audubon had also saved enormous embodied energy (in all of the existing building materials) by recycling its 1891 loft building designed by the renowned architect, George B. Post. In addition, many materials, such as old carpeting and lighting fixtures, were salvaged and reused, while items such as concrete and wood were recycled. All paints, adhesives, and glued wood products were made with low-toxicity materials. In the NRDC space, Croxton had installed a series of air filters and efficient HVAC equipment. The level of fresh air supplied to the space was six times higher than required by the prevailing standard; it even provided a slight breeze.

During the next two months I read anything I could get my hands on concerning environmental issues and went to the AIA Committee of the Environment's meetings—usually as the only nonarchitect in attendance. Heaped on my night table at home, the floor around my bed, and my dresser were all manner of environmental books. However, I found little literature on sustainable building. The best up-to-date environmental source was the Worldwatch Institute, and its annual industry bible, *State of the World*, along with its annual environmental trends report, *Vital Signs*, and dozens of white papers. These documents armed me with statistics on the ecological damage our postindustrial society was wreaking on the planet. Though depressing, this information about our shrinking natural resources and increasing pollution encouraged me in my quest. An informed person with the skills at hand in the building industry could make a real difference.

At work I pored over manufacturers' catalogs, looking for sustainable products. I became friends with people at the US Department of Energy's Office of Building Technology and EPA's Indoor Air Quality Division and Green Lights program. Green Lights urged energy efficiency in lighting—it was assisted in this effort by some utility companies, which offered cash rebates for installation of more efficient lighting fixtures, electronic ballasts, and mechanical system motors. As a result of such measures, the voluntary participants in the Green Lights program found their electricity bills reduced by as much as 50 percent.

Learning about individual governmental programs was a challenge. Each agency, and even divisions within a given agency, operated independently. At one point, I realized that I'd visited a dozen different agencies and divisions—probably I was one of few to ever to do this. I thought of publishing a directory for my new "green" friends at the AIA.

One day I trekked out to suburban Maryland to tour a house made of recycled-content materials. It was a hot day, and the house smelled a bit like the landfill it was made of. Even though it performed well as an example of waste diversion, the designers hadn't understood the greater importance of indoor air quality and hence occupant health.

Around this time the word *green* began to pop up as an alternative to sustainable. To me it had a broader connotation, incorporating the economic advantages of an efficient and healthy building, and one that could even make more money or have a higher value.

I learned that an environmental building could reduce annual energy and water costs to the end user or tenant, not to mention save on landfill and transport fees for dumping construction debris. Improved indoor air quality meant workers would get sick less—an enormous financial advantage for any company, especially since the cost of the average salary was about two hundred times the utility bill. Later I learned that this benefit fit into a field called occupant health and productivity. These were arguments that I hoped would impress Diane and other building owners.

I bought a forest green suit to symbolize my new creed. "There goes Mr. Green," coworkers would say to me as I rushed down the hallway at work. I didn't pay any attention.

Wanting to understand environmental laws and standards better, I asked around and was referred to Mike Italiano, an environmental partner in a D.C. law firm who also chaired the Environmental Assessment and Risk Management Committee at ASTM.

When I met Mike at his firm's fancy offices at Sixteenth and L Streets, I liked him immediately. He looked to be in his midforties, with an athletic build and classic Italian looks: slicked-back jet-black hair, a bushy mustache, alert dark-brown eyes, and olive skin. His stride was so fast that he swept rather than led me to his office from the reception area. And his office demonstrated his vigorous energy, with client files everywhere, regulatory books in piles on the floor, telephone messages scattered across the desk.

"We're thinking of getting into the environmental business at our construction company," I said. Mike pulled out a legal pad and entered the date and starting time of our conference. As I spoke, he scribbled words that to me were illegible.

"I've seen your signs," Mike said. If you lived or worked in D.C., it was hard to miss Jim's signs: they were on dozens of buildings and hundred-foot construction cranes throughout the city, with our firm name and logo boldly displayed in yellow letters on a bright-blue background. The signs were lit so they could be seen even at night.

As we launched into our meeting, Mike told me about ASTM and his environmental committee. ASTM was founded about a hundred and ten years ago. Its thirty thousand voluntary members develop thousands of standards for materials, products, systems, and services. ASTM standards for building products were cited in building codes, governmental regulations, and laws, as well as specified by architects in their building plans.

Under Mike's leadership, the Environmental Assessment and Risk Management Committee started in 1990 and now boasted about a thousand members. It created a standard that was one of ASTM's most successful, coming up with an efficient and cheap way for developers of commercial real estate to check a site for contaminants. Before the committee's standards were approved, an environmental site assessment cost about $25,000—afterward the cost dropped below $1,000.

Mike's specialty was environmental litigation—mostly Superfund work. He'd written a book on leaky underground fuel tanks. He advised manufacturers on product development and defense against liability, and had done some work with building owners. His depth of knowledge and enthusiasm were impressive—and infectious. "I can help you survey the environmental building industry options and formulate a strategic plan," he said as we shook hands goodbye. "If you're interested, I can pull together a panel of experts to help brainstorm. I'd also like to get you involved in ASTM."

Diane let me hire Mike to conduct the brainstorming session and write a summary report. But sport that she was, she was growing impatient. "David, you need to stop doing research and figure something out," she said to me one day over salads at Houston's Restaurant on lower Wisconsin Avenue. "This is costing us a lot of money." I lost my appetite. I'd been worried that this was coming, but was so enthralled with the research and networking that I'd delayed figuring out the question my employers were paying me to answer: how we could make money.

For the next week I holed up in my office, taking lunch at my desk. Diane came by several times a day to see what I was up to, but I wouldn't show her anything until I'd finished. I was hatching a plan for a sustainable building firm to be a subsidiary of Jim's construction company. The new firm would provide consulting services to organizations wanting a "green building" or office suite, with Jim's firm doing the construction work.

After Mike Italiano reviewed the plan for me, I printed it on green colored paper and, with my heart in my mouth, submitted it to our management team. We scheduled a meeting for the following week to discuss it.

As the week crawled by I grew increasingly nervous. The morning of the meeting I'd been unable to eat my Grape-Nuts or drink any coffee. When we assembled in the small glass conference room—I was wearing my green suit and a tie decorated with bright yellow flowers—everyone had my green document in front of them. I kept looking from one face to the other, trying to read their expressions. If they didn't like my plan, I'd have to go back to construction.

"Good plan," Diane said at once.

"I like it, too," Jim said. "What's the first step in setting up the new company?" Relief flooded through me. I reached for a bagel and started outlining my ideas, forgetting to chew what I'd stuffed into my mouth.

During the next few months we formed Katz Environmental Consulting, complete with new logo, letterhead (printed on recycled paper with soy inks), and a brochure describing our services. I set up a sustainable products library to use once I landed our first project. My title was Managing Director.

At that time—1992—there were just a few other green building consulting firms in the country: Rocky Mountain Institute's Green Development Services, headed up by Bill Browning, and E2 in Los Angeles, run by John Picard. Picard and I met on one of my trips home to visit my parents; he'd just started working with Southern California Gas Company on a green renovation project in Downey called the Energy Resource Center and also had a few clients in Hollywood.

A couple of weeks after our brochures arrived, Diane began to push me. Over take-out soup and salads in her office she said,

"Get out there, David, and find us some clients. This is a business." She pointed her spoon at me. I stabbed my tomato so hard that it splattered my green polka-dot tie.

I had been dragging my feet, not sure how to sell our new services. I'd never faced making cold calls before.

Mike Italiano assured me that I'd find the business. One night I joined him and four of his ASTM colleagues for drinks at the Marriott. They'd worked together for many years, and the bantering made them seem more like family than business associates. I saw a jovial and playful side to Mike that reminded me of my older brothers. I later learned he was the eldest of three boys, and I believed the eldest and youngest formed the best bonds.

"Hey, David," Mike said during a lull in the conversation. "How would you like to become chair of a new ASTM subcommittee on green building?" I flushed—in part because I was flattered, and even more because I was terrified.

"I don't know anything about ASTM or the standard setting process," I protested.

"We consider that a plus," Mike said. "Don't worry, we'll back you up. The next meeting is in Philadelphia. Why don't you join us? It'll be fun."

I told him so little had been written on drafting standards for green building that I had no idea where to start. "Just invent it," he said easily. "It's better to define it yourself than wait for the market. Speed is quality."

I must have looked doubtful. "Tell Diane that this will put your company on the map," Mike urged. "Being chair of an ASTM subcommittee is a big deal."

Diane agreed, and within a month I'd formed my group, with Bill Browning as vice chair. After several animated meetings, our green building subcommittee membership grew to well over a hundred, but we still had no product. I finally holed myself up for an entire weekend and wrote the first draft of an attempt to define a green building standard and its practices, covering areas like energy, water and resource efficiency, indoor environmental quality, and waste minimization. The draft even went on to outline ways to carry out green construction and building operations.

When I printed out the document, it was more than fifty pages long and was entitled: *Standard E-50.06.1, Standard Practice for green building*. Section 1.1, Purpose, stated, "This practice covers the design, construction, operation and demolition of commercial buildings which promote environmental and energy efficiency and performance. This is the meaning of green building." Under Section 1.2, Goal, it said that the Standard was intended to assist design professionals, contractors, building owners, managers, occupants, product manufacturers, and other industry professionals understand and evaluate green building design, construction, operation, and demolition. Little did I understand the tidal wave that would follow those draft words.

"I don't know how you pulled it off," Mike said. "You're scary when you focus. Like you've been doing this forever." The effort didn't seem hard to me; it was almost as if the words came from a higher place.

We sent the draft standard to our subcommittee for comments and, after revision, to Mike's full committee via a letter ballot. This is a formal procedure in which committee members have the opportunity to comment on the draft. All negative comments must be addressed—either by resolving them or by voting them as nonpersuasive. To my chagrin, we received dozens of negatives, and after an entire day of working on the revisions we still hadn't addressed all of them. Smoking was a big item of discussion. Three members tried to convince me that smoking was acceptable in buildings if a room was provided with separately ducted ventilation. Even though this solution was preferable to allowing unrestricted smoking inside, I fought it. From an investigative article in *The Washington Post*, I later learned that the smoking supporters were funded by the Tobacco Institute. They had unlimited funds to fight me, as did some of the large product manufacturers who wanted to slow us down, fearing that the standard would hurt their business. Another complaint came from a member from a major manufacturing firm who said that the information I'd written was "anecdotal" and needed hard statistics.

I agreed, but the data that he wanted simply didn't exist. It was better to start than wait for perfection. "Perfect is the enemy of the good" is a motto I'd learn to live by during the next two decades, as well as adopting the precautionary principle — to avoid the possibility of harm.

Mike had told me that the ASTM consensus process was powerful, but it also sure was laborious. I'd never been an especially patient sort, and the process began to wear me down. I understood that ASTM standards were important, becoming part of the building code and even law, but I found it frustrating that even a single dissenter with ample funds and time could significantly slow down the process.

I did enjoy one aspect of the ASTM work immensely, however, and that was the core group of passionate people I'd assembled in our green building subcommittee. They represented all sectors of the industry, many getting together for the first time: building owners, manufacturers, environmental consulting firms, insurance companies, government, architects, engineers, and contractors. The talks we had at meetings, and afterward over drinks and a meal, positively sizzled. Although we didn't know it at the time, we were inventing a new way of approaching the design, construction, and operation of buildings, which would later become a global marketplace. By looking at the building holistically, as a collective of individual disciplines, we could identify and lend strength to the interconnected areas, thus leading to a higher performing building.

Take energy efficiency, for example. Beforehand, this area belonged to the building engineers, who chose energy-efficient equipment and control systems to heat and cool the interior space so that occupants are comfortable whether it's snowing outside or one hundred degrees and humid. But, as I learned, if you want to minimize a building's energy use, you must start with its orientation and envelope, not with its mechanical systems. The architect and planner must first fine-tune the building's siting on the property, its orientation to the sun, its massing and footprint, the shading potential, wall and roof insulation, glazing performance, roof color, and daylight penetration. All of these factors change the design requirements and the building's energy systems.

Here's another example: the engineers typically viewed indoor air quality as a ventilation strategy, relying on the mechanical system to exhaust polluted indoor air. I learned from my new green architect friends that to provide for the highest level of indoor air quality, we first had to select and install building products that don't off-gas volatile organic compounds (VOCs). Selecting alternative nontoxic cleaning products is also critical. Little did I know that this concept would grow into a field of its own, with "red lists" of banned products from concerned and knowledgeable architects and building owners. In addition, in those instances where the outside air quality is poor — such as a location next to a freeway — a higher level of filtration will be required. The same is true for recirculated air within the building.

We began to ask manufacturers for more information about their products, like the off-gassing profile over time as shown in an air chamber test. Our concern about the environmental performance of building products and systems was new, and although a few of the more progressive manufacturers understood the importance of providing this data, the majority resisted. In many cases, the company didn't have access to the information itself, and the cost of obtaining it could add up to hundreds of thousands of dollars.

But we were asking the questions—and that's how change begins.

Meanwhile, I'd managed to interest a few companies—clients of Jim's—in finding out more about energy efficiency services. Calculating the return on investment for energy-efficient measures is easier than trying to sell a complete sustainable-building approach, so we started there: at the pocketbook. Each month these clients receive a utility bill. We suggested to them that if we made their lights and heating system more efficient, and the bill dropped 30 percent, they'd receive a good rate of return and be better off. The utilities also had begun offering rebates, which furthered the investment yield.

Return on investment is more difficult to calculate in other areas, such as improved indoor air quality (and the associated occupant health and productivity) and recycled-content materials. Yet I was determined to deliver a full green building menu. Seeing the projects that had been carried out for the Audubon Society, Natural Resources Defense Council, and Environmental Defense Fund convinced me that our best bet was nonprofit and environmental organizations. And Washington was the national headquarters for such groups.

Having narrowed my target audience, each morning I sent out introductory letters with our brochure of services to a dozen organizations, linking their specific mission to the environmental quality and performance of their office space. Finally, one took the bait: Greenpeace. To my disappointment, however, our meeting revealed that although there was interest, they were in the middle of a ten-year lease and not sure of their future office space plans.

Jim's firm, meanwhile, was bidding on the build-out of new offices for a branch of Blue Cross. We submitted two bids: one for the standard plans and specifications as designed, and my alternate environmental bid. I was distressed when they didn't even respond.

Still, specifying and sourcing out alternative green products was good practice for me. The products I'd entered in my bid included environmental carpets, adhesives, paint, ceiling tile, and ceramic tile with recycled content, and energy efficiency lighting systems with sensors (including both occupancy controls and daylight dimmers). Unfortunately, at that time, because of low demand those products were pricey. I had hoped that ecological- and health-oriented organizations would pay more for the chance to have their buildings reflect their principles. As the Blue Cross bid proved, that wasn't necessarily going to be the case. "This all remains to be seen," Diane told me with pursed lips after we lost that bid. "You may be wearing rose-colored glasses."

The turning point came when we bid a tenant improvement project for Worldwatch Institute. One day, while flipping through their latest edition of *State of the World*, I saw that they were located nearby on Massachusetts Avenue. I called them up and, amazingly enough, learned that they were about to renovate their offices. I scheduled a meeting with their chief administrative officer, Claudine.

A few days later, again dressed in my green suit with flowered tie, I drove to the office of Worldwatch, arriving ten minutes early. The walls were decorated with framed covers of their many books, including *State of the World* and *Vital Signs*. There were also photos of the Earth and many of animals and nature scenes. I looked up at the lights—they were inefficient fluorescents, and the wall sconces had incandescent bulbs (which consume energy to provide 10 percent light versus 90 percent heat). The air smelled stale. I looked down at the carpet and saw that it was old, then glanced over at the windows: they were inoperable.

Claudine walked into the reception area. She held herself straight, and her dress was D.C. conservative: long blue skirt, white blouse, and yellow scarf. I'd expected an outfit more Berkeley style: blue jeans and something flowery on top, with enormous hoop earrings. "I've got a meeting in about twenty minutes," she said, looking at her watch. "Tell me what you've got."

I took a deep breath. "I run the environmental division of Katz Construction," I said, trying to sound confident. I gave her my most winning smile and leaned forward. "I know that your new office space is already designed, but if you add us to your bidders' list, I'll figure out how to green it. We specify energy-efficient lighting systems, water-efficient fixtures for the bathroom, and healthy and resource-efficient building materials: carpeting, paint, cabinet substrate, ceiling tile. I will also calculate the PEPCO rebate you'll get for the energy-efficient items."

"We're on a tight budget," she said, chewing on her red pen. My head started to pound.

"A green approach does cost more, but the rebate helps and you'll save energy," I assured her. "The market for green products is just starting. It takes environmental organizations like yours to jump-start it. Your books speak to the enormous environmental impact of our buildings and the products we manufacture. Designing a green space would be an example to the public." I paused. She shifted in her seat, and my stomach lurched. "We could even do a white paper on the environmental benefits," I went on hurriedly. "It would be a great case study. The only other green space I know of in D.C. is the one we just built out for the Environmental Defense Fund." She looked at her watch. "I'd be pleased to give you a tour," I added hopelessly.

"We have published extensively on climate, but as I said, we have limited funds." Claudine began to shuffle her papers.

I exhaled in exasperation.

"Look, I'll add you to the bidders' list," she said reluctantly. She stood up, indicating that the session was over.

I walked back to my car in a daze. She'd showed little interest in our environmental services. I had thought she'd congratulate me or something, but no, it was all about the money. Could she have misunderstood? I stopped walking, realizing I'd gone right past my car.

The next week I worked around the clock developing two bids for Worldwatch: one for the plans and specifications as designed (nongreen), and the other, our recommended green upgrade. The green bid was 10 percent higher, though the rebate brought it down two points. I hoped they would see that paying an extra 8 percent was worth it.

I didn't hear anything during the following week. When Claudine didn't return my call, I phoned her construction manager. "We awarded the bid to another firm. You weren't the low bidder," he said.

"What about our environmental bid?" I asked.

"That was even higher than your base bid. Sorry."

I hung up the phone, missing the cradle. My legs felt heavy when I rose to go tell Diane the news.

If Worldwatch wouldn't pay to green their building, who would?

"I can't believe that we lost," Diane said. "They didn't even respond?" I remained silent and held my breath as she shook her head in dismay.

I went back to my office and picked up *State of the World* and threw it in the trash, then headed for the door. A few minutes later I was in the car, driving home. I slammed the door of my loft apartment behind me and double-locked it. My apartment felt foreign, as if I'd walked into someone else's home. When had I bought all that stuff? The black leather couch and sofa chair, Italian glass dining room table with its high-tech chairs, enormous Sony TV and component stereo. When had I started to need a $1,500 signature glass table to hold my mail? Glancing at the huge colorful ceramic bowl that Diane and Jim had given me for my birthday, I kicked off my Kenneth Cole shoes so hard that one slammed into the wall. I looked down at my clothes: a Hugo Boss suit and matching tailored shirt that together had cost more than $1,000; the Hermès tie I'd bought in Paris.

I changed into an old pair of jeans and a fly-fishing T-shirt from a trip to Montana I'd taken with my father and brothers several summers ago. My movements were jerky, my breathing ragged. I pulled out one of my favorite movies, *Mr. Holland's Opus*, and put it into the VCR. Seeing the difference Mr. Holland makes in the lives of thousands of students as their teacher and mentor had always warmed my soul. As it began to play, I took out the pint of Ben and Jerry's Chunky Monkey that I'd bought on the way home and shoveled the ice cream into my mouth. Although it didn't fit my health-conscious diet at all, for the amount of time it took to eat the million calories and large chocolate chunks, I felt calmer. Whoever invented the flavor must have felt pissed off like this, too.

I tried to concentrate on the movie. Mr. Holland was teaching his class about rock 'n' roll—a breakthrough in his once-boring teaching style. He'd figured out how to reach them. To the right of the TV I saw the photo of an old girlfriend, Lauren. We'd gone out for about three months, but it didn't work out. "You're too picky," my mother had told me when I broke up with her. "Unless you ease up, you'll be alone your whole life."

"I told you to go talk to the rabbi for names of single women," my dad added to the conversation. But how could a rabbi know who was right for me?

The phone rang, but I didn't answer. I wiped the sweat off my forehead. It was August and humid. What did I have to show for my decade here? I went to get a glass of water from the kitchen. The door of the closet in the living room was ajar. My eye fell on my blue suitcase.

"Do not confuse effort with results," my father had said a hundred times. That phrase came back to me as I threw my clothes into the bag. To him and almost everyone in real estate, money was one of the key measurements of success. But he had also quoted Polonius' advice to his son from Shakespeare's *Hamlet* when he'd sent me off to Stanford: "To thine own self be true." The more I solely pursued monetary success, the less I was able to breathe. Another voice was welling up inside me. With my whole being, I yearned for something different. But what?

PART TWO: GREEN BUILDING

WORLD GREEN BUILDING COUNCIL

"I know only that a life without cause is a life without effect."

— PAULO COELHO, ALEPH

6
JOBLESS IN SAN FRANCISCO

"Wake up, sad sack, it's morning," my college buddy, Jeff Davis, said. It was October 1992, 5:30 a.m. and still dark outside in San Francisco's foggy Marina district. I was lying on Jeff's apartment floor, which was cold, but the sagging couch had hurt my back. I pulled the blue sleeping bag over my head and shut my eyes. Jeff kicked me. I squinted up at his beaming face—his teeth were annoyingly white. My legs felt heavy and achy, my back, tight from sleeping on the floor, my head, thick with sleep.

Jeff prodded me again and clapped his hands in my face. "Come on, we're going to the gym." He wore black Lycra pants, Ironman T-shirt, and the latest Nike running shoes. Jeff was always training for a triathlon. On my last visit he'd taken me on what he called a "short bike ride." After five hours and three major hills, sweat streamed down my face and my historically fragile back was in spasm. I wanted to get off and walk, or even lie down or go to the chiropractor, but thought it better to endure the pain than admit my weakness. Jeff himself had hardly broken a sweat. "Isn't this fun?" he bubbled.

I'd met Jeff when we were both freshmen at Stanford. We'd joined the same fraternity, Sigma Alpha Epsilon, but I wasn't the ideal fraternity type. The nadir was Hell Week, when each of us was assigned some sophomoric task—letting a mouse go at a McDonald's at Fisherman's Wharf, painting UC Berkeley's big white C on the hill Stanford red, driving a golf cart naked through the library's first floor. Jeff's task was to drive in reverse through the tollbooth on the Bay Bridge. We thought this was hysterical, until the police gave him a $250 ticket. My assignment was to get on a United Airlines plane bound for Hawaii and nab a *Hemispheres* magazine—all without a ticket or getting arrested. I tried telling them my grandmother was on board and had forgotten her mink coat. I even had a mink coat that Cliff, my big brother at SAE, had lent me. When this aroused a security agent's suspicion, I leveled with him, and he got me a copy of the magazine. Today, with Homeland Security, they'd have thrown me in jail and x-rayed my shoes.

After Stanford, Jeff worked at IBM and, like many of our classmates, got a Harvard MBA. After a stint as general manager of Lucasfilm's THX division, he cofounded a software production company called Lumen Production Company. When I arrived that October he and his partner were still in the start-up stage, inventing products for kindergarten through the twelfth grade that merged the fun of games with learning.

I couldn't sleep while being kicked, so I let Jeff drag me along to the Bay Club, a fancy multilevel gym on Battery Street with state-of-the-art equipment, a basketball court, and a large swimming pool. Jeff pushed me onto a bike, the stair machine, and into the cold pool. I swam a few laps, then huddled on a bench watching him do lap after lap with a fancy flip turn, his little red swim cap a blur in the water. I looked down at my belly. I was carrying an extra ten or twenty pounds. When did I get that? My mind wasn't on getting fit. I felt more like curling up in a ball and sleeping for a month.

"Have oatmeal and a bowl of fruit," Jeff chided me at the gym's health food bar afterward, when I ordered a pastry and cup of strong coffee. I obeyed, then realized I felt better after the workout and healthy breakfast.

Jeff and I went to his office down Battery Street, between Green and Vallejo Streets, four blocks from the gym. He had leased a large space with high ceilings, windows that opened, and lots of light.

Jeff then gave me a tour of the suite; he finished by saying, "Here's your office, David," and pointed at a small bright room overlooking the street. It had bare white walls and was sparsely furnished with a desk, chair, and phone. "Use it as long as you want. We'll deal with the rent when you figure out what you're going to do. I'm just happy to have someone uglier than me on the premises, Sack-o." He patted me on the back and smiled.

Left alone, I sat down at the desk and, out of habit, pulled my Day-Timer out of my briefcase. The month of October showed no appointments and no to-dos. I had quit my job in D.C. I was thirty-two and unemployed.

After a while I went across the street to a small storefront selling fresh baked goods. The smell of coffee lured me in, and I bought a chocolate scone and a large coffee. The coffee was stronger and more bitter than any coffee I'd had in D.C., and the scone tasted granular and earthy. When I mentioned this to the cashier, she told me everything in the shop was organic, a word that didn't mean much to me at the time. Two guys at a table nearby were talking about a project deadline. "Do you think we can finish the code by Friday?" said a man whom I would have assumed was unemployed. He had on ripped blue jeans and sandals, and his T-shirt said, "Kill Your Television." In D.C. all the men wore a coat and tie, even at the height of summer's humidity and heat. Here in San Francisco, I felt like a square even wearing an oxford shirt and khakis—and people probably thought I was. I'd wear my David

Bowie T-shirt tomorrow, I thought pathetically, feeling more sorry for myself than ever. I took my coffee to a nearby park and sat on a bench. Several homeless people slept on the grass under some trees; their tangled hair covered their faces. "Save some room for me, boys," I thought. On the way out of the park I threw my coffee cup into an overflowing trash can. It fell to the ground, so I picked it up and plodded around the block until I found an empty trash can. Then I took the long way back to my empty office.

This was the first time in my life I wasn't sprinting toward a goal.

Diane and Jim had rescued me when I was fresh out of college and schooled me in the real world of business, as well as giving me loving and open access into their home, family, and daily lives. Even today I'm still reaping the benefit of not only what they taught me, but also financial gain from building ownership interests they'd generously granted me back then. I owe them a huge debt of gratitude. But it became clear that it was time for me to find my own path.

I'd scribbled about twenty names for a new green building consulting company on a legal pad. The only thing I could think to do was start my own green building consulting firm. I believed California, especially the Bay Area, was a better market than D.C. The best name on the list was ProTech—short for Progressive Technology Group. I'd already slashed a line through the others, and now I crossed out this last one, too. It sounded too much like the noise made by a frog in the night.

"Forget the green; you'll starve. Why not go back to real estate development?" my father had said—a tape that played continually in my head. But I couldn't go back to work for a nongreen company. Since leaving Washington I'd been unable to wear any of my suits, and was embarrassed to drive my BMW. The thought of working just for money seemed shallow. In fact, it made me nauseated. I'd been aimlessly calling past acquaintances who worked with environmental and real estate development concerns, trying without much hope to see if I could generate a green consulting project. "I'll call you in a few weeks when I have more free time," the last guy I called had said, brushing me off.

"No problem. I understand." My head was throbbing as I hung up.

I put the pad with the scratched-out names and a few papers into my briefcase. It was only three o'clock. I thought maybe I'd go back to Jeff's Marina apartment and take a nap or watch a video.

The phone rang. "Hey, David, it's Mike. How ya doing?" Mike Italiano was calling to check up on me. I'd reluctantly agreed to continue running the ASTM Green Building Subcommittee, but that volunteer effort was laborious and heavily political. What I needed was a job, not more volunteer work.

"When are you going to ballot your green building standard again?" Mike asked.

"We still need to beef up the document and collect more data," I told him, picking at the first pimple I'd had in eight years. "It's not ready yet." In fact, I had spent no time on the green building standard. I knew I was avoiding figuring out how, politically, to address a few committee members who still advocated smoking in buildings. I felt like David against Goliath on that issue, except I was out of stones.

"The best way to get the additional information is to send it out to ballot. Our Phase One environmental site assessment standard was the fastest in ASTM history," Mike said. "Remember, speed is quality."

"OK. I hear you," I said irritably. "I'll get on it. I was just heading out."

"Not so fast," Mike said. "There's something else." I gritted my teeth; Mike could be heavy at times, staying on one topic until he was sure you understood his point. "I had lunch yesterday with an old law firm buddy of mine, Terry Bevels." Terry, it turned out, was a high-powered lobbyist with the The Wexler Group, a full-service government affairs firm. His boss, Anne Wexler, had been a big shot in the Carter administration. Before that, Terry was with the Senate Appropriations Committee. "I told Terry about your ASTM subcommittee. He loves the idea of green buildings." I dropped my briefcase and sat. He had my attention now.

Mike said Terry had clients who wanted him to get money from Congress for new building projects. Terry's idea was to invent a demonstration green building program and include his clients' buildings in it.

"That sounds illegal," I said.

"It's done all the time. Perfectly legit." Mike assured me. "And Terry's the best." He paused. I opened my briefcase and pulled out my legal pad and a pen. I flipped past the crossed-out company names and turned to a new page. I would have dated the page at the top if I remembered the date.

"OK, shoot," I said, sounding more enthusiastic now.

Mike said Terry wanted our help in creating the demonstration green building program. He mentioned several phases of congressional funding, the first one starting at $1 million for five projects. Two of the five projects were buildings for Terry's own clients: the New England Aquarium and the Lamont-Doherty Earth Observatory at Columbia University. To placate the head of appropriations in the House and Senate, another one would be the Iowa Wildlife Center, and a fourth, Montana State University. The last project would be at the National Institute of Standards and Technology—NIST, a branch of the US Department of Commerce.

NIST would administer the green building program funds. I later learned that NIST had thousands of employees who did all types of standards and technical development and research; one of their divisions even specialized in construction and the environment. NIST's mission was to reduce the cost of designing and operating buildings and to make the United States more competitive internationally.

"What's the next step?" I asked Mike. After a short brainstorm on the phone, we agreed that we needed to talk with Terry about our role. We'd help him develop the congressional green building program, but in return, we wanted to be part of it.

After the call, I ripped out and threw away the page with the prospective company names, then read through the notes I'd scribbled while talking with Mike. I made a list of next steps—the first one being formulation of a plan we could pitch to Terry when we called him the following week. Then I went down the hall to tell Jeff the good news. That night, he took me out to celebrate at Greens Restaurant, my favorite vegetarian restaurant on the waterfront at Fort Mason.

The call with Terry the next week went well—in fact, he seemed very eager to have us work with him. The three of us would form a nonprofit organization to support the congressional demonstration program. Its purpose would be to find green building products for the five buildings. Our goal was to develop a method, based on life-cycle assessment (evaluating the environmental impact of products over their full life, from materials extraction to reuse or disposition) for selecting green products. I would also provide consulting services to the projects, helping them to define and implement "green."

We hoped manufacturers of green products would join the nonprofit as members. To fund the new entity, we'd charge them an initiation fee and annual dues. That part of the plan had particular appeal for me. It had been two months since I'd received a paycheck, and my real estate holdings in D.C. had soured with the down economy. I still equated income with success, and it was hard to shake that concept.

We agreed that since I was the only one who was unemployed, I'd become head of the new organization, working full time in Jeff's Battery Street office.

A nonprofit made sense, given the unknown business potential of the nascent green building field and our desire to focus on education and standards. And as I pulled away from my past, I liked the idealism of being part of a nonprofit, and of somehow leading the way for others without a profit motive. I could also finally devote myself to projects that adopted a fully integrated design approach.

I couldn't believe my eyes when a fax came from Terry's office a month later. It was a copy of the *Congressional Record* reporting the appropriation of $1 million for the green building demonstration program. Terry had pulled it off! Amazed, I sat in my office with a big smile plastered on my face, feeling like a kid after his first ride without training wheels.

During the next month I rose at 6 a.m. and hit the phone at the office by 7. I was calling building product manufacturers across the country, asking them to become part of our nonprofit and to help advise specification of products in the congressional demonstration program projects. The five projects and federal government linkage served as our bait to get them interested. Without this link, we'd never have tried to create the nonprofit: it was our catalyst. To get their attention, I'd fax the firms a copy of the *Congressional Record*. A few of the people I'd contacted pointed out that the congressional program did not mention our nonprofit and asked if we had an agreement with the program and any of the five projects. I could honestly say yes because of our partnership with Terry.

I'd printed temporary letterhead on 100 percent postconsumer brownish paper. We named the start-up the U.S. Green

Manufacturers Council: The qualifier *U.S.* linked it to the congressional program; our target members were product manufacturers; and the word *council* seemed fitting. I listed Mike, Terry, and myself on the left margin as the company officers. My title was President; Mike's was General Counsel; and Terry's, Vice President. We'd agreed that any start-up expenses would be paid out of future member dues. In my eagerness, I'd ignored my basic business judgment by failing to stipulate that the three of us would pony up equally for the expenses until we collected the money. Instead, as it turned out, I was the only one reaching into my pocket. As my monthly outlay increased, I became anxious. My future depended on this working out. All my chips were on the table to pursue this dream—to change the US building industry and make a difference in the safeguarding of the planet.

I looked for major manufacturing firms that had demonstrated environmental leadership. When I found a candidate, I'd mail, fax, call, and FedEx until the prospect agreed to meet with us or told me to bug off. I considered both responses a success. At least I was casting my fly to a fish. It would have been easier with the Internet, but that was 1992.

In December I flew out to visit Terry's clients, Columbia University's Lamont-Doherty Earth Observatory and the New England Aquarium. Terry had asked me to help them write their $200,000 planning grant applications, which had to be sent to NIST for approval. I came up with a green program for each of them. Columbia was planning a new laboratory building, and the aquarium wanted to expand and upgrade its outdated existing facility in Boston, at Central Wharf. These projects included setting performance guidelines in various areas of green building: energy, water, materials, waste, and indoor environmental quality.

Since there were no national green building standards, I used our ASTM Green Building Subcommittee draft standard.

I also incorporated the idea of a "green team" of outside experts—architects, planners, energy engineers, materials scientists, and air quality experts—who would guide the projects and, we hoped, would join the nonprofit as another membership category.

On my visit to the Lamont-Doherty Earth Observatory campus, each morning I woke up early, feeling invigorated. Its mission appealed to me: "To understand how planet Earth works, in all of its physical manifestations . . . Providing a scientific basis for the difficult choices faced by humankind in its stewardship of our planet." The 125-acre wooded campus, located along the Hudson in Palisades, New York, employed more than two hundred scientists and graduate students from all over the world. I sat with them in the mess hall and played Ping-Pong with them at night. I'd never met people who cared so passionately about our Earth's future. At night I'd lie awake in my dorm room staring at the ceiling. Was it possible that I'd been able to change my life so much in just a few months? The lack of direction and purpose I'd felt on arriving in San Francisco waned as I soaked up the pure air all around me.

As I moved along the winding paths connecting the various academic buildings on campus, I thought back to conversations some of my colleagues and I had in the office in D.C. during my development days. "How much do you think we'll clear on this building sale after expenses and payoff of the loan?" "What do you think about the new BMW 5 series versus the Porsche 928? I'm having a hard time choosing." At that time, of course, in the back of my mind I was calculating everything in terms of monetary and status value. Yet here, I'd overheard—and sympathized with—two scientists muttering in disbelief over rampant clear-cutting of trees in the Amazon rain forest and the increase in global warming.

Both clients ended up getting a $200,000 planning grant from NIST. I told myself that my turn would come soon. After all, I'd

7
COLD CALLING

In the next thirteen weeks, I hit my desk by seven, with two cups of strong coffee already jangling through my arteries. Coffee was an awful substitute for sleep. My eyes were swollen, with large bags under them. I skipped exercise and Jeff's morning gym invitations, and the jeans I'd bought at Gap a month ago were getting tighter and tighter. My hair was long and bushy, on its way to becoming an Afro. Piles of papers and packages to be mailed to prospective members covered every surface of my office.

One morning, as I was sifting through my calling list for new members, the phone rang. "Hello," I mumbled. My lips felt frozen. The phone rang, and I could not make myself understood.

"Ttanks for caalllling," I managed to get out. What was happening to me? Was I having a heart attack? I thought my chest or arm was supposed to hurt, but other than my mouth freezing up and being unable to speak, I felt fine — well, except for a racing pulse, as if my heart was in overdrive. And a twitching hand. After trying for a few more minutes to speak, without success, I finally managed to convey to my caller that I'd call him back.

Without another thought, I packed up my things, drove home, climbed into my sleeping bag on Jeff's floor, and slept for the entire afternoon.

The next day I was back at my desk at seven. I never did learn what happened to me. If I'd been less driven, I might have gone to see a doctor, but I didn't have the time. My only concession was to lay off the coffee for a while.

At the end of that period, in January of 1993, I took the red-eye to Washington. I'd lined up meetings over the next two days with five global manufacturing firms. Mike and Terry would join me.

The plane's wheels touching down at Dulles International Airport woke me. I rubbed the sleep from my eyes and put on my jacket and dark-green full-length wool Hugo Boss overcoat from my developer days. By the time the taxi pulled up in front of Terry's downtown building on Eye Street, we'd passed several of Jim's construction signs. His business was surviving the down economy.

Terry's firm, The Wexler Group, occupied the entire sixth floor at the modern office building. The elevator was crowded, yet all the passengers, men and women, looked as if they'd shopped at the same clothiers: they wore dark-blue or charcoal-gray suits with starched white shirts, even the women. I thought about what they would wear back home in California: shorter skirts without panty hose, and lots of color and skin showing. Most would have tans and look fitter. When I lived in D.C. people thought cool was pulling an all-nighter at work or working at the White House; in the Bay Area it meant doing something such as the Escape from Alcatraz Triathlon: a one-and-a-half-mile swim through the bay's frigid waters, an eighteen-mile bike ride through the hills, and an eight-mile run through the Presidio. Jeff had done it annually and had an array of medals hanging from his wall to show for it.

Terry's firm had its own lobby — marble floors with Oriental rugs, original art, an enormous floral arrangement, and deep leather chairs. I took a seat. I was early and Mike wasn't there yet. I looked at the wall of photos. There was Anne Wexler with Jimmy

Carter; underneath was a handwritten note from the president. The main phone was ringing off the hook while the receptionist struggled to keep up. The pace was faster paced than the West Coast, and there was no sign of the recession.

Just as Terry came out to greet me, Mike walked into the lobby. We all shook hands. Terry was about my height, five foot ten, with thinning black hair. His body was wiry, showing his runner's physique, and he moved with the lightness of an athlete. He wore a D.C. power suit: dark-gray wool with a thin pinstripe. His shirt was the latest two-tone—blue with a white collar, his tie was yellow with dark circles, his cuff links large and gold with the American eagle on each—the ones you get only from someone high up at the White House.

We settled into three black leather sofa chairs circling a coffee table in Terry's office. The walls held photos of Terry with various presidents, congressmen, and other top public officials. On his desk were pictures of his wife and two young children. Out the window I saw the White House a few blocks away. I smiled. It felt good to be affiliated with Terry's world. I sat up straighter, feeling a sense of purpose course through me. Terry fidgeted in his seat. His phone rang and he got up to take the call. Mike and I chitchatted while Terry advised a client on the status of a funding request via the latest House appropriations bill. It was as if he were speaking a different language. I was still amazed that Terry could get the government to fund his clients' buildings. That was quite a skill to have on our team.

Terry sat back down, landing heavily in his chair, and took a deep breath. He seemed to be under great stress. He'd told us he had about thirty clients, which seemed like much more than a full load to me. He had rings around his eyes and kept looking around his office, as if he was having trouble concentrating. "I've got some bad news," he said finally. Mike and I sat forward in our chairs.

"What's up?" Mike asked. I held my breath.

"I'm out." He slapped his knee

"What do you mean, you're *out*?" I asked. My pulse was racing and my body temperature felt as if it had risen twenty degrees in the past few seconds.

"I've got a conflict. I can't represent Columbia University and the New England Aquarium and also be an officer of an organization whose purpose is to help sell its members' products to my clients' buildings." Terry's shoulder was toward us, his legs pointed away. I clasped both hands into fists.

"That's it?" Mike asked. "Just like that?" He spoke slowly, trying to make sense of what he'd just heard. Sweat pricked the back of my neck.

"I'm sorry," Terry said. "I have no choice." He walked over to his desk, indicating that the meeting was over. I stood up; Mike had already begun walking to the door. There was so much I wanted to say to Terry. Instead, I followed Mike out of Terry's office.

Mike Italiano had given me *The Art of War*, by Sun Tzu, when we were building the council. He was a Chinese military general, strategist, and philosopher during the Zhou dynasty, around 500 BC. My mind searched for an apropos lesson from the book, such as: "All war is deception," or, "You have to believe in yourself." But it was impossible to embrace his sage counsel when we'd failed. How could I have been so dumb? My father had urged me to get a written agreement, but I'd decided to trust that it would all work out. I felt betrayed, especially since I'd spent several weeks and two trips helping Terry's clients receive grants. And I was thousands of dollars out of pocket in expenses for the new organization, not to mention lost salary. If this didn't work, it felt like I'd go broke.

We still had five meetings scheduled the next day with product manufacturers at Mike's office. Most of them were flying in to meet with us. What would we tell them, I asked Mike as we left the building.

"Let's just tell them the truth," Mike said. He showed a mouthful of teeth, then laughed. Our plans were in ruins, but he was cheerful. "You've got to love it," Mike said, hitting me on the shoulder. "If you take it too seriously, it'll kill you." I frowned, failing to see his point. "Just remember, we're alive and not in jail," he added.

I only saw the black side of things. Terry was our only connection to the congressional green building program and the five projects that were in the works. That was the main bait for the manufacturers. Why would they join a nonprofit membership organization without that link? They'd be angry that they had wasted their time and money coming to meet us. Maybe we could still reach them and cancel, I thought. I could take a late flight home and drown myself in videos on Jeff's couch.

The next morning, though, I was in early at Mike's office.

Soon I was tapping my pen impatiently on the table in Mike's law firm conference room with its glass walls, marble rectangular tables, black leather chairs. "It feels as if we're waiting for our own funeral," I said.

His bushy eyebrows arched. "It's not so bad. What else would you be doing on such a beautiful morning? Think of it as a great opportunity to learn about human nature." I shook my head. Where'd this guy come from? He looked at me the way my brother Glenn did when I was taking myself too seriously. I cracked a small, painful smile.

Mike's secretary escorted in Joe Smecker, our first meeting. He was the environmental scientist from Milliken & Company, a multibillion dollar private carpet manufacturing firm, one of the largest and most respected in the world. We stood to shake hands and then all sat around the table. I noticed that his eyes radiated intelligence. I'd heard high praise of his leadership as chair of the Carpet and Rug Institute's environmental carpet standard. It had taken me a few months to track him down and develop enough of a rapport to get him to meet with us.

Mike said, "We have some good news and some bad news. Which do you want first?" I bit my lower lip and looked down at my notes, which now seemed like a waste of time.

"Let's start with the good news," Joe said. He had taken out his notepad, but now put his pen down and took off his glasses and began cleaning them.

"Well, the good news is that David and I are here to meet with you."

He shook his head up and down and looked at us like we were a little crazy. "And the bad news?" What on earth was Mike going to say? — we're wasting your time, have a good trip home?

"Our third partner, Terry Bevels with The Wexler Group, resigned last night. He was the link to the congressional projects," Mike said.

"I see." Joe flattened his palm on the table. "What are you guys going to do?"

"We thought we'd get your take on that," Mike said. Joe leaned forward in his chair.

"Tell me what you're thinking."

I blinked in surprise. He was still here.

Mike nodded at me to take over. "Without the projects," I said, "we can broaden our base of members." Inventing my arguments as I went, I explained that when the focus was the five demonstration projects, we thought the council would be composed mostly of manufacturers and a few architects and engineers. Without a tie to the projects, however, we were free to build a more vibrant and integrated membership, one that represented the entire building industry. From my experience as chair of ASTM's Green Building Subcommittee, I'd learned the importance of having all parties at the table. Joe and Mike were nodding.

"The traditional adversarial position of environmentalists and manufacturers is changing," Mike said. "We've found at ASTM that a lot more can be accomplished by working together rather than suing each other."

"The nonprofits will embrace this concept," I added.

"That makes sense to me," Joe said. "We've had the same experience at the Carpet and Rug Institute. Legal action should be a last resort, not a first step." I looked at my watch, amazed that we were still meeting. Joe had even taken a few notes. Earlier I would have bet that he'd already be in a cab headed to the airport by now.

"Demonstration projects are important, but it's even more urgent that we define 'sustainable building' and set guidelines," I said. "There is still mass confusion."

"What do you have in mind?" Joe asked.

"We could help accelerate ASTM environmental building standards," Mike said. "A catalyst organization could shave years off the slow ASTM process by developing the standards in a fast, consensus-based manner." Taking turns, Mike and I went on to describe other programs we could create: a green building resource center, an economic benefits study, and even our own green building rating system, like the one recently inaugurated in England, called BREEAM. This was something I was particularly keen on. Rating systems, like the Good Housekeeping Seal and EPA's Green Lights voluntary standard, had helped their respective areas develop rapidly.

"What do you need from us?" Joe asked.

"We'll need your support with other firms," Mike said. "A letter would be great."

"We can do that."

"When we officially form, we'll have to charge dues," I said.

"Of course," Joe said.

"What amount would you pay?" Mike asked.

"Somewhere around $10,000," Joe said easily. "We pay even more to the Carpet and Rug Institute, but it's in our field." I grinned inwardly; Joe had thrown us a life preserver.

Mike and I were smiling as we walked Joe into the lobby and greeted our next appointment, Bob Johnston, a representative from Herman Miller furniture company, a multibillion-dollar global manufacturer. I had tracked him down at the AIA convention in Boston, where he gave a talk about the firm's progressive environmental wood purchasing and reforesting programs. When we sat down and he asked us how the meeting with Milliken had gone, I felt relieved that Mike could honestly say, "Great." Mike then explained that we saw the exit of the congressional projects as an opportunity to expand our organizational mission and, accordingly, our membership and activities base. When he nodded, I was elated. We brainstormed the new nonprofit industry council with him, coming up with even more good ideas. At the end of the meeting he, too, agreed to write a letter of support and told us he had no problem paying our dues and a charter member initiation fee.

By day's end, Mike and I had conducted three more meetings. One firm, Carrier Corporation, not only pledged its support but also said that the company's new head of environmental marketing, Rick Fedrizzi, would make a good founding chairman. They invited me to meet him a few weeks later at a media event Carrier was hosting in Squaw Valley in California. The other meetings were with Armstrong World Industries and USG.

At the end of the day Mike and I retreated to his office, which was cluttered with law books and client papers. A time sheet sat on his desk, and I saw that he hadn't billed a single hour during the past two days. I wondered how his firm felt about the new nonprofit. We later agreed that Mike would earn a monthly fee as general counsel.

I took off my tie and rolled up my shirtsleeves. "We need a new name."

"Something tells me you already have an idea." Mike took out his legal pad and picked up a pen.

"I still like the name we came up with previously, but let's just make one adjustment, and call it the U.S. Green *Building* Council." We'd drop the word *manufacturers* and swap it for the word Building now that we planned to represent the full array of sectors across the diverse industry.

"And I suppose," Mike said with a chuckle, "you also know where to get the founding members and good office space." My eyes lit up and I smiled.

As I walked back to where I was staying, it was difficult not to run. Despite the winter chill, I felt warmth pulsating through my body. I passed a big construction hole for a new project at McPherson Square. It took up the entire block. Why hadn't I noticed it this morning? I'd phone home to tell my parents the good news, now that we had a plan and supporters.

The world was sure looking up.

8
THE START OF A MOVEMENT

Our goal was to formally launch the U.S. Green Building Council in several months: April 1993. The American Institute of Architects would host the meeting in its D.C. boardroom. Although the AIA hadn't yet agreed to join, having the meeting at the national headquarters implied its support.

Now I had to get us to that goal. Mike and I hoped to have about forty firms in attendance, with at least one firm in each of a dozen categories of our diverse vision of membership for the new coalition. That meant finding leaders from the fields of energy, development, construction, homebuilding, architecture, engineering, planning, environmental organizations, government, manufacturing, property management, professional societies, and technical institutes.

I went back to working the phones and the postal meter. To attract new members, I faxed copies of all the letters of support we'd obtained to date. I aimed to create a snowball effect, as Mike had taught me. However, it wasn't always easy to find the right contact at a given firm — in fact, simply identifying which firms to get in touch with could be quite difficult. LinkedIn sure would have been helpful, along with email. One of my best methods was to attend the various national conferences and trade expos of the

AIA and the Construction Specifications Institute, a membership society of twenty thousand technical design professionals involved in the specification of building products and systems. Once I got a person's name, it would go on my hit list. I would then mail an informational package; after that, I would call every other week until the person either agreed to write a letter of support and attend the April meeting or told me to leave them alone. It was the same method I'd used for getting firms to meet with Mike and me in January, except now I had turned up the volume.

I met with Kathleen Cruise, a representative of Pacific Gas and Electric Company (PGE), my local utility, who pledged her support. I'd tracked her down because she was the project manager for PGE's Pacific Energy Center on Howard Street in San Francisco. The building showcased energy-efficient lighting and HVAC technologies and hosted industry training programs. She had contacts at Southern California Edison, in Los Angeles, and San Diego Gas & Electric. Soon I was on the phone with them; both representatives were enthusiastic and, after a barrage of my best sales tactics, both wrote support letters. Chuck Angyal, chief architect from SDG&E, agreed to join us at the kickoff meeting in D.C. The utilities had rebate programs to promote energy efficiency and immediately understood the benefit of supporting our green building. Little did I know that Chuck would play a big role in a later stage in my life as well as become a good friend. Many of those early pioneers I met in forming the USGBC became pivotal players in my life and each others' lives.

Getting building owners to support us was a greater challenge. They were, understandably, more immediately interested in the bottom line than in saving the planet. In my early public lectures to real estate groups, I made the mistake of focusing on the environmental degradation caused by buildings. The feeling in the room was dead. Later I learned to talk only about economic benefits, using the traditional financial analysis I'd relied on as a developer. I realized that for the business sector, what we needed to do was show them that green building had enormous financial benefits and was really a strategic lever to accelerating the business case.

The underlying ethic of all business is profit. This is the entity's responsibility to partners and shareholders. Another given is growth — growth in sales, stock price, market capitalization, number of products, workforce, resource consumption, and profit and net worth. That's America. Trying to fight this is impossible, like trying to move a mountain with a shovel. Building owners will only embrace green building when it is tied directly to their bottom line: rental rates, tenant leasing, lower expenses, higher occupancy rates, greater loan amounts at lower interest rates, higher building sales prices, and improved returns on investment. These parameters are the pulse of the business of real estate and dearest to the owner's heart.

Many environmentalists refused to accept this fact. Greenpeace may have shifted big corporations a few degrees in its normal course of business by staging dramatic strikes, blocking ships from delivering their goods, and other such efforts, but a more pragmatic approach would be to change how we make money and define financial value to include sustainability at its core. Later, many cities got into the green building game, using a "carrot" and sometimes a "stick" approach to lead real estate projects to green, the essence of long-term global value.

As we set out to build the council in 1993, we could supply solid information on the financial costs and benefits of energy, water, and waste efficiency. It would take two more decades to solicit and gather information in other areas of green building, such as impact on rents, building value, and overall financial return, as well as harder to document benefits, such as occupant health and productivity.

It's not easy to affect the momentum of the world's largest industry. It takes patience—a virtue that I was slow in learning to embrace. I want to sprint up the mountain. If someone tries to slow me down or stop me, I become frustrated and even furious. My basic nature is to look for ways to go around the obstacle and if necessary through it. This personality trait emerged repeatedly, for good and for ill, as we set out on our dream of creating the council and changing the US building industry—later expanding globally. To temper and expand my nature, Sun Tzu might have offered: "The general who wins the battle makes many calculations in his temple before the battle is fought. The general who loses makes but few calculations beforehand." Nevertheless, we prevailed and continued to steadily climb the sustainability mountain, whether equipped or not.

The leading design professionals in architecture, planning, and engineering understood the aims of the council at once. It was common for designers to use natural elements. They understood the wisdom of maximizing daylight and using solar shading to minimize heat gain during the summer months, and of allowing natural ventilation through operable windows and other measures. And of course, they were adept at adaptive reuse of older structures. Historic preservation is green at its core. Enormous materials and fabrication energy savings can be achieved simply by starting with an existing building. The key, and sometimes a conflicting challenge with the principles of preservation (for example, replacing old inefficient windows with new double-paned ones), is to then retrofit for resource efficiency and occupant health and productivity.

Engineers who were already trying to maximize energy efficiency and enhance air quality and thermal comfort also thought the council was a great idea. The first to jump on board was Alan Traugott, a principal with Flack + Kurtz engineering firm of New York (later becoming part of WSP). His firm had worked on both the NRDC (Natural Resources Defense Council) and Audubon projects in Manhattan. Finding kindred spirits like him made all the difference.

The first environmental organization to sign up was the renowned Rocky Mountain Institute. Bill Browning, head of green development services there, was still vice chair at our ASTM Green Building Subcommittee. He watched as our plan took shape. "The council is exactly what the country needs," he said when I first explained the idea to him at the end of 1992. "What do you need us to do?"

NRDC was next. I had been referred to one of their lead international energy experts, Rob Watson, by the staff scientist, Ashok Gupta, who led me through their New York building the year before. "This is exactly the type of group we've been looking to join forces with," said Rob. He and NRDC became a pivotal force in building the USGBC and global sustainable building marketplace.

It made an enormous difference to get those two powerful environmental organizations, RMI and NRDC, on board. Their names had clout and credibility with the government, manufacturers, and many of our other targeted industry sectors. Politically, they fell in the middle of the environmental movement. Unlike those to the far left, these organizations understood the value of working with manufacturers, even firms that produced toxic products or were on the EPA's Superfund cleanup list. As Bill put it, "If we are going to green the world, we need to show business that green is profitable."

After Jim's construction company built out the tenant improvements for the Environmental Defense Fund (EDF) in Washington in 1991, I'd met with one of EDF's senior scientists, Richard Denison. He told me that the year before they had established an environmental partnership with McDonald's. That collaboration led to a recycling program, in which McDonald's purchased hundreds of millions of dollars' worth of recycled-content materials for its stores and packaging and diverted thousands of tons of waste from the landfill. The recycling effort not only helped environmentally, but it also saved McDonald's considerable amounts of money. By working with an enlightened industry leader, EDF was able to create a new market overnight. I never forgot this important lesson, and tried to use it in our formation of the USGBC.

In essence, Mike and I had invented a new way of doing business as an industry. There was no precedent for such a coalition and its integration across traditional boundaries. Generally, membership within a specific sector was highly restricted. Environmental organizations were never invited to join manufacturer trade associations, for example—and vice versa.

Many industry trade organizations were essentially lobbyists. I had a visceral reaction to some of them. The mere definition of lobbying meant trying to influence legislators in favor of special interests, whether or not what they wanted might be good for the environment. A nonprofit organization could serve as a shield for its members to take on controversial issues without exposing their personal corporate brand. Our vision, in contrast, was to build an organization of leaders who demonstrate constructive action through bricks-and-mortar methods: by constructing buildings that optimize environmental performance and are healthy for occupants and the planet. We excluded trade organizations. These groups were different from the industry professional societies we embraced, such as the American Institute of Architects and Construction Specifications Institute. These member-based groups proved to be quite progressive on sustainable building issues, leading their memberships forward into new practices that were not only good for the Earth, but were good business as well.

As firm after firm signed up to attend the kickoff meeting, I felt invigorated. I carried their support letters around in my briefcase as if they were priceless heirloom jewelry passed down by my grandmother. Each letter that came in renewed my sense of commitment.

Money continued to be a problem, though. I was still working without pay and writing checks to cover the council's bills. My bank account continued its steady slide. For the first time in my life, I stopped eating out, opting to fix meals at home. Buying new clothes was out of the question. I'd even driven to L.A. to visit my folks instead of flying.

"You'll starve." The words of my father when I'd set out on this journey reverberated late at night in my head. Whenever I heard them, I'd get out of bed, get dressed, and head to the office to send out more faxes and prepare more mailings. At 5 a.m. I'd be on the phone, calling people as they arrived at their East Coast offices. "What are you doing up at this hour?" one man asked me. "Are you crazy?"

Mike was a steady support and shoulder to lean on as he continued working full time at his law firm. "You're doing a great job, David. I don't know how you do it," he'd say before giving me a list of a few more people to contact. His enthusiasm and tactical strategies were important, but I still felt isolated and insecure without proper funding, staff, and a committed board and membership.

I'd feel a lot better when we had a chairman to legitimize our nascent organization. Mike and I wanted to recruit a progressive leader from a global manufacturing firm. In late January 1993, after our encouraging round of meetings in D.C., I trekked out to Squaw Valley to meet Rick Fedrizzi, director of environmental marketing at Carrier Corporation. I knew the hundred-year-old firm from my construction and development days; it was the world's largest manufacturer of heating, ventilating, and air conditioning products, with forty thousand employees in 170 countries. Rick had helped Carrier adapt its products to reduce ozone depletion, boost energy efficiency, improve indoor air quality, and reduce packaging. The Squaw Valley meeting was an environmental press briefing on their products for about forty trade publications.

I tracked Rick down in the lodge. He was decked out in ski clothing: dark-blue overalls, black after-ski boots, a multicolored sweater. About forty years old, six foot two, with sparkling deep-green eyes, he looked like an oversized teddy bear. Over a beer, he told me that as the father of two young children, he was inclined to look more broadly at his life purpose. "My kids love this stuff," he remarked with regard to his environmental role at Carrier. "It's the first time they've ever taken an interest in my work."

When I told Rick why I was there, his response was enthusiastic but tentative: "I don't know what it means to be chairman of a nonprofit. But I'd like to learn more." Clearly, I would need to do further explaining. And what better place than on the slopes at Squaw?

"I've only skied at Syracuse with my kids," Rick said the next day as we rode the chair lift to the top of the mountain. We'd been warming up on blue runs, chatting on the lift rides up about the USGBC and his potential role as our first chairman. Now, though, it was time for a more serious workout. "I do the black diamonds in Syracuse, but they're not nearly this steep," he said, as he eyed the steep mogul run beneath us. It looked fun to me. I was eager to test the soft demo skis I'd just rented at the hotel's posh shop.

"I'm sure it'll be no problem," I said with a grin. Rick tightened his grip on the safety bar.

We got off the lift and I egged him on toward the easiest black diamond slope. I'd grown up skiing at Mammoth Mountain with my brothers. We'd been to Squaw Valley several times as a family—flying there in my father's plane. Mom and Dad also liked to ski. Once I had to ski down KT22, one of the steepest and iciest runs at the resort, carrying my brother Glenn's skis. He'd fallen at the top and slid halfway down before coming to an abrupt halt with a dislocated shoulder. My older brother, similarly named Richard, and about Fedrizzi's age, was a graceful skier.

"You can do it," I urged Rick, who stood staring down the nearly vertical face, the tips of his skis barely protruding over the edge of the run. "It gets easier as you gain momentum." I jumped off and made a turn into the soft powder below. This was my first run of the year, and it felt great to be skiing again. Rick proceeded slowly but steadily to make his way down the mountain. His form was good and his legs strong. I made a few more turns, then waited for him at the bottom.

"That was awesome," he said with a smile as big as the mountain. "I was thinking about the council on my way down. I'd like to be the founding chairman."

"Fantastic!" I sidestepped a few paces up the mountain to shake his hand and pat him on his big, parka-encased shoulder. That ski run changed the world and both of our lives in ways that neither of us could anticipate at the time. Good thing Rick hadn't fallen and hurt himself! I'd learn that he was always up to conquering a new slope, no matter how steep or full of moguls. And even today, he's still solidly balanced on his skis.

The truth is that none of us had the experience to design and construct what we dreamed of building. As in a steep mountain climb, our strategy was to gather a balanced and inspired team and the necessary gear, and simply set out on the journey. We tried not to focus on the height of the mountain or the ruggedness of the terrain, but just to progress, one step at a time. Of course, we were doing it where there were no trails, because nobody had been up this particular mountain before. We were building the first industry coalition of its type in the world. The key was to keep our sights on the top and never stop climbing or look down. In practical terms that meant working to change the way we designed, financed, constructed, and operated our buildings.

What we didn't understand was that in changing our relationship to the world, we would also change ourselves and build life-altering relationships.

Even though Mike's and my decision to appoint Rick as chairman was quick, almost intuitive, during the next decade our faith in him was validated a hundred times over. Rick provided exactly the leadership and strength of character and vision that we needed. He was also the perfect foil to Mike and me, with our hot tempers and brash manners. In those days, if we didn't like someone, we labeled them "darksider" and plotted over drinks how to "take them out." If Rick was present, he'd calm us down and get us to agree to release our aggression by laughing more over drinks or going out for a run with him. Through his solidity and evenness, mixed with vision and insight, he got the best out of us, stabilizing us and goading us onward. He went on to become the peacemaker for the council as our momentum increased and we began to encroach on sacred turfs on all sides. We couldn't have found a better leader than Rick.

Finally, April 1993 rolled around. We had sixty firms confirmed for the kickoff meeting of the council and a stack of support letters from leaders in a dozen sectors of the building industry.

Once the taxi had dropped me at AIA's headquarters on New York Avenue, I straightened my green-patterned tie and tried to smooth the airplane wrinkles from my trusty green suit. I ran my fingers through my hair. It was longer than when I lived in D.C. My hairline had begun to recede, but there was no gray yet. Glasses wouldn't come until later. I was thirty-two.

I hurried into the building and headed upstairs to the boardroom. Caterers were setting up a continental breakfast in the reception area outside. Should I eat something? No. My stomach was unsettled. My notes, with three-colored highlighting, burned a hole in my pocket. I'd reviewed them so much on the plane that the paper was worn at the edges. Would I return home as president of a new nonprofit organization? Would the attendees agree to become members and fund us?

The stakes were high for me personally. I'd put everything I had into the council. It was my best creation, with the greatest potential of anything I'd ever done. What if they didn't want it? I had no Plan B.

I entered the boardroom, and something in me relaxed when I saw Mike already there, setting up the overhead projector. He looked up and saw me. "Hey, David. Ready for the show?" His broad smile flashed white teeth. His black hair—less of it every time I saw him—was parted and slicked back. He was in his early forties, but moved around the front of the room with the vitality of someone a dozen years younger. I cracked a wan smile and tried to say I was, but the words caught in my throat. My legs felt heavy.

Soon people began to pour into the boardroom. Mike and I stood together up front as Carl Costello, the director of AIA's Committee on the Environment, offered words of welcome. Game on.

"Welcome to the founding organizational meeting of the U.S. Green Building Council," Mike began. "Today is the start of a revolution in how we make buildings." As he spoke, I looked out at the attendees, recognizing about half of them. The others I knew only by the sound of their voices on the phone. It was a profession-al group, the men dressed in suits and ties and the women in skirts and dark blazers. A couple of guys were wearing jeans. I guessed they were from the Environmental Defense Fund and Audubon;

they'd agreed to come only last week when I told them that Rocky Mountain Institute and NRDC were on board. Rick, sitting upfront, winked at me. My buddy Reed, a real estate developer, was off to the left; I lifted my chin at him gratefully. Chuck Angyal from San Diego Gas & Electric sat in the back; he'd already loosened his tie and rolled up his sleeves. He and the guy next to him, Alan Traugott from Flack + Kurtz, were laughing, probably at one of Chuck's jokes. A chill of excitement shot up my spine. I'd gotten them here! They had come because they believed in our vision, and in me. I could feel the collective electricity of the participants, like a thunderstorm just before bolts of lighting flash through the sky.

Then it was my turn. I took a deep breath and began. "Your presence here," I said, "makes you visionaries of a new movement—Green Building. We are honored to welcome all of you, representing about a dozen sectors of the industry. Although our council will comprise individual voices that function independently, together we'll be an orchestra, speaking with one integrated and holistic voice for the industry. Our mission will be to transform building design, construction, and operation from conventional practices to sustainable ones that optimize profit for both business, the environment and its people." I paused to catch my breath and take the pulse of the room. Several people nodded intently. Everyone was paying attention.

When I'd finished, Mike returned to the podium. "This is going great," he whispered as we exchanged places. He launched into the first of his two white papers on recommended council activities. Calm and poised, he walked the group through several overhead slides. The first paper had to do with accelerating ASTM green building standards. We believed the council could independently develop critical standards at a fast pace, and then introduce them into ASTM as appropriate. Mike's second paper was on the concept of developing green product standards for the building industry. It was difficult for product specifiers to determine the pertinent green product attributes and then obtain comparative information from manufacturers, and our thought was that the council could take a leadership role in this area—a field that today is still rather nascent, given the complexity of environmental attributes and data collection and reporting.

When it was my turn again, I presented two papers I'd written. One was on the need for us to develop a building rating system—like England's BRE or BREEAM (Building Research Establishment Environmental Assessment Method). It had been introduced in 1990 and was beginning to make a market impact, having been used to certify about 5 percent of new commercial office buildings. Canada was developing a rating system, too, but it was complicated and ultimately failed. My second paper was on establishing a green building resource center. As I'd found while working for my cousins, it was a full-time job to track down and assemble information on green building. We could be a one-stop green building informational clearinghouse.

Mike and I then cleared our throats for the most crucial item on the agenda: organizational formation, including membership and dues. I was determined not to let them out of the room until they agreed to join our coalition and pay up.

We launched into the topic by introducing the first year's budget, which included staffing—myself as president and Mike as our outside general counsel—and the expense of our headquarters and some new staff in San Francisco. An overhead slide showed our proposed dues levels. We planned to limit membership to organizations, thus avoiding individual members, who in other organizations paid lower dues yet required the same level of service in terms of mailing costs, staff time, and meeting costs. Strategically, we wanted the organizations' commitment as well. According to our proposal, product manufacturers with revenues of more than

$1 billion would pay $10,000 annually, plus an initiation fee of $15,000. At the lowest end, but still having the same vote and organizational representation, were environmental nonprofits, with annual dues of $300 and no initiation fee. All other dues fell between $500 and $5,000, depending on a firm's category of membership and organizational size. Payment of all fees up front would allow us to rapidly capitalize the new group.

Mike took his place by my side. "And now I'd like to take a vote on the formation of the U.S. Green Building Council," he said. "All those in favor, raise your hands."

Silence fell over the room. Standing at the podium alongside Mike, I felt as if my heart had stopped. On the far side of the wall a cart creaked and dishes rattled. I looked, and all over the room hands were in the air. Joy and relief hit my backbone. I almost staggered. "Yes! Thank God," I whispered to myself. I felt my face break into a smile the size of the Grand Canyon. Rick winked at me and his face glowed as if the sun had come out. Ours was an idea whose time had come, but I thought his welcoming remarks as founding chairman, representing UTC/Carrier, had added great credibility.

9
BUILDING THE USGBC

"The goal is to collect $100,000 by the end of June," I said to the group at the founding meeting. I had sixty days to collect and deposit the pledged dues in the bank—a difficult task even for a skilled fundraiser at an established nonprofit organization.

That first weekend back from D.C., I switched all the inefficient incandescent light bulbs in my apartment to compact fluorescents and installed water-saving devices in my sinks, shower, and toilets. Recycling I'd done since I moved in. I'd recently moved out of Jeff's apartment, which was nearby in San Francisco's Marina District.

On Monday morning, I rose with the sun. I bolted down the three flights of stairs from my apartment and opened up my garage door. The morning light bounced off the BMW I'd bought during my developer days. I couldn't drive that anymore. I dusted off my bike, pumped up the tires, and pedaled off downtown to work.

As I rode through the Marina Green I reveled in the fresh morning air. Beyond the furled masts of the boats in the harbor, the water in the bay was calm. Seagulls hovered, occasionally plunging into the water in hopes of catching their morning breakfast. Could I do it? Could I climb the mountain in sixty days? Would the attendees at our kickoff meeting really cut a check and join an organization with no programs, no track record, no official office, no money—just me as the staff, a man with no nonprofit experience whatsoever?

Hitting the grassy hill leading up to Fort Mason, I shifted into my lowest gear, popped out of the seat, and stood on the pedals to pump my way up the incline. I'd do it just like this, pedal stroke by pedal stroke. Soon I'd crested and was zooming down the hill toward Aquatic Park. Fishermen were already out on the long pier, and dedicated cold-water swimmers with little red caps were doing their laps. I felt the exhilaration of speed and wind on my face.

During the next weeks, I expanded the target list to include firms that had previously expressed interest but were unable to attend the founding meeting. I brought in a temp to help with the mailings. Stacks of packages ready to mail teetered on every surface. Slowly, the list of those who said they would sign up grew. We were building the organization one member at a time.

I flew to Chicago for AIA's national convention: two days to hit three hundred booths in a room the size of several football fields. First I sat down and highlighted the names of large product manufacturers that I knew could contribute to green building—makers of energy systems and of products that could contain recycled content, such as drywall and carpeting, or those that impacted air quality (paint, glues, laminates)—and that could pay our dues and initiation fee.

"Is your product environmental?" I asked the sales representative for Southwall Technologies. I knew that they made an energy-efficient coated film.

"Of course," he said. "We have a new product: Heat Mirror. Have you heard of it?"

I pulled out a small pocket notebook and wrote down the company and product name. The salesman described its energy efficiency properties, giving me a lecture on windows as well. Apparently, Heat Mirror was developed by NASA to protect astronauts from the sun's radiation. The thin film is placed in the center of two panes of glass and enclosed with krypton gas. It minimizes heat gain and loss while maximizing insulation. He showed me the National Fenestration Rating Council seal for a window with Heat Mirror encased in the middle, certifying its properties. The NFRC had done for windows what we wanted to do for entire buildings: created an accepted national certification system. I launched into my spiel, linking my sales pitch to his product, then handed him a newly printed council brochure and my card. It listed my new title: president. The address was still 901 Battery Street, San Francisco — Jeff's space. I was hoping we could move into our own green space once I collected more than $100,000. I had started compiling a list of manufacturers I wanted to hit up for product donations. I made a note to add Southwall Technologies to the list.

When I got back home, footsore, having given my sales pitch hundreds of times, I sent out a mailer to the new list of targets. Then, as usual, I followed up with phone calls, faxes, and a second round of mailings. I did use a lot of paper, but at least it was environmentally friendly paper, and our brochures used nothing but the finest soy inks.

By the end of June, I had raised $125,000. The council was a reality.

I could now draw a salary and hire staff. The first thing I did was bring on Lynn Simon as program manager. Shortly after we'd launched the council, several people encouraged me to track Lynn down. Not only had she been president of the AIA's national student organization under an environmental banner and started the San Francisco AIA's Committee of the Environment, but she'd also mastered in architecture with a thesis on sustainable design. She was perfect for our first hire, and to this day is an active contributor to the council and to the industry. We then hired a designer to develop the council logo, hoping that in time it would be considered a brand or seal: two concentric circles with an oak leaf floating in an olive-green background.

Mike and I had handpicked the council's founding board of directors based on the individuals' enthusiasm and the type of organization they represented. We wanted at least one representative from each of our dozen sectors. Our board and about forty founding members provided testimonials and help with the recruiting process. Our top priority was additional capitalization (through memberships) to offset our increasing overhead. Rick brought in several large manufacturers, including Johns Manville, the insulation company, which was a supplier to Carrier.

Shortly after our official launch we received checks from two trade organizations, each for $300—the same fee our environmental organizations paid. Although on paper both groups were nonprofits, one represented thousands of firms, and the other about two dozen billion-dollar powerhouse corporations. Mike and I moved quickly to get our board to prohibit trade associations from becoming members, and we returned the two checks. Otherwise USGBC would become a council of trade organizations, killing the pioneering spirit that our visionary and progressive corporate members stood for. Years later, we'd reverse this policy when the council became a much different force.

The going was not always easy. "Aren't you primarily an organization of product manufacturers?" Terry McDermott, CEO of the national AIA, asked Mike and me at a meeting in 1994. He'd just been brought in after serving as president of Cahners Publishing Company, and we'd approached him about partnering in the area of sustainable building. McDermott stiffly extended his hand when we were introduced. I perched on the edge of my seat, tapping my right foot under the table. "I've heard a lot about your new group. Tell me about your mission," he said as the meeting began.

I explained that we were an open and balanced coalition of the entire building industry. "What's your dues structure?" he asked. I told him the amounts were distributed according to the sector's ability to pay, as well as tiered according to an organization's size.

McDermott listened skeptically. "Who pays the most?"

"Large product manufacturers with sales over a billion pay an annual fee of $10,000 plus an initiation fee in the first year," I said. "But they only get one vote, same as an environmental organization paying $300. All parties have agreed to this structure, and it's working." I pointed out that we had about eighty firms, only about 20 percent of which were manufacturers. It's true that I'd spent more time recruiting big firms because of the greater financial contribution, but others joined more readily, therefore keeping our membership in balance.

McDermott remained unconvinced. I felt my heat rising. "What will be the role of architects in your group? I see that the AIA San Francisco has joined," he said. While the national AIA had been deliberating on whether to offer us its support, Lynn Simon had helped me recruit Bob Jacobvitz, the executive director of AIA's San Francisco chapter. He'd even hosted our first San Francisco board meeting in 1993 at his office on Sutter Street, which years later played another exciting role in our history.

"We have thirteen sectors of membership. Architects only represent one category," Mike offered. "We also have another category for professional societies. Both ASID (the American Society for Interior Designers) and ASLA (the American Society of Landscape Architects) have joined." He paused.

McDermott shuffled together the various documents we'd given him. "We'll stay in touch," he said as he rose. It took all my will to extend my hand to shake his on my way out. I couldn't look him in the eye, and stomped out of his office. I shake my head now to imagine what he must have thought as he watched the head of the

USGBC comport himself like an overwrought teenager. The next year we negotiated reciprocal memberships between USGBC and AIA's COTE, and our collaboration has grown yearly since then.

In early 1994 we signed the lease for a new office space to be built out in a building being renovated on Sansome Street, part of the Transamerica Pyramid building complex, overlooking a beautiful little urban park with a waterfall. The landlord agreed to house us temporarily in an adjacent building until the construction was finished. That gave us time to design our own green space and solicit product donations from our members. I couldn't wait to sit in Herman Miller's new award-winning, ergonomic Aeron chair and use its executive stand-up adjustable desk. USG agreed to give us the drywall, and Armstrong provided the ceiling tile we needed (both had recycled content). We'd have to install three carpets — by Interface, Milliken, and Collins & Aikman Floorcoverings — to showcase our members' latest environmental carpet tile. Flack + Kurtz engineers helped design superefficient lights, and we were talking to Andersen about installing their latest windows, with the best energy-efficiency values. Meanwhile, we camped out on an enormous vacant floor. My old Stanford best buddy Jeff, whose own lease had been terminated, came along and staked out a corner in our temporary space. It was comforting to have him around, and I was glad I could pay back some of his hospitality.

One of the ideas Mike raised during our early formation was a pollution tax on building products. Products would be taxed based on their level of pollution, such as the amount of carbon dioxide produced in the manufacturing process. If two carpet tiles, for example, were produced by different processes, the "greener" carpet would get a tax break. Its "green" determination would come from a more environmentally enhanced process: use of recycled-content materials, "clean" manufacturing plant energy derived from solar panels or hydroelectric, or other green features.

and then quickly innovate by releasing version 1.1 and then 2.0. Lynn Simon helped in that regard by implementing such program initiatives as researching the viability of our own resource center at Southern California Gas Company's Energy Resource Center, and establishing local government and annual conference committees.

As a result of this Silicon Valley entrepreneurial-type approach and our own philosophical bent, the board ended up being a collection of mavericks in an industry that was traditionally conservative and slow to change. Building invests less in research and development than almost any other industry—0.5 percent versus 5.0 percent for high tech. We were out to buck that trend.

I was with Mike on pollution taxes. As he put it, if we didn't take on the hard issues, who would? But it was becoming clear that I had to get him to pull back on that issue. If I didn't, we'd lose our some of our mainstream manufacturers on the board, and they wouldn't help me raise money—and money was crucial. This was the kind of conflict I was most afraid of. The group came from all sides; the only thing we agreed on was the need to boost the environmental performance of our buildings, thereby saving the environment as well as reducing building operating expenses. How could I keep everybody from disagreeing as their natural inclination toward the left or right surfaced on an issue? If we couldn't get along, the council would be split in two.

One morning when I was in D.C. for meetings, Mike and I went for a bike ride in Rock Creek Park. He had on cut-off jeans, an old Syracuse University T-shirt, and dirty tennis shoes. Still partly my developer self, I was decked out in black Lycra biking shorts, a multicolored Pearl Izumi jersey, Shimano shoes, and yellow mirrored Oakley sunglasses. His bike looked as if it had spent the last thirty years stacked with a lot of other junk in his garage.

I led the way, being more familiar with the trails. Every time I looked back, Mike was right behind me, even though I thought I was the more conditioned one—I'd been biking a lot in the steep hills of Marin County, just over the bridge from San Francisco.

As my tires crunched over twigs and rocks, I vowed that I'd speak to Mike at our next break. At the top of a hill, I pulled off the trail for a drink from my water bottle. Mike caught up to me and dismounted, then took a long gulp from his bottle of Gatorade. It was hot and humid. Under my helmet my hair was dripping with sweat. "Mike," I said.

"What?" Dirt streaked his face.

Another rider swept by, standing on his pedals as he crested the hill, his helmet a shock of blue and yellow against the dark trees. He lifted a hand, and I did the same. Mike was waiting.

"Nothing." I stuck my bottle back in its holder. "Ready?"

Mike was like a brother to me. I didn't want to hurt his feelings. And I hated the idea of giving in to outside pressure.

As was bound to happen, however, the issue boiled over a few months later, at a quarterly board meeting. A scientist at the National Audubon Society had just begun his report on a grant application that they'd been working on for the pollution tax committee, when Bill King interrupted. "Why are we taking this on?" he asked. His eyes were steely behind his large-frame glasses. "We have many other more 'apple pie' priorities."

Several others agreed.

"This is chicken shit!" the scientist declared. A new board member, he was responsible for Audubon's pioneering green building in Manhattan. He looked like a professor, with tweed coat and thin strands of hair pasted over a high forehead. Now his face and even his balding pate were bright red. He hit the table with his fist, the thump resounding throughout the room. "If we don't have the guts to take on something as important as pollution taxes, then I quit. None of these folks here are environmentalists; they're just a front for the industry." He started stuffing papers into his briefcase and making his way to the door.

I sat there open-mouthed. His display reminded me of Khrushchev pounding the table with his shoe at the United Nations. Several people looked at me. I was there to provide leadership, but I had no idea what to say or why he was so angry. To date, we'd made it through all controversies by staying at the table until we resolved our differences. Achieving consensus was one of our sacred values. I willed myself to speak, but nothing came out.

Then Bill Browning jumped up so suddenly his chair tipped over. "Screw you. I can't believe you'd say that," he said. The board member wheeled around to face Bill, whose face was contorted and crimson as his own. All around the table, mouths dropped open with surprise. Bill was among the most soft-spoken and thoughtful person on the board.

The new board member reached for the door. A rush of voices remonstrated with him. He just shook his head and walked out. We never heard from him again.

I later learned that there was much more to the story. I still am not sure of the truth. Like most misunderstandings, it was likely a gray area. Yet curiously, the feeling that flooded me at the time was gratitude. A committed board member had walked away. That was bad. But if Bill and Rob Watson (representing our other two environmental organizations) had not stayed at the table, our coalition could have fallen apart then and there. Two decades later I still feel appreciation at the willingness of our fellow members to embrace, support, and expand on our vision—for similar incidents did occur, many times over the years, and yet we remained together despite our differences and behind-the-scenes feuds. Those early charter members of the council who joined when it was hardly more than an idea were change agents and pioneers across all industry sectors, passionate stewards of the planet and its natural resources. They not only had vision, but the tenacity and will to make our dream a reality as well. All my life I had felt like an outsider, never comfortable with any club or society. Here, among the other members of the council, I experienced a sense of belonging I had never known before.

In late 1994 we held our first annual green building conference, in partnership with NIST (the National Institute of Standards and Technology) at its Gaithersburg, Maryland, campus. Again, they'd taken early leadership by standing with our nascent organization. Having such an esteemed governmental agency partnering with us lent the council credibility right out of the gate. The Institute deserves great credit for helping launch USGBC and, accordingly, the green building industry for the country and beyond.

I walked around mingling (or simply eavesdropping), and most of the remarks I overheard were animated as the participants eagerly shared their thoughts on green buildings. "This is incredible," one man told another. "I'm the only one in my firm who cares about sustainability. It's amazing to see all these other passionate professionals. I'm going to go home and tell my boss that this is going to be big."

The keynote banquet dinner speakers at the conference were Bill McDonough and Paul Hawken. Bill shared his thoughts on waste as feedstock for new products and on the need to make things that aren't toxic to people and the planet. These concepts were later detailed in his books, *Cradle to Cradle* and *The Upcycle*. It was the first time many had heard him speak. I noticed many heads bobbing up and down; a few others stared at the ceiling in complete shock, and a couple of people left.

When Paul's turn came to speak, he said enthusiastically, "I love the council's coalition model—there's nothing like it in the world." A few years later he told me that he thought our open and integrated sector model of membership would work not only in greening the building industry, but also in greening the business world. Paul was renowned for his provocative best seller *Ecology of Commerce*, advocating the need for business to lead the sustainable revolution. Paul went on to cowrite (with Amory and Hunter Lovins) the next important industry bible, *Natural Capitalism*, and later on, *Blessed Unrest*. It was encouraging to receive this affirmation from such a towering figure in the movement who also later became a good family friend.

In addition to the AIA, I wanted to bring the Construction Specifications Institute in as a professional society member of the council. While attending a CSI conference in Houston to solicit members, I had learned that the organization wanted to expand its standard manufacturer product information template to incorporate green characteristics. This was a shift with national implications.

In 1994, I was elated to receive an invitation from Ross Spiegel, an officer of CSI, to address its board at its national convention in San Francisco. I planned to talk off the cuff, presenting the history of the council and making a case for CSI's membership. When I walked into the room, I was shocked by the formality of the setting. About a dozen tables were joined together in a circle. In front of each board member was a microphone and nameplate. It looked like the United Nations.

Fortunately, I was not asked to present first, which gave me time to scribble a few notes and learn the protocol. Each party addressing the board had five minutes. I noticed the speakers handed out a copy of their spoken remarks in advance, then presented a formal reading of the text. A queasy feeling in my stomach told me this was a time I should have been more prepared.

Soon my name was called and I took the visiting presenter's hot seat at the roundtable. To my embarrassment, my voice cracked slightly when I introduced myself, as it had at my Bar Mitzvah twenty years before. I caught my breath, then felt my strength of will kick into gear as I told them about the council's programs. "We'd like to work together with CSI to incorporate the principles of sustainable building into its standard specifications," I finished. I returned to my seat exhausted, with no idea what I'd said.

"You did a good job. They were impressed," Ross told me afterward. "Our president wants you to sit with us at our banquet dinner."

That evening, I climbed up onto the stage and joined the head dinner table. I'd dusted off my tuxedo, bought during my D.C. days; it felt tight, but the color was right—nice and black. Seated below us were thousands of CSI members (eight thousand had attended the convention). Would USGBC ever fill such an enormous room?

The president of CSI, William Riesberg, spoke, lauding the work being carried out by Ross and his environmental committee. "And to further our environmental commitment, we will be joining the U.S. Green Building Council as a charter member," he announced before the thousands—to my utter surprise. Ross looked over at me and winked. I simply beamed.

Ross ultimately became a board member of the council, bringing not only his depth of knowledge in the greening of building plans and specifications, but also his decades of organizational experience. He served as our parliamentarian and beacon for organizational professionalism. He would have made Bill King from Armstrong proud, but Bill had retired, having been replaced by Steve Piguet, a baby boomer like me. The council went on to form a long-term partnership with CSI, cosponsoring several trade expos, which boosted our credibility. Ross further accelerated the environmental platform for both organizations when he became CSI's president in 2001. He later coauthored a book called *Green*

Building Materials on environmental specifications that further solidified his leadership in the green building movement.

I continued to send out new membership packages and call prospective firms, but after the first rush of charter members, only a fraction of the building industry seemed open to our message. Finding the right contact at the right firm was like panning for gold. The big money lay in bringing in large manufacturers, but the recruiting process for that was difficult and slow. It had taken me a year to enlist several of our latest members. Dozens of others were on the sidelines watching to see if we'd fold or continue to grow.

It was March 1994. I'd increased our overhead significantly since funds started coming in the preceding June. I'd hired Lynn and an assistant, and was trying to pay myself a full salary—though that had worked only for the first few months (for the past seven I'd been paid nothing). We also had several interns. Mike's law firm billed monthly for his services as general counsel, but we also accrued their payment. The travel budget added up as I flew around the country to attend board meetings, deliver speeches, and continue to recruit new members at big conference trade shows.

At every council board meeting and during officers' conference calls, I brought up our sinking finances. "Let us know who to call and what to say," people would say. But this was not the way to get new recruits. Even the best-intentioned board members were reluctant to make solicitation calls. "David, you're the best at bringing in members," a board member from a large company said at one board meeting. I would update them on our progress at meetings, and they'd give me a round of applause. I'd smile for a moment and then tense up, thinking of the two-weeks-overdue office rent and our accumulating debts. Every month I paid a fraction on each bill from a long list, trying to remain in good standing. I'd begun to feel a little desperate, especially when I found myself writing a personal check to cover council expenses.

Eventually the council owed me more than $70,000 in expenses and unpaid salary, and the bills were still piling up. I decided to take the weekend off, and went up to Mt. Shasta to do some fly-fishing. I pitched my dome tent at the Ah-di-na Campground along the McCloud River, just up from the Nature Conservancy land. I assembled my four-piece fly rod, put on my waders, dirty boots, and old green vest, and made my way, a wading staff in my other hand, through the trees and into the swiftly flowing river filled with slick boulders.

I worked my way upstream, casting as I went. The night of mountain air and morning of focused fishing gave me perspective on my situation.

By the time I packed up my tent, sleeping bag, and gear and drove home on Sunday, I'd made my decision.

In April I flew to D.C. for a board meeting. This time, as I walked off the plane, my eyes were on the tarmac, not in the clouds. I was no longer wearing "rose-colored glasses."

Once in the boardroom, I passively shook hands with my cohorts. I did not work the room as I had in the past (pumping members with information about our progress and growth). I'm sure everybody there was aware that something had changed in me.

I told them about the dismal state of our finances. "The council can't afford someone at my salary level," I said.

"What are you saying?" Bill King asked quietly.

"I have to step down." I took a deep breath and exhaled for several long seconds. Disappointing people who relied on me tore at my insides. "We'll also have to close the San Francisco office and move our operations to D.C."

The board members exchanged glances. The silence felt like the aftermath of a bomb. I stared at a painting on the wall. It depicted a small whaling ship heading into an enormous wave;

the seamen were being thrown all over the boat, but kept hold of a large whale they'd harpooned.

At Rick's suggestion, the board voted me a nonstaff vice chairman role (instead of president) and lifetime board member. A D.C.-based association management company would oversee the council's operations. They gave me a round of applause for the work I'd done on the council's behalf, and pleaded with me not to abandon my commitment now that I was a dues-paying volunteer. I nodded, but inside I felt deflated.

Immediately after this meeting, I flew to Los Angeles, where my dad was in the hospital recuperating from lung cancer surgery; he'd had half of his left lung removed after forty years of smoking.

Just a month before, he'd flown in his Beechcraft Bonanza up to the Bay Area for a visit. The plane's number read N41RA. Dad's first name is Ira. As I waited on the tarmac, he jumped lightly down the plane's stairs, wearing his old black leather flight jacket that had about a dozen patches from air shows. Shoved up on his head were the headphones he used to talk to the tower. He carried a piss pot, which he handed to me to hold.

Now when I walked into his room, Dad lay in bed in a light-blue hospital robe, his bare legs sticking out. A respirator was taped to his face, a heart monitor beeped away near the bed, and the TV was on. On a side table lay his reading glasses, James Michener's *Space*, and the Airline Owners and Pilots Association magazine, *AAOP Pilot*. Despite his pallor, he looked strong. My mother was asleep in an armchair next to the window, but lifted her head and smiled when I came in. Her face was drawn, and her hair looked like it needed a wash and setting. I could feel the tension in her body when she got up and gave me a long bear hug. Tears rolled down her ashen cheeks. I choked up, but through an effort of will managed not to cry. I couldn't remember the last time I'd cried. It was probably around the time Glenn beat me up for burying his coveted Matchbox racing cars in the sandbox.

I had filled my father in on what had happened with the council. "Now you can go out and make a buck," he said "What's your plan?"

I told him I was again thinking of starting my own green consulting company. That was the best I could come up with, to stay in green building and be independent.

"Well, I wish you well with it," Dad said. "You know consulting provided a wonderful life for me." He stopped and took a deep breath. "But it's important for you to follow your heart." A warm, peaceful feeling surged through me.

"How are you?" I asked.

"I won't be climbing Everest anytime soon, but they think they got all the cancer out. How are you doing?" my father asked me.

"Not so great," I said. "I'm scared." I reached out to grab his hand.

"I don't want you to worry. No matter what happens, I've lived a full life. I have no regrets." More tears started to stream down Mom's face. I wished I could cry, too. "I want you to take care of your mother."

But my father didn't die. Like an old bull, he grew stronger. After his surgery he asked me to fax his clean bill of health to the Federal Aviation Administration so he could get back the pilot's license they'd suspended when he'd been diagnosed. A few years later, he traded in his plane for a good-size motor boat and set a record for his speed in taking the Coast Guard Auxiliary exams — passing about twenty-five different technical exams in his early eighties. The last certification he passed was called Assistant Life Raft Inspector.

I hoped I'd be strong like him when the time came.

10
WHAT NOW?

When I arrived back in San Francisco, I closed the council office and Lynn Simon opened up her own green consultancy. I would work from home—if I found work to do. Each morning I got up and went out for a muffin and coffee on Chestnut Street. I found it hard to walk the block back home and get to work. I had no clients, no projects, and no income.

I worked the phones for a few months, calling just about everyone I knew in green building to see if they had any consulting work for me. Then one day I got a return call from Annette Osso at Public Technology, the nonprofit arm for the National League of Cities, a membership organization comprising hundreds of local governments. Annette managed the environmental program and wanted my help producing a process-oriented book on how to make a green building, to be called *The Sustainable Building Technical Manual*. In addition, she wanted the council to serve as a peer-review entity and to lend its name to the book. The lead funding source was the US Environmental Protection Agency, with additional funds contributed by the US Department of Energy.

And so I landed my first client. I'd be the managing editor for the book and contribute some chapters. My first tasks were to arrange the council's peer review and endorsement and bring in Lynn Simon as my project manager. She knew the content experts we needed to round up in each of the sixteen areas of green building we identified and was good at project management. When it was finished, the manual filled a void, defining the components and process for creating a green building, as we had tried to do in our ASTM standard. It also provided a checklist of recommended strategies and resources, and a few case studies. The book later became a standard for the new industry and went through several rounds of publication.

Then in late 1994, the project of my dreams fell into my lap. I'd been invited to a cocktail party in San Francisco, a gathering of Public Technology's West Coast members hosted by Annette, who was becoming something of an angel in my life. A heavyset fellow in his early sixties sat down next to me. I introduced myself, and he said his name was Rich Hays and that he was director of the Environmental Services Department for the City of San Diego.

"What do you do?" he asked.

"I'm a green building consultant."

"Really! That's a coincidence. I just bought a building for my department and we want to green it."

"Tell me about the building," I said, almost licking my lips in anticipation.

"We bought a vacant building in the Kearny Mesa area of the city. It's about seventy-five thousand square feet and needs a full renovation." He paused. "We've just brought on an architect and some engineers. Green was part of their contract, but tell me how you can help us."

A week later I flew to San Diego at Rich's invitation. I was so excited and nervous that I hadn't been able to sleep the night before. I needed this project, but didn't know what to expect, having never done a green building project from start to finish. As a developer, especially in the early years when I lacked experience, I'd succeeded by identifying and diligently managing the best technical professionals. I hoped I could do the same here.

Chuck Angyal picked me up at the airport. He'd been an active founding board member of USGBC throughout the years. As chief architect and head of new-construction energy-efficiency programs at San Diego Gas & Electric, he would, I knew, be a valuable resource for the project. About ten years older than me and balding, but with an athletic build and can-leap-buildings energy, Chuck wore a flowery tie, the kind an architect would wear. That's when everyone wore ties. His smile was Buddha-like—lighting up all those around him.

As we walked to the car, we had a lot to talk about. In discussing the San Diego Environmental Services Department building project the previous week by phone, Chuck had raised an interesting possibility. He told me that SDG&E had wanted to build an energy demonstration center, but the utility's public-good funds within the state had dried up for such projects. Now, Chuck thought, we might be able to make this building into a mini-energy center, complete with displays and a tour given its high visibility, since it included the building permitting function for the city.

We drove north on the freeway to the tired-looking brick-faced building, which was located at the end of Ridgehaven Court on a hill overlooking Interstate 15. About fifteen years old, it had been vacant since the tenant, General Dynamics, moved out several years before. The building had an east-west exposure, receiving San Diego's strong morning and late afternoon sunlight through its long rows of tall ribbon windows. It had two mirror wings connected by a common lobby on each of its three floors, all of which needed some sprucing up. I'd read the engineering inspection report and knew that all of the systems required replacement: mechanical, electrical, plumbing, fire, and life safety. The city had paid $3 million for the property, totaling only $40 per square foot. That seemed like a good deal to me. However, their $20-per-square-foot budget for the full building renovation was too low. I'd mentioned that to Rich when we last talked on the phone. He said he had other resources if necessary. His department ran the Miramar landfill and collected the waste disposal fees. That gave them a separate source of revenue, as opposed to other agencies that relied solely on the city's general fund. He then told me about the project's tight schedule. The department was leasing space with a termination date less than a year away. The lease called for double rent thereafter.

Chuck and I met Rich and his project manager, Adam Saling, at a construction table set up on the building's first floor. The ceiling tile had already been removed, as had the carpeting, doors, and most of the walls. Rich and Chuck immediately started brainstorming about creating the best green building in the city, a showcase project for the city and the utility. A jolt of energy pulsed through me as I imagined hundreds of people touring the building to learn about the green features I'd helped specify and install. "Did you recycle the demolition debris?" I asked.

"Of course," Adam said. "We're salvaging and recycling almost all of the materials that come out of the building." As the environmental services department, waste reduction was one of their mandates.

Later that morning I met the project architect, Alison Whitelaw, as we toured the building along with several other members of the design team. "I've heard a lot about your work at the council," she said to me in a British accent. Her firm had won the city's bidding competition to become the architect of record for the project. I had worried that, given my late arrival, the project design team would be hostile, since they were fairly far along with the plans, but I needn't have been concerned.

I walked into the first-floor men's room. It would need a full renovation — new tile, floor, fixtures, toilets, paint. It smelled from lack of ventilation, making my stay brief. Next we took the elevator to the top floor. The elevator worked fine, and they planned to keep it intact. The main office space on both sides of the elevator lobby had lots of windows. I breathed a little easier seeing the high level of sunlight penetration into the core of the space. Heat gain through the untinted, single-pane windows would, I imagined, be something of a problem, with the afternoon sun beating on the western façade. Adam later confirmed that the southwest corner offices were more like greenhouses than office space.

I followed the team up the metal ladder to the roof. It was black, with patches everywhere, and needed replacement, as did the old cooling towers, boilers, fans, and motors. "Are you thinking about installing a cool roof and a high level of insulation?" I asked Alison. A cool, or light-colored, roof would incur less heat gain from the sun, which in conjunction with more insulation would mean a lower air conditioning requirement on the top floor.

"That's a good idea," she said. "We hadn't thought about the impact of the roof's color yet."

We clambered back down the ladder to the third floor. "What about the mechanical heat pumps?" I asked, looking up at the inefficient old boxed units mounted to the ceiling.

"We'll buy all new heat pumps but keep the ducting," said Mitch, the mechanical engineer. I had contacts through the council with several of the major manufacturers of heat pumps and thought that I could help out with their specification and purchase. I made a mental note to add procurement assistance to the consulting services I'd pitch later in the day to Rich and Chuck.

"What are your thoughts on lighting?" I asked, surveying the old T12 two-by-four-foot fluorescent fixtures stacked on the floor. I was told that they would be recycled for scrap metal and glass. When I mentioned the new daylighting sensors that dimmed the lights to Pervez Mobin, the electrical engineer, he was enthusiastic.

After the tour, we assembled around the makeshift tables on the first floor. Alison said that the construction drawings were already 75 percent complete. My stomach muscles clenched. That wasn't so great. Rich saw my concern and asked what I was thinking. I told everyone that I thought the building was ideal for a green demonstration project, but that if I came on board the schedule would be set back two months. To my relief, all parties agreed easily to this. Chuck then said that if the building achieved a high level of energy efficiency, with displays installed on the first floor, his utility would pay my bill and even finance the energy upgrades. Rich grinned at this news. It was all I could do to keep myself from jumping up and down.

After the meeting, Rich and Chuck asked me to put together a consulting proposal to make the building into the leading green building demonstration project. "No problem," I said. "I can get it to you next week." I didn't have a clue how to do that.

That night after flying home and climbing into bed, I pulled out *The Earth Summit Strategy to Save Our Planet*, the book summarizing the agreements (known as Agenda 21) made at the 1992 Rio de Janeiro Earth Summit. In the introduction, editor Daniel Sitarz writes: "As humanity approaches the end of the century, it is poised at a crossroads of unmatched magnitude. The very existence of human life on Earth may well depend upon the direction which is taken in the next few years." I looked up and thought, "At least I'm doing my best." We'd make the building green, and we'd cut energy use by at least 50 percent.

I had never bid a project as a green building consultant or hired a green team of outside subcontractors. I called my dad for help, hoping to benefit from his thirty years of consulting experience. He gave me a one-hour crash course that proved invaluable: helping me figure out a scope of work, who to hire for help, deliverables, pricing, and a schedule for our services.

Somehow, despite my doubts, I managed to put together a consulting plan. It called for two brainstorming rounds with the full team; several iterations of energy modeling; life-cycle costing of the energy package; procurement of green items via an industry partnership program that I'd invent; utilization of the utility's custom finance program; ongoing review of the project's plans and specifications; a commissioning review of the finished construction work; and drafting of a green operations manual and a case study at the end of the project. All of this work was pre-LEED, which came out in 1998. Otherwise, the work scope would have included LEED certification.

I identified a good team for the energy component of my consulting work: Clark Bisel at Flack + Kurtz engineers (now part of WSP), and Steve Taylor, who would do the energy modeling and building commissioning. I tacked on the markups as my father suggested and sent off my proposal: $110,000. It seemed like a huge amount to me. If it was accepted, I'd finally be making some money. Even more important, I would have landed my first real green building project.

Chuck called the next week to tell me that the contract had been approved. His firm would split the cost with their membership association, EPRI (Electric Power Research Institute). I was on my way.

Although in future project proposals I would also include the cost of getting technical advice in the selection of green building materials, Alison had already hired Lynn Froeschle for this purpose.

A sufferer from multiple chemical sensitivity (MCS), Lynn was allergic to most traditional building products—adhesives such as carpet glue, the binders used in cabinet substrates, and finishes like paint and varnish. Her charge on the project was to find products that not only were attractive but also had limited toxicity and low volatile organic compound (VOC) emission levels. Later, this focus became part of a bigger field, including what they now call a "red list" of products, something very important to Google, Kaiser Permanente, some governmental agencies, and other progressive companies and professional firms. It was spawned by the Living Building Challenge Rating System.

At our meeting, Chuck's firm had set a target level for energy consumption of 9 kilowatt hours (KWh) per square foot. I didn't even know if that was possible under the best of circumstances, much less given the city's limited budget and a tight schedule. General Dynamics, the last tenant, had operated at an average of 21 KWh per square foot. That meant I had to come up with a 60 percent reduction over previous actual use. I'd asked Clark Bisel what the energy requirements would be under California's Title 24 energy code. He passed the question on to Steve Taylor, who did some analyses and came up with 18 KWh per square foot—still making our goal of 9 KWh a 50 percent reduction relative to the legal standard.

As a result of two brainstorming sessions held in early 1995, we decided to buy new high-efficiency water-source heat pumps, thereby raising efficiency by about 40 percent. We'd install a comprehensive lighting system with both direct (downward-pointing) and indirect (bouncing light off the ceiling) fixtures, using only one light tube (instead of four), an efficient electronic ballast, and both occupancy and daylight sensors. Our lighting goal was 0.73 watt per square foot, over 50 percent less than code. Most of the day, the lights would be powered down, since the extensive daylight would provide plenty of illumination. Clark suggested that we install and link the occupancy sensors with the mechanical system in all large rooms, since unoccupied space does not require lighting or temperature conditioning. Due to San Diego's mild year-round climate, it wasn't necessary to replace the windows with superefficient double-paned windows. Instead we decided to install a solar film made by Llumar on the windows. Now we have dynamic windows that can automatically compensate, going from clear to dark, when the sun and glare levels become too intense.

We'd replace the two rooftop cooling towers with new ones with variable-frequency drives for added control and efficiency. The employee workstations would have adjustable and energy-efficient fluorescent task lights and smart power-surge strips, also with occupancy sensors. Because a good deal of the city's computer equipment was too old to meet the EPA's new ENERGY STAR guidelines, the sensors would help with the old monitors. Any new purchases would be ENERGY STAR compliant. We also set a policy that employees could not install their own space heaters, which consume a lot of power. In any case, if the new heat pumps worked as designed, space heaters wouldn't be necessary.

Efficient lights, window film, and new equipment would lower the building's heat gain, allowing a reduction in the load requirements of the heat pumps. That translated into savings of more than $100,000. We also saved money when we downsized the fluorescent lighting fixtures to single tubes. Now, some years later, I'd suggest LEDs, which are now market ready and becoming cost effective. Taking advantage of the ample daylight streaming in the windows eliminated a quarter of the fixtures.

Next we turned our attention to water use. Our water goal was a 30 percent reduction from the code requirement. We started by installing efficient fixtures in all bathrooms and a waterless urinal, which can save about forty thousand gallons per year for each unit, in the first-floor men's room. Although they use no water, they are reliable and clean. Outside, a mix of indigenous and desert plants meant the landscaping would require minimal watering. We discussed installing a cistern to capture rainwater off the roof, but San Diego's annual rainfall is so low that we couldn't justify the expense. We also talked about installing a dual-plumbing gray-water system to capture sink water, but decided against this, too. We didn't need recycled water for our landscaping, and it would be too expensive to filter it for reuse in the building.

Waste reduction was next. This was an important goal for the building, especially since Rich's department was responsible for both recycling and waste minimization within the city. They'd already salvaged a lot of the original tenant improvements, and the low-bid contractor would be charged with doing the same. Later, a case study was published showing that the project had diverted more than 50 percent of its waste from the landfill — 186 tons of construction debris, for a total cost saving of $93,000. This was a high level at the time, though not many years later it would be considered the minimum, as leading projects in the state began hitting savings figures of more than 90 percent. After the building was completed, ongoing recycling would remain a high priority. For this purpose we included numerous recycling areas and a collection system in the design. The choking of landfills with construction and demolition debris propels local governments and waste agencies into green practices.

Lynn chose products with high recycled content — ceiling tile, drywall, insulation, ceramic bathroom tile, toilet partitions, fiberboard — and products that were themselves recyclable — carpet tiles, walls built for disassembly, movable workstations. When it came to paints, glues, fiberboard, wood finishes, and cleaning materials, she found products that promoted good air quality with minimal off-gassing. We also specified dual air filters and flushing out the building with 100 percent outside air for two weeks after construction to get rid of pollutants resulting from any off-gassing of materials and finishes. Some of the doors and other items would be spray-painted off-site to further lessen contamination of the building itself.

Steve ran a new building energy analysis after we'd made all of our selections. We found that the overall energy consumption projection had fallen to 8.3 KWh per square foot. We'd beaten the goal!

Now we had to figure out how to get the money for all this. The total project construction cost was just over $3 million, plus the previous purchase of the building at another $3 million. The largest budget item was the new HVAC and electrical systems—27 percent of the total cost. Clark and Steve had calculated that the incremental add-on for the higher-level energy items (relative to conventional systems) would cost about $270,000, though they'd pay for themselves in less than three years. The problem was that the city didn't have the funds for the measures we were proposing (a common problem, I later learned). As a result, it was necessary to come up with an alternative method of financing and procurement, something that I named "green finance."

In the realm of energy, we got lucky; SDG&E agreed to finance $230,000 of the $270,000, with a loan that the city would pay back over five years through the savings from the building's monthly energy bill. The remaining $40,000 would be paid by the city. We projected a high rate of return on that relatively minor net investment.

We still had to solve the problem of higher-priced green materials, and for this we created the City of San Diego Ridgehaven Building Industry Partners Program. We persuaded the city attorney to let us sole-source products that had unique environmental performance—meaning, we could purchase directly from individual manufacturers who specialized in certain green product lines. Lynn Froeschle selected the qualifying materials—paint, insulation, floor tile, ceiling tile—while Clark and the project engineers came up with the energy items, such as lighting, sensors, heat pumps, and window film. In return for publicity that included signage in the building and being showcased in a display, we asked that the exclusive manufacturers knock 25 percent off their normal market prices.

I was in charge of designing this program and getting the manufacturers to go for it. To my delight, the task proved relatively easy, and we soon had eight firms signed up. By going straight to the manufacturer, we cut out four levels of markups (the usual supply chain for our industry being from manufacturer to distributor to supplier to subcontractor to contractor to owner), saving about $130,000. This approach also enabled us to skip the public bid process that allows contractors to include in their bids "or equal" substitutions, which often aren't equal in performance.

The city didn't have the money for carpet tile, which is more costly than broadloom carpet. Carpet tile, however, has numerous environmental advantages over traditional carpeting. For one thing, it lasts longer and, because it comes in individual eighteen-by-eighteen-inch squares (as opposed to the twelve-foot-long sections of broadloom), is much less wasteful to replace if it is damaged. It often includes recycled content from old carpet and is itself recyclable. Finally, installation is easy and requires a no-VOC tack strip. In the end, we arranged to sole-source Interface's carpet tile (13 percent postindustrial recycled content) through its five-year Evergreen carpet leasing program—the second building in the country to participate in this innovative plan. The city was happy to divert the $130,000 initial payment, and savings from our energy-efficient design would easily offset the monthly lease payment. Private companies gain an added advantage from such a leasing program, since they can write off the lease payment each year, as opposed to having to amortize the carpet over a longer period. Such an arrangement can work for all types of building products and systems, yet it has rarely been undertaken in the building industry. One key to making leases work is the interest rate embedded in the deal. It has to be equal to or less than the loss of capital.

After we'd finished the plans and specifications, the green renovation project went out to public bid. Alison and her team had written green guidelines for the contractor's waste recycling and salvaging, indoor air quality during construction, and other measures. Unfortunately, the city is required to accept the low bidder, whatever their qualifications in green building. I'd prefer that governmental agencies first start with a request for qualifications and then prepare the ensuing financial bidders' list only from those that are highly skilled in green building. Later, I worked on a State of California project that was able to go with what they called "Best Value," as opposed to lowest price. Best Value can take into consideration obtaining the highest life-cycle measures and associated benefits, and for a given fixed price. This is a smarter approach and can lead to improved building performance, occupant health and productivity, and environmental savings. Low bid creates a setup for future disagreements over change orders.

Some years later, in 2002, I took a tour of the building with Ken Jordan, the engineer selected by the city to monitor the building control system and make sure it worked as designed. The Interface carpet tiles still looked good, as did the environmentally friendly paint from AFM and the ceiling tiles from EuroStone (no man-made fibers, formaldehyde binders, or organic materials). The lighting system from Genlyte/Lightolier was still considered cutting edge. Computer screen glare was minimal due to the bounced light from the ceiling-mounted fixtures. The occupancy sensor went into action when I entered one of the conference rooms, turning on the lights and air conditioning. It would turn them off again when the room was empty for a predetermined period.

After reviewing the six years of operating data that Ken provided, I was ecstatic to see that the building had averaged 8.3 KWh per square foot in energy consumption (the same number Steve Taylor had projected in 1996). During the energy crisis in 2000, when the city's utility rates more than doubled, the building virtually coined money for the city, and it is still saving about $80,000 in energy costs every year. That's about $1.10 per square foot of space. Ultimately, the city achieved a 57 percent internal rate of return on its $40,000 investment. I imagine this was one of their better investments, and it continued to pay dividends for the city. After solar panels were installed in 2003, the annual energy savings increased to about $100,000.

Ken told me that city employees have loved the building. At one point, the city shifted employees who complained about poor air quality in other city buildings into Ridgehaven, and the complaints faded away.

Behind Ridgehaven is a mirror-image sister building occupied by the Sheriff's Department. For five years after we finished Ridgehaven, it was the same on the surface, but without our green elements—and we used the energy consumption in that building as a baseline to gauge our building's performance. Whereas we had cut our utility costs by more than half, the other building continued paying the full bill. A few years ago, they'd had enough of our showing them up and renovated the building, incorporating many of our green features.

According to the city, the new building's water-efficient appliances and landscaping save approximately five hundred thousand gallons of water each year, 45 percent more than before. The reduced electricity consumption has lowered CO_2 emissions by about 500 tons annually, SO_2 by 1.4 tons, and NOx by 1.3 tons.

As a demonstration project, about seven thousand enthusiasts visit Ridgehaven each year, from more than forty-five countries. Other San Diego city buildings went green, and in 1997 the mayor passed a green building ordinance. The city later adopted the U.S. Green Building Council's green building rating system at the Silver level. We had proven that green building could be achieved even with the constraints of a city budget, a tight schedule, and city low-bidder procurement laws.

As Ken and I walked through the lobby, I spotted a thirty-foot cabinet filled to bursting with environmental awards and trophies the building had won. Among them was the US Department of Energy and US Environmental Protection Agency's ENERGY STAR Building Label: Ridgehaven was the first building in the country to receive that coveted award. It also won the governor's environmental award for California, AIA's top ten green buildings in the United States, and about twenty others.

Ridgehaven taught me that finishing a successful green building is like competing in an Ironman triathlon. After the open-ocean 2.4-mile swim, you have a 112-mile bike ride, and then you finish with a full marathon. The goal is not merely to participate in the race, but to cross the finish line. With Ridgehaven, as with most projects I later learned, we moved two steps forward and one step back throughout the project. Money was always an issue. At one point Rich went to the City Council for more money and was turned down. We did get the money later, with the help of SDG&E—and even later, not surprisingly, the mayor and the City Council had no qualms about accepting the ENERGY STAR Building Award.

My next project, in 1995, was among the first demonstration green buildings for the US Navy, its Building 33 in southwest Washington, D.C., along the waterfront. I assembled a small green team that helped me advise the designers on energy systems and green building materials. The former gun turret plant was being renovated into a 150,000-square-foot four-story office building. It turned out to be another award-winning green building, with a high level of performance—30 percent below a conventionally renovated building, with $135,000 a year in energy savings. The payback period for the incremental energy investment was less than one year. Its features included Heat Mirror high-efficiency glazing, insulation with an R-value of 30, light sensors, and low-VOC building finishes. The building's energy-efficient design provided for a reduction in the conventional HVAC system by 36 percent, resulting in $200,000 of first-cost savings. Afterward, an order stipulated that all future Navy construction projects be green as well.

Next was the conversion of Kansas City's 1914 Union Station into a science museum, restoring the structure back to its original glory. My client was Kansas City Power & Light, which tried to copy my arrangement with San Diego Gas & Electric on the Ridgehaven project. They paid my fee and then donated my services to the museum's development and design team as a customer benefit. The utility also wanted to make the million-square-foot building into a showcase for renewable energy and other state-of-the-art energy systems. However, in contrast to the Ridgehaven situation, where the city was a determined advocate, in this case the owner wasn't able to embrace green building. The project was strictly cost and schedule driven. I led a green brainstorming session for the entire team, but few of my green team's suggestions were adopted. It was a frustrating experience after the success of Ridgehaven, especially given the opportunity that the building's history and intended use offered. Years later, the developer turned on the "green building light" and advanced the industry through active leadership. It often takes time to change standard practice, including having the right personnel on a given project.

In late 1996 a woman named Kath Williams approached me at the annual USGBC conference, held that year in San Diego. "I want to know everything you know about green building," she said. "We're going to set the standard for university green building." Kath, it turned out, was the project manager for a new campus laboratory building (later named EpiCenter) to be built at Montana State University. She told me that she was finishing up a PhD in education at MSU and had also taught at Stanford. As tall as I was, and probably stronger, she had a bold voice, thick glasses, and curly brown hair. I got the impression that whatever she wanted, she got. She had heard my keynote address at the conference, had toured Ridgehaven, and now was interested in having me fly out to meet the top brass of the university. I already knew something about the project, since Montana State University was one of the five NIST grantees for the congressional green building demonstration program several years earlier. They had gone on to receive several rounds of additional funding from Congress.

The next month I arrived in freezing Bozeman. I joined Bob Berkebile, the lead architect for the new building, and his young architect, Jason McLennan. Bob and I had first met through his leadership at the AIA Committee on the Environment. A broad-based team had already been assembled for the project—one that included many of my colleagues from the council—and several design charrettes (intensive and integrated team brainstorms) had been conducted over the previous two years.

I was delighted to have the opportunity to work with Bob. His team's vision for the project was decidedly forward-looking: fuel cells that ran off hydrogen generated by a solar-powered water-splitting machine, solar algae ponds to treat wastewater from the lab on-site, unprecedented levels of daylighting, locally sourced materials, low-energy fume hoods for the labs, wireless equipment, an enormous vision wall for students to observe ongoing lab experiments, and dozens of other innovations. The team wanted this to be the global model for campus green building.

I worked for MSU for the next two years, and helped put together an industry partnership program that was adopted by the state. But the project soon ran into problems. As the team's wish list grew ever longer, the budget fattened. The university simply didn't have the name, infrastructure, or experience to raise so much money. Meanwhile, the only new funding that had come in was a multimillion-dollar technology innovation grant, given by Congress as the last installment in the demonstration program funding. All of us consultants were paid out of the congressional funds when the university flew us in for a dozen or more meetings. Much of the rest of the money was spent on mapping local materials resources, developing the technology for the low-energy fume hood, and the closed-loop energy system for converting water into hydrogen fuel—fantastic ideas, but probably not the best use of the limited project budget.

In the meantime, I did the work I'd been hired to do: bringing thirty companies to the university to partner at a 25 percent product-cost discount, and working with Kath to get the industry partnership program that I'd drafted passed by the governor. But I couldn't help make the project happen. Due to financing problems, it was clear that my work was fruitless, and that didn't feel right. As a team we'd done what my dad always advised against: confused effort with results. But that's OK. We had pushed the bar forward. Sometimes it takes failures to get quantum leaps in results, and sometimes efforts become results. It's not always possible to succeed when a high level of risk is involved. After all, venture capitalists remain highly profitable hitting about a one in ten return on their company investments.

Shortly afterward, the university put the project on hold. The university's allocated project funds were used in renovation of its main library and the student union, and a portion was returned to the university's general fund. The team's inventions were published in a report by NIST with a CD-ROM, so others can benefit from the hard work and creativity of the team. Some of the prototyped technologies are still operating as MSU's nearby technology office park. However, the green passion remained, as faculty members developed new green research projects and several students graduated and formed a construction waste management company. Kath finished her PhD at the university and went on to open her own green building consulting firm. Just after we started working together she joined the USGBC board of directors as our university representative. Her strong take-charge approach and people skills led her to become one of our two vice chairs and helped push through our research and education agendas. The rest of us went on to do more projects, using many of the innovations we arrived at through our creative brainstorming and extensive technical research for MSU. One of the resulting highlights was Jason McLennan's creation of the Living Building Challenge out of many of the project principles we'd brainstormed. The new rating system introduced the concept of a building with net-zero energy, waste, and water usage, as well as other important health-related performance metrix, extending the reach of best practice for the industry.

In September 1997 I visited my parents for Rosh Hashanah services at University Synagogue in Los Angeles. Before having a family of my own, I'd go home for one of the two Jewish high holidays each year to honor my parents, listen to the beautiful voice of the cantor, and say hello to some old friends. Years later, temple would take on greater meaning to our family, as a way to build our community and slow down on Shabbat. We're all so busy. At least one day a week it is nurturing to stop.

After the holidays, I went over to pitch new consulting work to the City of Santa Monica. The year before, I'd put in a bid to the city to develop green building guidelines, but lost to a lower bidder. Still, that bidding process had allowed me to become friendly with Susan Munves, the city's environmental manager. Her office was on the Santa Monica Pier, where I'd learned to fish at twelve, riding my bike from our house in the hills near Mount Saint Mary's College, just behind the J. Paul Getty Museum.

Susan and I eventually did start working together, after I'd dreamed up a new program called BuildingFutures, based on the Ridgehaven success. Its focus was on optimizing the development process in five steps: (1) project definition and management, (2) identification of best-practice design areas, (3) life-cycle investment, (4) building performance assurance, and (5) communication of results. The main feature was BuildingCamp, a highly interactive brainstorm session. It was my version of the green charrettes that projects now included, but it was results driven. Susan wanted me to do a BuildingCamp for Santa Monica's new $30 million public safety facility. The project was just getting under way, and the city wanted to showcase its new green building guidelines.

The site was tightly sandwiched between City Hall and the Santa Monica Freeway. It was hard for me to imagine a multistory 150,000-square-foot building and parking deck going up here, but that was the plan. The new complex would house the city's police, fire, and public safety departments, as well as a jail, shooting range, cafeteria, and offices.

Susan had arranged for me to meet her boss, Craig Perkins, head of Public Works, to discuss the project. The morning of our meeting was just perfect: the sun was shining brightly, and there was a fresh ocean breeze. As I walked along Palisades Park, a grassy stretch studded with huge palm trees, I was transported back to my childhood and the picnics my family used to have there. In those days, one could hear Spanish, Yiddish, Russian, and Hebrew all along the greensward.

When I arrived at Craig's office, Susan was sitting at his conference room table with a cup of coffee, and Craig was on the phone at his desk. He was slender and fit, his wiry energy making him pace back and forth during the call. "Tell him I want it done by tomorrow," he said to the party on the phone. "He's had enough time." Craig hung up, but before I could say hello, his secretary bolted in to give him his messages. "Tell George I can't meet this afternoon. I'm in hearings."

Finally he turned to me. "How can you help us with our project?"

Great. There was a fish there, but how was I going to land it? "Go steady, David," I told myself, then launched into my sales pitch, outlining the services I'd developed for BuildingFutures. I handed Craig a copy of the booklet, hot off the presses, explaining the program. The cover resembled a blueprint, light blue with a thin line drawing showing the C. K. Choi Building at the University of British Columbia, solar panels perched on the roof (something I still hoped to see installed in one of my projects). Craig flipped through the booklet, nodding his head. Then he went to the white board and began scribbling categories for the environmental goals of the new public safety building: energy, water, and waste. "What levels do you suggest?" he asked.

"A 50 percent reduction for energy, 30 for water, and 75 percent waste diversion," I said. Today I'd push for much higher goals, but that was 1997 and green building was still nascent. The pilot for LEED hadn't been released yet and was still in committee.

The meeting was relatively brief but dense. Craig asked good questions, and my answers apparently satisfied him because I went home with a new client. He'd bought the full menu of services, including my first BuildingCamp and green procurement assistance.

On this job I needed even more outside expert help than I had at Ridgehaven. I retained Anthony Bernheim, an architect with SMWM Architects (which later merged with Perkins + Will), whose San Francisco Public Library project had been a pioneer in green building, featuring significantly boosted daylighting and indoor air quality. I also retained Malcolm Lewis, president of Constructive Technologies Group, to do energy modeling, indoor air and systems analysis, and peer review of the drawings. Both Anthony and Malcolm became frequent participants in many of my future projects.

I opened a new office in downtown San Francisco on New Montgomery, right at Mission, a small tenth-floor suite with a view of the bay. I installed Interface carpet tiles, AFM paint, and efficient lights with sensors. More projects came in: the Marin Community Foundation, Starbucks, DreamWorks, and a high-rise residential development for Kent Swig. I hired staff to help out.

11
USGBC CPR

The association management companies that we'd brought in to take my place running the U.S. Green Building Council didn't work out. Members were not renewing, complaints were rising. Eighteen months passed as I continued building my consulting business.

"Can you meet me in L.A. for dinner next week?" It was April 1996, and Rick Fedrizzi, who was still chairman of the council, was on the phone. He was flying out for a Carrier meeting from his base in Syracuse.

"What's up?"

"I'll tell you when we get together." Something in his tone alerted me that this was not going to be a purely social dinner. Was it his job at Carrier, or his family? The council?

At seven sharp I walked into the Ivy at the Shore, located on the beach in Santa Monica. As I waited for Rick in the entry area, watching the hustle and bustle of the decked-out patrons and fast-moving staff at the lively restaurant he'd selected, I wondered if I'd changed since leaving L.A. at 18—half my age. I was still single and didn't yet own a home. But Stanford, my D.C. real estate years, and now the promise of green building were part of my story.

When Rick came into the restaurant, he grinned and came over to give me a bear hug. We caught up over the meal. He was about to celebrate his eighteenth wedding anniversary, and his two kids were growing up fast. Even though we were only five years apart in age, I reflected sadly that I had yet to begin that part of my life.

When they brought dessert and coffee, Rick leaned back in his chair and looked away. "I'm going to tell you something you're not going to want to hear," he said, as if announcing an omen to come. "Don't get angry."

I put down my fork, a chunk of chocolate cake still clinging to it. "I'm listening." I inhaled deeply and leaned forward. A waiter hurried by with a loaded tray of clanking dishes.

"If you don't come back to run the council, we'll be bankrupt in a month," Rick said.

Words of protest rushed to my lips, but I had promised to listen. The spicy taste of tandoori chicken rose in my gullet.

"The management company is killing what you, Mike, and I created."

"It's out of the question, Rick. The first round almost killed me," I said.

"You can call the shots," Rick pleaded. "Just let me know what you need and I'll make it happen."

"No," I said.

As we parted to go to our cars, Rick again said, touching me on the shoulder, "Think about it, Buddy. You know you love it."

Later that night I got into bed at my parents' house in L.A. The ceiling of my old bedroom still looked like cottage cheese. I wondered who'd invented that. Grandpa Izzy's vinyl sofa chair stood in the corner; it had cracks running all through it and was faded to a light plum color. Mom would never give that old thing away. I finally fell asleep, and soon I was having a familiar nightmare. I was at the council board table in D.C. Our vice chairman was yelling at me, "I told you, we'll help you with fundraising when you get our policies and procedures manual in order, and your buddy Mike in line!"

Everyone else looked out for themselves. Why couldn't I? I was finally making money, and at what I wanted: greening buildings. Why did I need to do anything more for the council? Hadn't I done enough already? At 6 a.m. I finally gave up trying to sleep and went for a run around Mount Saint Mary's College, beating my previous time by five minutes. Then I showered and called Rick at his hotel along the beach in Santa Monica.

"I knew you couldn't say no," Rick said when I told him I'd accept.

"I'm going to keep my consulting business. The council will have to be a client of my company," I said.

"Whatever you want."

Over the next few months I moved quickly to stabilize the council. I assigned two of my staff members to it full time and personally called all the members who hadn't renewed their annual dues (about 40 percent of our 125 members). I nominated board members to take on critical committee assignments: the building rating system we'd been developing, our stalled upcoming annual conference, the jump-start of our state and local government committee. We hadn't selected a location for our annual conference, so I chose San Diego, given my connections with the city and SDG&E, with the lure of the Ridgehaven building as a place to tour. Since we were broke, Chuck got SDG&E to pay $15,000 in advance registration for fifty of his program's building owners to attend.

In mid-1996 I flew to Washington for a board meeting. The day before the meeting, Mike and I met for dinner at Meskerem, my favorite Ethiopian restaurant, in Adams Morgan. Having settled on large pillows on the wood floor, we ordered a couple of Ethiopian beers. We'd share food from a large round plate, eating it with our hands, using flat injera bread to scoop up the spiced vegetables and tender beef and lamb. The weather was hot and humid, and we were both wearing shorts. Mike had on a patterned Hawaiian shirt, and I wore a golf shirt from Bajamar, a great course ninety minutes south of the border in Mexico. It was one of Chuck's favorites, and we'd played there a few times.

When our second round of beer arrived, I glanced over at Mike. "You need to let the pollution taxes effort go, Mike. It's not worth it."

He put his beer down. "Who got to you?"

"No one in particular. Everyone thinks the timing is still premature." Mike studied the colorful pattern of an adjacent pillow. I'd hurt my friend. "It's the wrong time. We've got to revive the council first." I listened to the melodic Ethiopian music on the loudspeaker for what seemed like an entire song.

"I understand," Mike said at last. He took a long pull from his bottle of beer. "Another time," he said. I breathed a sigh of relief.

12
LEED ROLLS OUT

Rob Watson, our board member from NRDC, took over the leadership of the building rating system committee. In 1997 he'd arranged for an initial grant of $200,000 from the US Department of Energy (DOE), under the leadership of Mark Ginsberg, for a rating system pilot program. During the next two years, DOE added another $600,000. The committee gave the rating system the catchy name of LEED—Leadership in Energy and Environmental Design. It provided a point system that is sophisticated, yet easy to use. LEED quickly became both a powerful building design guideline and a certification system for commercial new construction and major renovation. It is also effective for use in brainstorming sessions on project greening, a game of sorts.

While using the pilot version of LEED to rate a prospective project, the goal was to earn the highest number of points in six defined environmental categories: Sustainable Sites (14 points possible), Water Efficiency (5 points), Energy and Atmosphere (17 points), Materials and Resources (13 points), Indoor Environment Quality (15 points), and Innovation and Design Process (5 points). There are four levels of awards distributed according to the number of LEED points earned by the project: Platinum–a minimum of 52 points (out of 69 total); Gold–39;

Silver–33; and Certified–26. These relative points levels changed in later versions of LEED.

Obtaining LEED certification requires registering a building project with the council and then, after the project is completed, submitting an application with supporting data to USGBC. It's a complicated and lengthy information-gathering and documentation process that the whole team supports. Buildings are given a certificate and LEED plaque at the award level achieved, once approved by the council. The idea was that building owners would proudly mount the plaque on the outside of the building, or display it prominently in the lobby.

LEED provides the green building benchmarks, but doesn't tell applicants how to get the points; that's up to the team. For example, a building project can earn one point for using 20 percent less water than the minimum set by the Energy Policy Act of 1992, while a 30 percent reduction tacks on another point. Generating a minimum savings of 5 percent of energy through on-site renewable energy systems is worth one point, 10 percent adds another, and 30 percent yet another. The most cost-effective points are those for energy-efficient performance (receiving four to six of ten available points, the most of any credit category). Additional credits are earned for installing renewable energy into the project and developing a building monitoring and verification plan, including continuous equipment metering. Materials credits are achieved for reusing an existing building, managing construction waste, and specifying building materials that include recycled content or are local or rapidly renewable. Indoor environmental quality credits are earned for actions such as specifying low-emitting construction materials, providing for occupant thermal comfort, and maximizing daylight penetration into the building.

Soon after it was rolled out, LEED inspired a type of green building Olympics, with cities and private projects unofficially competing to see who could earn the highest LEED award. The federal government was one of the first to require its use for some of its leading agency projects. The US Navy mandated a LEED Silver level, as did the City of Seattle for civic buildings. Dozens of other cities adopted the system, including New York, Los Angeles, San Diego, and Portland, Oregon. The council posted the LEED guidelines on its website so that building professionals could download them for free.

I began using LEED on all of my consulting projects, starting with Santa Monica's public safety facility. A few years later, I used it as a multiproject design tool for Foothill-DeAnza Community College District. I was hired to help develop a sustainable design strategy for their two campuses with nine building projects being designed at the same time. In April 2001 we assembled one hundred professionals, representing all of the district's project design teams, as well as district staff and some students, in one large room at DeAnza College. Day one was dedicated to setting district-wide campus greening goals, while day two was entirely LEED focused.

On the second morning, the assembled teams brainstormed their way through LEED's credits in each category. I bounced from team table to team table. "Team One got six points for a 30 percent reduction in energy from code," I said to Team Three. "How come you guys are projecting a measly 10 percent reduction?" Team Three would then vow to beat Team One, redoubling its efforts.

Afterward, I reassembled the full group and had each team call out its LEED points in each of the six categories. The wildly different answers led to a dynamic competition that made everyone hot to beat the others. As I watched the participants (including the presidents of both colleges and the district chancellor) eagerly debating the merits of a higher energy efficiency level, on-site generation of renewable energy, and a higher level of waste diversion from the landfill, I felt chills moving through my body, and goose bumps on my arms beneath my tailored blue oxford shirt. Yes! This was my dream, I said to myself as I pumped my fist. I recalled a meeting seven years earlier in the AIA boardroom, when as a younger man, I had nervously presented my white paper on the need for a US building rating system to sixty professionals.

LEED soon became the standard definition for a green building in the United States. It did what we'd hoped to do years before in the ASTM Green Building Subcommittee. In two words, a concerned party could communicate a new building's or a city's green performance level, as Seattle's Mayor Paul Schell did in 2000 when he announced (at one of our board meetings hosted by the City in Seattle) his goal of LEED Silver for all new building projects in the city. That kicked off a competition among cities, states, and federal government agencies to use LEED as a benchmark and in many cases, a requirement. They'd offer incentives for private projects to use LEED at a specified level, such as Arlington County, Virginia, which offered the option of extra density, or in later years, an investment tax credit in New York State and a real estate tax credit in Nevada. In time, the list of participating agencies grew to the hundreds.

That all happened once the LEED program was well under way. The early years of the process, however, required some fine-tuning. When the first few LEED applications were submitted to the council, we were shocked at their size: each application write-up was a foot thick, bound in several large notebooks. Apparently the LEED documentation requirements were burdensome, and led green building professionals to charge owners high fees for collecting, verifying, and organizing the data—a cost that naturally made building owners unhappy. The council took note, and the fees came down a bit with the release of version 2.1, which included time-saving standard templates in which the professionals could certify that the given LEED minimums had been met. Over the years, things became more streamlined.

Eventually the council built up the LEED program into a full suite of products: training courses with approved faculty, LEED reference guides, an extensive LEED website, and a LEED professional accreditation exam. Soon I began seeing "LEED AP" (Accredited Professional) on members' business cards, letterhead, and marketing materials. It made my heart swell with contentment. I, too, took and passed the LEED AP exam, on the theory that I should practice what I preach. Years later, USGBC added a LEED Fellow designation that was difficult to earn, creating an elite cadre of LEED experts. USGBC also built in a continuing education requirement as a prerequisite for AP accreditation maintenance and offered a lower level entry: LEED Green Associates.

By 2003, LEED had become the key to the greening of America's buildings. Its use had also spread overseas. Even private companies such as Ford, Toyota, Pottery Barn, Pier 1 Imports, PNC Bank, Adobe, Office Depot, and Starbucks used it. However, one of the greatest barriers to green building lay in obtaining accurate information on costs. In 2003 the council and a private consulting firm, Capital E (run by my good friend Greg Kats), surveyed thirty-three green buildings and found the average cost increase for the LEED-certified buildings (certified through Platinum levels) was only 2 percent. Seattle and the State of Pennsylvania, where LEED Silver was required by law for public buildings, reported almost no cost increase as they gained increasing project-based LEED experience. The study showed that the cost of green has been coming down every year, falling 38 percent from 1995 to 2003. With more experience using LEED, the cost can fall further, and even more importantly, buildings can receive a high annual return on the relatively small incremental investment.

Though most of the savings in green building come from improved energy and water efficiency, studies by the Rocky Mountain Institute and Joseph Romm in his book *Lean and Clean Management* found that in six green projects, employee productivity (including reductions in absenteeism) rose anywhere from 6 to 16 percent. Each year, employers pay more in salary than an entire building costs to construct. Over the course of thirty years for an owner-occupied building, Romm notes, only 3 percent of the total cost outlay is for the building's up-front design and construction, 6 percent goes for ongoing building operations, while 91 percent pays building-occupant employee salaries. A productivity increase of just 1 percent is double the savings of the entire annual energy bill; at 6 percent, the productivity savings is almost the same as an average rental payment. Occupant health and productivity represent the smoking gun of green building, but are hard to measure.

In the early years of green building, it was difficult to define and source out "sustainable products." LEED's credits helped here, too. Soon, leading manufacturers were informing architects and building owners about their products' contributions to LEED credits. The council has always steered away from certifying products as "green," but LEED did provide a measure of guidance to the marketplace. Most of the council's manufacturer members have gone on to introduce sustainable products. When Armstrong came out with a ceiling tile recycling program initiated on a Microsoft project while working with one of our board members at Selen Construction (the project's construction manager), I felt like a proud parent. They had introduced a revolutionary product that would not only make the world a better place, but also save the client money.

LEED allowed me to lower my consulting fees. Before the program was instituted, I was often hired to define "green building" for a fee that could top $100,000. Afterward, I was hired to implement LEED, rather than having to start from ground zero by defining it. It took the mystery out of green building. Now many mainstream design teams are thoroughly versed in LEED and green building, limiting the need for green building consultants. I consider this a sign of success.

No one could have predicted the enormous impact of LEED on the global marketplace. Rob Watson and the hundreds of other LEED committee volunteers are to be thanked, as well as governmental agencies that mandated the standard. And the thousands of pioneering building owners and teams of dedicated professionals who promoted and advanced its use helped build an entirely new green building industry with the LEED standard as its foundation and the glue that holds it together.

13
GROWING UP

In the summer of 1996, Ray Anderson, chairman of Interface carpet tile company and a man known as the "green CEO," put on a conference in San Francisco called "The Power of One." A hundred top building industry professionals and environmental leaders from around the Bay Area were there. He had asked seven environmentalists to speak; two of them were my idols. David Brower was the first executive director of the Sierra Club; had started four other environmental groups, including Friends of the Earth and Earth Island Institute; and had written four books. And Paul Hawken was the author of the best seller The *Ecology of Commerce*, and later *Natural Capitalism*, which he coauthored with Amory and Hunter Lovins, and *Blessed Unrest*. Visionary, concise, and able to speak the language of business and merge it with environmental needs, he is, for my money, the best speaker in the green movement.

But I wasn't there for the pleasure of hearing these towering figures speak. I was supposed to get up on the same stage with these guys!

I had only a month to prepare. When I asked our sponsor what I should talk about, Nanci Scoular of Interface froze my blood by saying, in her South African accent, "Daaavid, we want you to talk about yourself. What drives you? Why did you quit development and start the council?"

I'd never been asked to speak about myself before. No pictures of green buildings or PowerPoint slides to hide behind, no building case studies to present. Just me. I was terrified.

The night before the event, I filled a sheet of paper with crossed-out thoughts. What could I possibly have to say that these people would want to hear? Somehow, I wanted to talk about life, point out that it's short. I wanted to tell them the planet is our only home, and we need to take care of it. It was nothing they hadn't heard before, but these were the ideas that stirred my soul.

The next morning, still not at all sure what I was going to say, I sat in the third row, mesmerized. "What we are all missing are operating instructions for the Earth," David Brower was saying. "I propose CPR—Conservation, Preservation, and Restoration." At eighty-four, with a full head of gray hair and bushy eyebrows, he was the elder statesman of the environmental movement. In his prime, he had climbed the world's highest mountains alone (with sixty first ascents); now, a large stooped figure in old-fashioned walking shoes, slanting a bit to the right at the podium, he still conveyed that same energy and passion. His blue eyes radiated hope and enthusiasm.

David spoke about turning the lights on for our future. He told his famous World War II story, about a time when turning lights on had saved his life. The war had just ended, and when the sun went down, the Germans began to shell David's battalion (the infamous 10th Mountain Division). Clearly, the Germans hadn't heard the news. So in order to avoid further casualties, David's unit turned on the headlights of their vehicles. No one had ever consciously done this while in battle. No doubt realizing that something odd was going on, the Germans ceased their fire.

When David finished speaking, I stood and clapped with the rest until my hands hurt. Then they were calling my name.

I blundered up to the podium on autopilot, taking in as much air as possible, then slowly letting it out. I'm sure the audience could hear the air hiss from my lungs over the large overhead black speakers. The video camera operator flipped a switch, and the light changed from red to green. I was on.

I put my hands in my pockets and looked out at all the upturned faces. My silence had captured their attention. I could hear plates being cleared in a room across the hall. The air conditioning system was humming. I looked up at the skylight twelve stories up and took a deep breath.

"It's not too late," I began, and immediately felt the words start to come, start to tumble from my mouth. I went on, hardly knowing what I said. All I did know was that my heart was full, and as I spoke, heads were nodding all over the room. I finished with a quote from one of my favorite Jewish scholars, Abraham Joshua Heschel:

> As a tree torn from the soil, as a river separated from its source, the human soul wanes when detached from what is greater than itself.
>
> Without the holy, the good turns chaotic; without the good, beauty becomes accidental.
>
> It is attachment to what is spiritually superior: loyalty to a sacred idea, devotion to a noble friend or teacher, love for one's people or for humankind, which holds our inner life together.
>
> Unless we aspire to the utmost, we shrink into inferiority.

The applause was loud, the audience on its feet. Ray Anderson came over and hugged me. Then a dozen others did. "I love the way you think," David Brower said as he wrapped his huge arms around me and squeezed. Wow. Incredible. Something huge had happened, but I wasn't sure what.

By mid-1999, membership in the council was growing (it hit 250 that May) as was interest in the LEED green building rating system. Since the San Diego conference three years earlier, Kristin Ralph Douglas had run the council's day-to-day activities, first out of my office on New Montgomery Street in San Francisco, and then out of new offices at 110 Sutter Street, where I had a seventh-floor suite and she had set up the council's office on the fourth floor. Two other staff members helped out, but we were always shorthanded.

"You need to be more constructive with me," Kristin blurted out one evening at the office. I'd been admonishing her to bring in more members and make more public appearances. She tended to stay in the office with her head in the paperwork. "I'm doing my best. If you think we need someone else for the job, then bring in somebody," Kristin went on. She was red and shaking. She looked tired, as if she hadn't slept for a week.

I stared at my shoes, keeping silent.

On my drive home, I realized that I'd pushed Kristin as far as I could. She'd done a tremendous job, but the council needed something more. I was spending time I didn't have supervising her instead of dedicating it to my clients.

The next day I wrote a memo to the board, saying it was time we brought in a president (we hadn't had one since I'd resigned from that role in 1994). I showed it to Kristin, hoping desperately that she wouldn't quit. Without her, we wouldn't have an organization worthy of bringing in a president.

When she finished reading it, she looked up. "I've always wanted what's best for the council. Send it out."

Several months later, in late 1999, the board assembled in San Francisco for a quarterly meeting. We'd rented the Carnelian

Room, on the top — 52nd — floor of the Bank of America building near the council's offices. Everyone was in a good mood; we were excited to see each other, the panoramic views of the city below were spectacular, the coffee and the food were good. But the cause of our good spirits went beyond that.

Steven Winter, our newly elected chairman who'd just replaced Rick Fedrizzi after his six-year reign as our founding chairman, nodded at a smiling woman sitting to his right at the board table. "Our new president and CEO, Christine Ervin," he announced. Everyone clapped and beamed. Kristin was clapping, too. Christine, who was in her midforties, had been President Clinton's Assistant Secretary of Energy, overseeing nearly a thousand employees. Before that, she'd been the director of energy for Oregon.

She'd spoken in 1996 at our third annual green building conference in San Diego, an event we cohosted with AIA and NIST. "I envision every building as its own renewable power plant," she'd said then; and now, stepping gracefully into her new role, she said, "The council has always been dear to my heart. I'm flattered and excited to lead this incredible organization and group of pioneers into the next century."

14
PUSHING LIMITS

In June 1998 a new office tower was being designed for California's EPA headquarters in downtown Sacramento. The twenty-five-story building totaled more than one million square feet and would take up an entire city block. As reported in the *Los Angeles Times*, many people wondered whether the building would be green.

One day, I received a call from the office of state Assemblywoman Deborah Bowen. The state wanted to hire me. It took me several seconds to find my voice. I couldn't have been more flabbergasted if I'd seen a hundred-foot-long purple dinosaur float past my tenth-floor window. The biggest new public building in California, and I was being asked to steer it green!

Unfortunately, I got so caught up in my messianic passion that I came very close to screwing up the project and jeopardizing my consulting future with the state.

The state's Department of General Services issued a press release announcing my contract: "Gottfried is a leader in environmental design. We are pleased to bring such forward-thinking people with expertise on environmentally smart buildings into this process," Cal/EPA Secretary Peter Rooney was quoted as saying.

I hired the largest green team I'd ever assembled — two energy experts, two green architects, and my own cost estimator. I wasn't going to hold back on this one, even if it meant I didn't make any money. I asked my team to develop three levels of green: ideal, middle of the road, and low. Of course, I wanted ideal.

Thomas Development Partners (TDP)—later renamed Thomas Properties Group, a major firm based in L.A.—was the developer. Jim Thomas was a friend of Governor Pete Wilson's and owner of the Sacramento Kings NBA basketball team. His company had already been working on the project for years before I came along. The building's exterior and base building design, after many hearings, had been publicly approved. That made it nearly impossible to change.

TDP had an agreement with the state providing for shared savings from any cost reductions below the guaranteed maximum price of $170 million. The last thing in the world they wanted was me in there driving the costs up. But that was something that, initially, I deliberately cast aside. I was all about green, and the more the better, especially for my state's flagship environmental headquarters building. I envisioned another *Los Angeles Times* article, several years out: "The State's Greenest Building." The photo would show a fuel cell on the grass roof, with translucent photovoltaic solar cells integrated into the façade. Naturally, there would be a picture of me as well that talked about "green" results in a language that would make my father proud.

"This is the one," I told my green team on a conference call. "I want all of your most creative ideas." Our initial building energy analysis showed that the building as designed was at 24 percent below the energy code. I was surprised it was that efficient—the state and TDP team must have made energy a priority. However, it only scored fourteen LEED (version 1) points, twelve short of the lowest certification level. We could boost that score, we discovered, by redesigning some systems and going stringently green with the tenant improvements, which hadn't yet been designed.

My team soon had developed several different plans for the building. One of them hit LEED Gold, increasing energy efficiency to 41 percent below code with the help of an underfloor air distribution system, solar cells, a fuel cell, and individually tuned windows on every side of the building. We'd even brainstormed a mechanical solar tracking panel on the roof that would follow the sun's movement during the day.

Then John Goleman phoned. He was the state's Department of General Services manager for the project and my client. To my surprise, he wanted to come over the next day to talk to me. I'd been sketchy about keeping him up to date on our work, and I hadn't gotten around to mentioning my goal of hitting LEED Gold. (I'd read the state's design-build agreement with TDP, and the contractual references requiring Thomas' creation of a green building were weak, requiring only a "best efforts" approach. In my experience, that type of language never added up to much.)

John showed up at my office at around three the next afternoon. He sat stiffly at the Italian glass conference table, his arms crossed. "What are your plans for the brainstorm?" he asked.

I told John that we'd come up with three tiers of alternatives and were going to recommend LEED Gold. He gasped. "David," he said, "most of the building is already designed. We've been working on it for five years." I sat back in my chair and bit the end of my pen so hard I thought the ink would squirt into my mouth. "The only thing open for consideration is the tenant improvements. They haven't been designed yet."

"The building should have an underfloor air distribution system, more efficient glazing, and a higher level of insulation," I countered. "It's a good investment over the life of the building. The underfloor air system boosted energy efficiency by 8 percent in our Santa Monica project. It also improves indoor air quality and user flexibility."

He visibly struggled to stay calm. "That's out of the question."

I turned red with rage. "Assemblywoman Bowen brought me in to do a good job. I'd hoped that you would give me the latitude to do that." I was struggling with my own anger now, let down that I'd be unable to deliver a showcase green building.

"You work for me," John said.

There was silence. Out of the corner of my eye I saw a red and white tanker glide up the bay. "Do you know Joe Rodota?" I asked. Joe was deputy chief of staff for the governor. We'd met twenty years ago at Stanford, and I'd last run into him in 1990 skiing in Vail. "Joe's an old fraternity brother of mine. I assume you know that Anne Sheehan is his wife?" (Anne was acting secretary of the State and Consumer Services Agency. Her immediate boss was the governor. John's entire agency, the Department of General Services, fell under her command.)

John looked at me like I'd hit him. "We can work this out ourselves," he said. When I said nothing, he rose. "Well, I hope you understand where I'm coming from."

Two days later my project manager, Huston Eubank, and I drove to Sacramento for a BuildingCamp brainstorm session for the Cal/EPA building, chitchatting the entire way, excited and nervous. I'd even put on a green tie. We expected about one hundred people: the full building design team, including the architects, AC Martin, and engineers, Levine/Seegal Associates; the developer; and representatives from the various EPA agencies that would be tenants in the building, such as the Integrated Waste Management Board. We parked outside the SMUD (Sacramento Municipal Utility District) building. I'd chosen to meet there because it had an underfloor air system and other innovative green building technologies — hoping it would inspire the attendees. SMUD had also enthusiastically participated with my green team to generate renewable energy ideas and incentives for the building.

The room began to fill up. I said hello to a few people I knew and was making my way to the front when my way was blocked by Mike Smith, senior vice president for TDP. We'd never met before, but I knew who he was. He was thick and burly, with a big neck below a bright-red face.

"This is my project," he spit out, his face close to mine, "and I'm setting the ground rules." I took a step backward. "The base building design is not up for discussion. If you want to accomplish anything, you'll stick to the tenant improvements."

I felt the wind go out of me. As my lungs emptied, my anger shot up. "It may be your project, but it's my meeting. I was brought in to brainstorm, and you've no right to limit the discussion." He stomped to his seat. I realized I was shaking.

A few moments later, we called the meeting into session. I started off by having several manufacturers talk about renewable energy systems that would work for the building, a topic of interest to all. "We can design the building so that a fuel cell can plug into the building at a later date when it's feasible," said the lead architect from AC Martin. The mood in the room was cautious and edgy, and discussion remained limited — making the session more presentational than participatory. My team of experts offered suggestions, the developer's design team took notes. There couldn't have been more of a difference from the vibrant, almost jubilant integrated dialogue we'd had a few months earlier on the Santa Monica Public Safety Facility project, where the team was pushed up the sustainability mountain by the building owner.

At sunrise the next morning, I put on running shoes and headed out on a trail along the American River near our hotel. I ran for an hour, and to my surprise, my stride and breathing were in harmony. My thinking was clear. As I showered after the run, I felt a rare sense of peace. I dressed and returned to the meeting room for round two. "Today, each of us faces an opportunity and a choice," I said quietly, grabbing hold of the lectern and staring deep into the eyes of my listeners, hoping to reach deep into their souls. "When you go home tonight and your head hits the pillow, I want you to ask yourself if you pushed yourself toward greatness, or mediocrity."

That day we brainstormed dozens of wish-list ideas, including lighting at 0.8 watts per square foot, product emissions testing and imposing off-gassing emission limits, end-use electrical metering, permanent air monitoring, building commissioning, and a dual-plumbing gray-water system for the bathrooms. Meanwhile, both my client and the developer sat silently with their arms crossed. The next time I looked over, John Goleman's seat was empty. I never saw him again.

"You're a zealot," remarked one of the EPA participants in the parking lot afterward. "Even if you try, you can't control yourself."

Me? A zealot? The label irked me, but over time I came to recognize the truth of it. Once when I played football in high school, the nose guard for a competing team decked me. After the play, I got up and slowly and shakily made my way back to the team huddle. I sucked in air and chanted "Kill!" in my mind. On the next play I drove straight at the three-hundred-pounder, hitting him an inch above the ankles. He fell over, bounced once, and settled to the ground. Even as pain shot through me, I smiled. I'd done it. I put both hands on the ground to push myself up, then screamed in agony. I'd dislocated both shoulders. It was the end of my football career.

Had I done a similar thing here? Even as I wondered, I didn't care. I reminded myself I was on the side of the angels.

A week later I received a harsh letter from Mike Smith telling me that in his "wildest dreams" he couldn't fathom why we continued to demand changing the building to accommodate an underfloor air delivery system and other base building design changes, like the windows.

I shot an answer back to John Goleman; "My wildest dreams," I wrote, "are unfortunately big. I dream for a state of California that demonstrates environmental leadership through its actions and boldness, not words. I dream of team collaboration and integration to create healthy, productive buildings that consume minimal energy, contribute to a world of less pollution and waste." I then added, "I believe we can do all of this and still have it work on a life-cycle costing basis at a rate of return higher than the state's cost of capital." I copied the letter to the state secretaries of EPA and State and Consumer Services, Assemblywoman Bowen, and Jim Thomas.

In my fury, I'd forgotten one of the famous ancient warrior Sun Tzu's key lessons: "Supreme excellence consists in breaking the enemy's resistance without fighting." I was not mature enough to understand. I was still making diving tackles that brought down not only my opponent, but myself as well.

Anne Sheehan called when she got my letter. "Let's meet and resolve this thing, David," she said. "In the meantime, I assume you'll hold off from sending any further letters."

"Yes, of course," I said, feeling elated. "Green" would now receive a hearing at the highest level.

The day before the meeting, I went for a sunrise bike ride in the Marin Headlands. I crossed the Golden Gate Bridge and climbed the steep hill, shifting into my granny gear. Sweat dripped down my face and back. At the summit, I stopped and looked at the city skyline, all Mediterranean whites and pastels except for the black rectangle of the Bank of America building. It was so quiet and peaceful there. A breeze cooled my brow and rustled the manzanita. Why did I need this fight? I didn't own the building. I breathed in the salty air. Once it had filled my lungs, I exhaled—letting it all go.

Later that morning in the office, I directed Huston Eubank to select only the most practical ideas, those that respected the stated project constraints. I then trekked out to Sacramento to apologize to Mike Smith for the letter I'd written. He said, "We'll do our best to add as much of the green as possible. You have my word."

A few years later, in late 2001, I stood in front of the tower. Its massive size overwhelmed my senses. I pulled out my camera and took several digital photos. The developers had installed the solar panels on the roof of the building and incorporated many green finishes into the tenant improvements: low-emitting paint, carpet tile with a high level of recycled content, and superefficient lights. The building ended up 29 percent more energy efficient than the code requirement.

Years later, the building became the first LEED-EB (Existing Building) Platinum building in the country. And thereafter it continued to lead through green performance and demonstrating new products and systems. That project also planted seeds for future collaboration between me and Thomas Properties Group.

Other projects for me followed. One of the tenants of the Cal/EPA building was the California Integrated Waste Management Board (CIWMB). Ralph Chandler, the board's executive director, and Arnie Sowell, the assistant to board member Dan Eaton, had been at the two-day Cal/EPA building brainstorm session, and had hired me as the CIWMB's green building advisor. During the next three years, on their behalf, I went on to advise the greening of seventeen projects for local governments in the state.

I was also involved in the state's next major project, the Capitol Area East End Complex: a $400 million, five-building, 1.5-million-square-foot development. Here, we learned from the Cal/EPA and other projects by including a strong green requirement from inception in the bidding requirements and evaluation criteria for hiring the design-build contractor. As a result, the finished project beat the energy code by 30 percent by installing "cool" roofs, environmental systems furniture, an underfloor air-distribution system, and dozens of other green building enhancements. One of the five buildings earned California's second LEED Gold certification.

In 2000 I was hired by another waste board, Alameda County Waste Management Authority, representing fourteen cities in the East Bay. Ann Ludwig, the senior program manager, challenged me to design a course on the greening of city contracts for retaining architects, engineers, contractors, and developers. When I told her I'd never done such a thing, she said, "I know. That's why I hired you." I later helped the agency buy and renovate its own LEED Platinum building in Oakland, California. A few years after that, in 2013, I held a solo art show, displaying about twenty of my own modern art paintings in the building's art gallery. I even did a talk called "The Art of Green."

I spent the entire next month, including several all-nighters, working to write a three-hundred-page manual, illustrated by 120 slides. It entailed a training manual on how to green a six-hundred-page design-build contract that Alameda County General Services Agency had given me to use as a prototype. Contract greening was a rewarding new task that allowed me to draw on my experience in many areas: development, construction, legal issues, building design, and green building performance.

When the government starts throwing money at anything green, it's human nature to get in line. I am not immune to this. In a sense, that helped steer me into green building, when Congress was funding those early green demonstration projects, and Mike and I formed the council in part to get in on the action. Yes, I was already passionate about green buildings, but bucks are green too, and I'd be lying if I said I never noticed that.

Even more boldly, I firmly believe that green needs to be the economically preferred approach, earning a higher rate of investment return, while boosting health and productivity.

But I was not the only one who followed the federal money. In mid-2002 I was invited to Bozeman, Montana, for a two-day green brainstorm meeting at the hunting lodge of a developer named Bill Lamb. A dozen other "greenies" had also been invited—experts in the areas of energy, water, development, and design. We were met at the Bozeman airport by one of Bill's project staff. On leaving the main highway about an hour's drive outside of town, we drove for about ten minutes on a dirt road, through thousands of acres of vegetation and man-made lakes, toward the hunting lodge. We passed deer, wild turkeys, and, in the marsh areas, statuesque white cranes. We drove by several farms and ranch houses. As Bill assembled his kingdom, he'd purchased some twenty-five individual parcels, allowing many of the sellers to retain their homes free of charge, if they agreed to work for him on the compound and on miles of newly created preserves, including a hunting and fishing resort.

Emerging from the woods, I gained our first view of the palace. It was massive, an oversized mix of hunting lodge and fortress constructed of enormous logs and boulders. The dark structure stood adjacent to a huge man-made lake, which visitors were compelled to drive completely around to access the compound. The lodge's entrance was twelve or more feet in height, looking like the front of a castle with its four-inch-thick wooden door. To the left was a retinal scanner. "Sometimes he can't find his key," the driver remarked.

On entering the building, I found myself in what felt like a medieval great room: about two thousand square feet, with ceilings thirty feet high. The floors were all stone. Dozens of huge log beams were exposed throughout, some up to eight feet in circumference. Full-size canoes and other antiques hung from the beams.

We toured about a half dozen rooms on the second floor, each with a different theme. They, too, were massive, with high ceilings and large private bathrooms. They looked like miniature houses in their own right. The decorating budget could easily have been $150,000 or more per room.

Our group of experts had been assembled to provide strategic guidance in the greening of a project Bill envisioned creating outside Dallas: the world's largest shopping mall, along with a dozen hotels and office buildings. The mall alone would be ten million square feet—an artificial city under a single roof. And he wanted it to be better than LEED Platinum. "I want Dallas Center to use zero fossil fuel and be a net energy generator," he declared when we had all convened in a well-appointed conference room, next to the thirty-seat state-of-the-art theater. "It will be the greatest showcase for renewable technology in the world. The cost is over $2 billion." The sketchy renderings of the envisioned project made it look like a mix of Disneyland and Biosphere 2.

"I have the money. I have been fortunate. My children are successful in their own right and they don't need my money. I am prepared to put in whatever it takes, even if the green adds hundreds of millions. What I am missing is the knowledge; that's why I invited you here. What you have been missing is a committed owner with the capital and connections to make things happen."

He took a sip of water and surveyed the room. "I am seeing the governor on Sunday. I need your help in figuring out what points to emphasize. He loves this project and is very supportive. When it's finished in twenty years, this project will bring one hundred thousand jobs and fifty million people each year to Texas."

Next he turned to the need to eradicate our dependence on foreign oil, becoming passionate, raising his voice and waving his arms. He almost couldn't contain himself. All of the green experts in attendance were firm advocates of reducing America's energy consumption and boosting renewable energy generation. However, we weren't billionaires. Most of us couldn't reach top politicians. We didn't own thirty million square feet, as this man did, and so we couldn't create our own market as we "greened" fifteen million square feet of commercial space.

We were each invited to make recommendations for the mall, its other buildings, and how to make its energy systems self-sufficient and renewable. But we never got a chance: the agenda seemed to change every minute, despite the careful advance preparation of the staff. Bill kept switching direction, listening for awhile, and then, when he couldn't sit silently any longer, launching into another speech — making it clear that we weren't getting at what he envisioned. Some of the participants had questioned the volume of traffic the project would attract and our ability to achieve net-zero energy, given its unprecedented size. "I want you to be positive and creative," he admonished at the end of the first day. "I don't want to hear why we can't do this, but what we can do."

Despite Bill's urging that we redouble our efforts the next day, again the opportunity to do constructive work never arose. First thing in the morning he sat down with our panel and asked us to come up with the presentation for the governor's meeting on Sunday. But when we tried to do this, he changed tack and decided we needed a mission statement for the various project components.

At day's end, I still had not presented my ideas for the project, so one of Bill's staff called him over to see the slides I'd been asked to prepare in advance. It was my main opportunity to reach him, and to contribute to the project. "You have two minutes," Bill told me. "They're waiting for us to come to dinner."

I tried to focus and speak as quickly as possible. Already with the first slide, though, I saw that he wasn't with me, but was looking off to the hallway where others were talking. I quickly and mechanically read him the titles of my slides and finished before the two-minute deadline.

Bill's project manager approached me a short while later at the dinner table. "David, can you come with me?"

"What's up?"

"We want you to come to a press briefing upstairs. The local media want to learn about the project. Can you tell them your thoughts about the development, from the perspective of the founder of the U.S. and World Green Building Councils?" Immediately I felt flushed, as my stomach dropped to the floor. They hadn't told us that we'd be asked to provide a testimonial to the media. I wondered if Bill had assembled us "greenies" much as he had the stuffed animals that he'd shot and the antiques adorning his castle. I imagined that with his wealth he could do whatever he desired.

"Sure, no problem," I managed to get out softly, wondering if I'd be stuffed if I refused. I understood I was expected to be supportive and say that both projects were credible world-class examples of sustainable building—even though we had not seen any plans and the first team of architects had been fired. Other than hearing the enormous goals and vision of the owner, I really knew nothing about the project. We were necessary in order to affirm his credibility with government and the press, and even more important, to get enormous governmental subsidies.

It all came down to making his project the biggest, grandest, greenest vision imaginable, attracting the right people—politicians and idealists with deep pockets—and then opening the sluice gates so the money would pour in. And it would: this man was a true marketer, with the know-how and the connections to make his vision reality.

I kept my cool and made the most of the social interaction with my colleagues until it was time to leave the next morning. I had a hard time falling asleep that last night, as I tried to make sense of the extravaganza while staring at a stuffed turkey, beaver, and wild boar above the gigantic stone fireplace in my room. I'd learned at Cal/EPA that it's important to accept gray, rather than always push for white (with the strong likelihood that all you'll get is black). Dallas Center, however, was too close to black from the outset, and I decided to watch from afar. Later on I heard that they'd received a multibillion-dollar tax credit for the development.

15
GBC GOES GLOBAL

"It is my great pleasure," I said, "to welcome the formation of the Japan Green Building Council!" I was standing on a stage in Tokyo; it was April 22, 1998 — Earth Day. I wore a new lightweight sage-colored wool suit and a sparkling gold-patterned tie. My host, Takatoshi Ishiguro, had only seen me in my California wardrobe of jeans and Gap shirts and suggested that I should dress up. He was with PES International, a green building design and consulting firm.

On my head were headphones so that I could hear the proceedings translated into English. It was my first time giving a speech through a translator. It seemed to take three seconds for them to turn my every one second of speech into Japanese, making me select every word carefully. Takatoshi had warned me to not tell jokes: "American humor doesn't work in Japan." I found his command difficult to obey, preferring to stay loose on my feet.

Seated in front of me were about three hundred Japanese businessmen and government representatives, almost all of them wearing dark-blue suits with white shirts. It felt like the United States twenty years earlier. Several reporters took notes in the front row, and a video camera and an impressive array of movie-studio overhead lights shined brightly in my eyes, making me self-conscious.

I'd met Takatoshi Ishiguro three years earlier at the 1995 Big Sky, Montana, membership summit, the council's first exclusive gathering of its members. We were all surprised when Jane Fonda showed up and Ray Anderson led a hiking trip up the mountain. Previously, we'd hosted large conferences that were also open to the public. The summit concept excluded formal presentations; instead, we led discussions on critical green building topics. The session opened with an attempt to determine the council's first state-of-the-world summary of green building. Each of the three hundred attendees spoke for about thirty seconds on their efforts in green building. Hearing the collective stories of triumphs, challenges, obstacles, passion, and growth charged me. At that meeting, Takatoshi wore a suit and tie, while I had on shorts and a lightweight fishing shirt with "CalTrout" written on the pocket. He introduced himself in the formal Japanese way, extending his business card toward me with both hands and a slight bow of the head. I pulled out one of my cards and gave it to him the American way—in one hand without a bow. I later learned to be more sensitive to cultural differences.

"I want to found a green building council in Japan," he told me. "We are a different country and culture, but I think your model will work. Can you help me?" Earlier I'd noticed Takatoshi taking notes on a pad of pink Post-its. (I later learned he'd been studying us for several years.) His thick black-rimmed glasses were dirty, and his hair on top of a tiny body was disheveled, as if he was too intent on business to take the time to notice such unimportant details. On his jacket lapel was a round green pin with a Japanese character.

As we spoke, I learned that he'd started an environmental discussion group in the city of Nagoya, where he lived, and wanted to expand beyond its hundred members, by adding from all parts of the industry, and to form a green building coalition like ours. They planned to create green building guidelines and host educational events. His assistant, Shisano Takeuchi, often translated for him; although her English was easier to understand, his was quite good. He was an architect by training, and had worked for Syska Hennessy Group, a medium-size US engineering firm in New York (and an early member of the council).

Takatoshi and I stayed in touch for the next few years. We would meet in San Francisco during his frequent trips to the United States. He had scoured the country, tracking down many of our leading green building experts and projects. He had probably toured more American green buildings than I had. He'd also met many of the early pioneers, who were also my friends in the industry, and paid a few of them to lecture in Japan, as I was now doing.

He'd asked me to welcome the Japan council at this event, its inaugural meeting, and to give a talk on the economics of green building. "It's all about increased building value," I said as I was wrapping up. "If a building is efficient in its use of resources, then its value will increase." I saw many heads nodding, but only about thirty seconds after I'd stopped speaking, while the translator caught up.

And here came my "kicker:" "Now that we have green building councils in the United States and Japan, I'm announcing my formation of the World Green Building Council." I had come up with the idea on the flight over, figuring that if Japan was interested in the council model, other countries would be, too. "The global building industry needs to work together to share knowledge, standards, and technologies. I hope you will join me." I looked out at the quiet room, feeling the way a ship's captain must have felt in the 1400s when landing on soil as yet untouched by Europeans.

I smiled broadly and held my head high. The next day my photo appeared in the newspaper. I'm not sure what the caption said, but it made me grin. Unfortunately, my only glimpse of Tokyo was from the enormous Hilton Hotel, which was not much different from Hiltons in America, just bigger.

Takatoshi asked me to repeat my talk in Nagoya, and he also arranged for a dozen or so meetings with government officials, architects, and large product manufacturers. "What's the purpose of this meeting?" I asked Shisano early on in our schedule, as we headed into a small meeting room at the hotel after a quick breakfast of salad, fruit, and sushi. I was surprised to see about a dozen business executives waiting for us. "They want to meet you," Shisano said. "Well, OK," I said, unsure of the intent and business purpose.

We quickly got down to business, though for the most part I had little role to play in the meeting. Occasionally they would have a question for me: "David," Shisano translated, "they would like to know about the cost of green building in the United States. Is it more?" For much of the discussion, however, I simply sat there, trying to figure out what was going on. I heard my name mentioned occasionally, and the term "green building," but that was about all I understood. Takatoshi was smiling and shaking his head, talking fast as he led the discussion, occasionally glancing down at his pink Post-it notes jammed with Japanese writing. I began to feel as if I was the wriggling bait on the end of his fishing pole.

"I'm not sure what you're up to," I said to Takatoshi and Shisano that night over dinner in the hotel restaurant. He'd had three drinks already. Then he was yelling at her, or at least that's what it sounded like to me. I sipped my Sapporo beer, not knowing what to think. "We keep going to all these meetings. And it looks as if you're drumming up work for your consulting business," I said.

He and Shisano jumped into a long exchange in Japanese. I sat and waited. Next time, I'd hire my own translator. The waiter had brought out a metal bowl and a small gas burner. Firing it up, he added water and about a dozen spices to the bowl. In no time it was boiling. He then placed a large platter of green vegetables and thinly sliced slabs of Kobe beef on the table. They called this dish *shabu-shabu*—which Shisano interpreted as meaning the "washing" of the vegetables and meat in the hot water.

"We're very interested in working with you," Takatoshi said at last. "What is your standard billing rate?"

"Two thousand five hundred dollars per day," I said. "Plus expenses." I was actually billing at $2,000 per day at the time, but given the distance and cultural strain, I upped the amount.

"I see. That's expensive in Japan," Takatoshi said. Then he launched into another exchange with Shisano. Meanwhile, I "washed" more food in the hot water and stuffed the cooked items into my mouth. It was delicious.

"What services do you provide?" Takatoshi asked. Should I be frank? I was providing a free education, as I'd done over the past few years, coaching him on how to build a council. He'd paid me an honorarium and expenses for this visit and my talks, so at least I'd seen some cash, but for the most part all my advice had been free of charge. I hesitated, and then decided to trust him. Pulling out a pen, I made a list on the paper tablecloth of the various services I'd invented as part of my BuildingFutures program: the BuildingCamp brainstorming session, energy modeling using DOE software, life-cycle costing financial analysis, green materials research and selection, product procurement, peer review of building drawings at several levels of completion and building commissioning. "Can I keep this?" he asked once I'd finished, already beginning to fold up my work of "art." I nodded, and he put the paper in his shirt pocket along with the notes he'd scribbled while I was outlining my offerings.

For a year or two, I continued to meet with Takatoshi and Shisano when they came through San Francisco. During an international building rating system conference in Maastricht, Holland, I learned from two representatives from Takanaka, a large Japanese construction firm, that Takatoshi had trademarked the English term "green building" in Japan. That meant that anyone who wanted to use the term needed his approval. A few international green building leaders said I should not have permitted this. "If you want to be involved with the WorldGBC, you must release the trademark," I told Takatoshi and Shisano at lunch one day in San Francisco. A year later he had transferred the trademark to the Japan council, now a governmentally recognized nonprofit organization. Years later, Japan's membership in the WorldGBC shifted to a government- and university-backed organization, which was the inventor of CASBEE, Japan's green building rating system.

After Japan came Korea. I'd heard about the formation of the Korea Green Building Council in 1998. From their material on the Web I could see that they'd copied the USGBC's organizational format and programs and Green Building Council name. The next year, three representatives from Korea came to my office. After an hour quizzing them about their ownership structure and bylaws, I'd learned that the Korea council was privately owned. "If you want to affiliate with us, you'll need to spin the council out into a nonprofit organization," I said. "Our model is open, consensus based, and strictly nonprofit." I was surprised when they agreed to do this, explaining that they hadn't fully understood our nonprofit requirement.

A year later, I was pleased to hear from a governmental contact in Seoul who was now the chair of the newly established nonprofit council. Like us, they had started off by creating green building guidelines and a building rating system. I received photos of their first demonstration green building, housing the government's energy efficiency and research department. It looked as if it was from the 1980s, rather square, without much design detail, but it had extensive south-facing glazing with large solar shades and superefficient energy systems.

Next was Spain. In spring 1999, I'd had frantic emails and calls from a man named Aurelio Ramírez-Zarzosa, who wanted me to grant him the exclusive right to be the founder of the Spain Green Building Council. I was evasive; I'd never met the man, knew nothing about him. The WorldGBC was still just an idea in my head, even though I had announced it publicly. True, we had councils under way in the United States, Japan, and Korea, but no formal commitment to work together or a binding code of ethics. Nor, as I was acutely aware, did we have funds, staff, volunteer members, or a dues structure. I was holding the group together myself and personally funding the start-up costs.

He and a fellow Spaniard came in July, and I met with them for two days. We had an enjoyable time and they seemed credible, so I agreed to work with them. Of course, they said that because they were just starting out, they had no funds to commit to the WorldGBC.

Just after the meetings with Aurelio, I got a call from the environmental director at Gap. She had $5,000 of extra funds in their foundation's year-end budget and wanted to donate it to my council work. I told her about a founding WorldGBC meeting I was planning to hold that November in San Francisco, and she agreed to sponsor the event. It would be the first time representatives from the various countries with councils (plus a few others I had met over the years) came together.

About thirteen people representing six countries flew in for the two-day meeting. I had invited Nigel Howard, director of the Center for Sustainable Construction at the Building Research Establishment (BRE) in England (BRE developed the BREEAM green building rating system), to attend, and from Australia came Che Wall, a green building consultant I had met a few years earlier in Mexico when we lectured together for the Asia-Pacific Economic Cooperation Forum. Takatoshi and Shisano came from Japan, bringing their new council chairman. Aurelio returned with the partner I'd met previously from the Spanish green building council. We also had a representative from Russia whom I'd met the month before. Rick Fedrizzi and Mike Italiano represented the USGBC. It felt great to have my comrades present as we incubated the next creation.

The evening after our first day of meetings, I hosted a celebratory dinner. "Thank you for bringing the vision of the green building council to your countries and for standing up as founders," I said to the group in our private banquet area at E&O Asian Kitchen on Sutter Street, one of my favorites. The sound of the jazz pianist playing an old Benny Goodman tune wafted up from downstairs. Everyone was jovial, enjoying drinks after a productive day spent educating each other on their respective green building efforts. Those who already had councils shared their start-up experience with the newcomers. I felt at home with these kindred souls from many countries.

The second day was more difficult. I'd set a demanding agenda, hoping to address critical organizational issues: membership, founding board, rules of conduct, priority programs, and dues. "What's the purpose of the World Green Building Council?" Takatoshi asked at the beginning of the meeting. Since I'd known him for four years and he'd heard more than anyone present about the WorldGBC, I didn't understand why he was asking that, especially in such a challenging tone. I frowned at him, hoping he'd back down, but he met my look impassively. All eyes were on me.

"The WorldGBC is the umbrella organization for national green building councils," I replied. "Now, let's — ."

Takatoshi had his hand up again. The room was tense. Our hostess came in with a pitcher to fill our water glasses. I waved her away. Finally I acknowledged Takatoshi with a curt nod of my head. "Whose hand is holding up the umbrella?" he asked.

I knew what he was implying, and I resented it. "No one country or person will own the WorldGBC. Each of us will have a seat on its board."

"But who will control the board?" he persisted. The others squirmed.

I had already explained to him several times that no one person or entity would control the nonprofit coalition's board. We would have officers, but the assembled group hadn't yet elected them, though I hoped that would happen by the end of the day. It was clear he thought that the USGBC and I would control the WorldGBC. To the contrary, I had taken great effort to prevent such a thing from happening. Instead of founding the world council from within the USGBC, I had set it up as a separate entity, inviting the US council to assume only one seat on its board. The USGBC had agreed not only to this structure, but also to the principle that the world council would be rating system neutral: USGBC would not mandate that the WorldGBC use only LEED, opening the door for each country to determine which rating system approach was best for its country's climate and culture.

"You need to get control of yourself," my assistant, Michelle Crozier, whispered to me when I'd shown my rising frustration at the interruptions — and our overall lack of progress. I took a few deep breaths and plowed forward, managing to keep the rest of the meeting under control. In the end, we didn't come to any conclusions, but had a good discussion about the issues, and a few countries agreed to help develop a website for the WorldGBC. I tracked their progress and when they went home, almost all of these pioneers ended up founding their own green building councils, following the lead of the USGBC. They'd also invent their own green building rating systems, or would use LEED, which became available internationally.

There were other signs of growing interest in green building overseas. I went to China as part of a small US group that had been invited by the Shanghai Overseas Returned Scholars Association to participate in the Sustainable Shanghai conference in July 2000. Accompanying me were Ray Anderson of Interface, and Amory and Hunter Lovins from the Rocky Mountain Institute. We each gave a short lecture to the four hundred or so assembled scholars and government officials. Amory and Hunter spoke about *Natural Capitalism*, the book they had just released with Paul Hawken. It had already been translated into Chinese, and I saw many of the scholars carrying it. (The word *capitalism* in the book's title had to be finessed, as it didn't translate well into the culture of our hosting country.) At a small session with several government officials, I talked about our experience in the United States with the USGBC and challenged them to create a similar entity in China. A few years later, I was pleased to learn that they had formed the Shanghai Green Building Alliance, in partnership with the Green Building Alliance of Pittsburgh, one of our early council members. Years later I helped form the China Green Building Council with the government's Ministry of Housing and Ministry of Urban-Rural Development.

From Shanghai I flew to Hong Kong. I had set up several meetings with professors at the University of Hong Kong and was scheduled to deliver a few lectures on green building, including one for a small group from the Hong Kong Institute of Architects who were interested in forming a Hong Kong council. (Years later, in June 2003, the Professional Green Building Council of Hong Kong held its inaugural meeting.) I then had lunch with

Gordon Ongley, managing director of Swire Properties, a global developer of high-rise buildings. Swire's interest in green buildings surprised me. The firm owned an enormous chunk of land near the international airport and was working with the city, which required use of their BEAM green building rating system (Hong Kong's version of England's BREEAM system), to make it into a model green community. During my meetings at the University of Hong Kong, the head of the journalism department asked me to accept an academic fellowship: I'd be able to teach, green their building, and write the book I had begun thinking about. The thought was appealing, but I still had things to do at home and wasn't ready to move halfway across the world.

Just before Christmas 2000 I flew to Madrid to meet with Aurelio and the three other founding partners of the Spain Green Building Council. They had sent me an airplane ticket, saying they had a business proposition to discuss that would help fund the WorldGBC.

In our first meeting, we exchanged progress reports on our respective councils. Membership in the USGBC was growing rapidly, having surpassed five hundred member firms and moving toward a thousand. The Spanish council had yet to officially form and had no funding, though they'd been at it for a year and a half. In that same time, the USGBC had raised more than a million dollars.

Something was amiss.

One of the partners, Sergio Cruz, worked in a midsize legal firm in Madrid. Tall and about fifty pounds overweight, he'd walked in that morning wearing a shiny light-brown leather coat. We met in his firm's conference room, which stank of the cigarettes he was constantly smoking. When he wasn't lighting up, he was talking on his cell phone or with his secretary, who repeatedly interrupted us. I'd thought New Yorkers were wired, but this man and other Spaniards I met made them look like vacationers chilling on a beach. "Do you mind not smoking?" I'd asked him at the beginning of the meeting. "Sorry," he said equably, continuing to puff away. What kind of an environmentalist was this? And the others weren't much better. Ricardo García owned a family fish business in Biko, a small fishing town northwest of Madrid, and the third, Alfredo Rios, owned a landscape business. At least that was sort of connected to buildings. Aurelio was an engineer, and had been running the day-to-day business of the incipient council while carrying on his one-person consulting firm. His small, cluttered office in a shared suite reminded me of my own early days as a consultant.

I excused myself to go to the bathroom. A few seconds after I entered, the door opened and Aurelio came in. I turned to him. "What's going on?" I asked. "I've had enough of this bullshit." He didn't answer. The air smelled of urine, and paper towels littered the floor. Then he said in his thick Spanish accent, "They're playing with you, trying to figure out your position. They think you're weak, and they want to take advantage of you." He had bags under his eyes, and his tweed suit was wrinkled. "They've tied my hands for the past year. That's why we've accomplished nothing since we were in San Francisco."

"Why didn't you level with me before I flew all the way to Spain?" I asked, touching his shoulder to take the sting out of my words. I wanted to be angry with him, but he seemed defeated and in need of help.

"They said they wouldn't give me any money unless I got you here." He gazed at the floor for a few seconds, shaking his head. Then he looked at me. "I'm sorry that I wasn't honest with you. If you help me get rid of these three bozos, I'll make it up to you."

I studied the peeling paint on the toilet partition nearest me. "OK," I said after a minute. "Let's do it."

As we entered the conference room, the three partners stopped talking. Maybe they sensed that something had changed.

"It's time you get to the point," I said in my Dirty Harry voice. "Why did you ask me here?" They looked at one another uneasily. "We propose to form a new business with you here in Spain and, if it works, expand it to cover the full European Union," the fish salesman said. Aurelio sat with his head down and his hands covering his face. He wanted me to handle this alone.

"I'm listening," I said to draw them out.

"We'll give you 20 percent of the new business, and we'll put in all the money."

"Uh-huh," I said after a few moments of silence. "What do you expect me to do for the 20 percent?"

"You deliver the LEED building rating system to us for Spain," he said. I sat back in my chair. This was the missing piece to the puzzle. Ironically, the USGBC had authorized me to negotiate a LEED licensing agreement with them.

"What are you going to do with it?"

"The private company that we own will license it to the Spain Green Building Council. They will be required to hire our firm to do the building inspections," he said with a smug look. "We've run the numbers and believe this will be a lucrative business for all of us. Our government will pay a lot of money for this system."

"There's no way I'd be part of a boondoggle like that," I shot back. "It's against our principles and it's unethical. Maybe this is how you do business in Spain, but in the United States we are careful about conflicts of interest. The council model requires that it be owned by a nonprofit in which all programs are open and consensus based. No one group can influence our standards or profit from our products." My words sounded pompous, but I meant them.

"You shouldn't dismiss our generous offer so quickly," the lawyer said sourly, his words mingling with smoke as he exhaled. "If you remain such a purist, you'll never make any money." He pointed his cigarette at me to emphasize his point.

"You've wasted your time. And you'll be receiving a bill from me for mine." I stuffed my papers into my briefcase.

"Aurelio?" the fish man asked. Aurelio's head popped out of his hands.

"I agree with David," he replied. "You guys are no longer part of the council." We left together with no goodbyes. When I glanced back, the three ousted members of the council sat shaking their heads and talking in rapid Spanish.

Ultimately, things didn't work out with the resulting Spain green building council leadership, and the WorldGBC recognized another more established organizing group. We learned that it was hard to perform adequate due diligence in a foreign culture, which led to the WorldGBC creating an extensive eight-step road map for working with new country GBC candidates. In 2007 we established a Secretariat in Toronto and brought on Jane Henley as our CEO to help guide the process, as well as to steer the WorldGBC's growing global activities. Jane had previously been the CEO of the New Zealand GBC, where they'd licensed Australia's Green Star rating system.

16
THE FIRST GREENBUILD

Two years had now passed. I'd gone on three speaking trips to Australia and helped launch the Green Building Council of Australia. Another GBC in Canada was in process. I had plenty of consulting projects, including the California Integrated Waste Management Board and Alameda County Waste Management, Starbucks, DreamWorks, Williams-Sonoma, Genentech, and Stanford University—its first campus green building, at Jasper Ridge Biological Preserve.

It was a decade since that cold night on the floor of Jeffrey's Marina apartment. I was now one of the longest-tenure tenants in my three-story walk-up, which had a partial view of the Golden Gate Bridge. I'd never imagined I would be there an entire decade, and still single. I was now forty-two. My eldest brother, Rick, had gotten married five years earlier, and he and his wife now had a beautiful son. Glenn had been married seventeen years; we'd just celebrated his son's Bar Mitzvah, and his daughter was twelve. I found myself wondering if I'd ever make it to the altar and have the chance to speed in the middle of the night to the delivery room.

In November 2002 I traveled to Austin, Texas, for the USGBC's First Annual Greenbuild International Conference. As I walked from my hotel along the Colorado River, I made my way to Sixth Street. Everywhere I looked, I saw bars and clubs. It was 6:30 and the streets were fairly empty, though they would soon be filled with revelers: the University of Texas football team had won earlier that day. It was a party town, for sure. I had last been in Austin during the early days of USGBC for a talk hosted by the state government. Even then I was amazed at the level of green building activity and thoughtful leadership of the city, propelled by the great work of Pliny Fisk and Gail Vittori.

I turned off on Red River Street, looking for the restaurant where I was meeting some colleagues. Above me, my eyes fell on a huge banner strung from lamppost to lamppost, at least fifty feet long and ten feet high. I figured it was announcing some local event, but the green and white graphic in the upper left looked familiar. I stopped in my tracks, a dazed joy spreading through my body. It was the council's round oak leaf logo, and the sign was announcing our conference in the Austin convention center. I trotted to the next main street and saw another banner swaying in the Texas sunshine. My heart beat rapidly. I got out my digital camera and shot a dozen photos. At one point, I stopped a passerby and asked him to take one of me in front of the sign. "I founded that group," I told him. He glanced at my jeans, at the banner, then shrugged and snapped the photo.

The next day, standing at the head of a large conference table, I welcomed twenty representatives from eight countries to a two-day WorldGBC meeting I'd organized to precede the USGBC conference. This time, I vowed I'd let the others lead the meeting, not drive the agenda myself as I'd done three years earlier. Instead I would be the courteous host and quietly guide us forward to my goal, as Sun Tzu would advise.

We were in the Lady Bird Johnson Wildflower Center. It was the perfect spot: the flowing and colorful wildflower exhibition gardens were spectacular, and the scattered brick and concrete passive solar buildings were water and energy efficient, and included rainwater captured in a self-contained cistern that was as beautiful as it was effective. The room we were meeting in was lit by daylight, and the air smelled fresh and clean.

All that day, as founders of councils in Australia, Japan, Spain, the United States, Canada, Brazil, Mexico, and India described their progress, I listened like a proud parent. The councils were at all phases of development, ranging from the USGBC, growing stronger by the day after almost a decade, to Brazil and Mexico, which had come to the meeting with the intention of learning the basics of a green building council.

At each break, I walked around, listening to the conversations. Despite the many organizational and cultural differences, the participants had a remarkable rapport. Over the two days we met, I marveled at the strength of the bonds being created. These people shared passion, a pioneering spirit, and a determination to bring green buildings to their countries, despite the expense or hardship of the struggle. It was like we were inventing a new religion together, after having seen the light of the burning bush.

That first evening, USGBC (the lead sponsor of the two-day WorldGBC meeting) hosted a banquet dinner for the international coalition, with welcoming remarks given by USGBC president and CEO Christine Ervin. Rick Fedrizzi was there, too, continuing to lend his support and grounding leadership. Christine enthusiastically supported our assembly and pledged the USGBC's full commitment as a founding member. After several years of a wait-and-see attitude, our council had finally embraced the concept of the WorldGBC, agreeing to assume a leadership role and contribute seed money of $25,000. The WorldGBC (a "United Nations" of country GBCs), they realized, was a powerful way to share information and green building tools, and expand the GBC model globally. The USGBC already had an international base, and many of its members were glad to see our vision spread.

On the second day I woke up early, worrying. How could we get everyone to agree on our common organizational principles and structure? Our failure to accomplish this at the San Francisco meeting three years before was heavy on my mind. Despite my resolution to let things take their course, I had to do something, so I fired up my laptop and, gulping coffee, proceeded to list the dozen key organizational priorities as PowerPoint headers. They included mission, main programs, organizational structure, location, funding, founding board, officers, and strategic partners. This time though, I left the text blank. I'd let the group fill that in.

I had asked Maria Atkinson, CEO of the Green Building Council of Australia, and Nigel Howard, a vice president of the USGBC, to help me lead that day's discussion. (Nigel had moved from England to the United States to direct the LEED rating system program and its rapidly expanding staff in our D.C. office. It tickled me that he had been responsible for the BREEAM rating system — the first in the world of its kind.) To keep myself from assuming control, I walked around the room with my camera, taking pictures. I also took numerous bathroom breaks and sat on my hands a lot in the back of the room, chatting with Rick Fedrizzi. At one point, Nigel said that we'd have to let each country organically develop its own version of a green building council, one that fit its culture. I wanted to interrupt and talk about common guidelines for all, but somehow managed to keep quiet. It wasn't my meeting; it was theirs. If there's one thing I had learned during my early years at the USGBC, it's that you can't bully people into moving faster than their natural pace — and you can't do everything yourself.

To my amazed delight, by the end of the day we'd progressed through almost all the topics I'd written down on my laptop that morning. People jumped into the discussion with enthusiasm, ideas came fast, and agreement followed quickly. "Raise your hand if you're in favor of the formation of the World Green Building Council," Maria said. I looked around the room. There was Raghu, the council founder from India—his organization, the Confederation of Indian Industry, represented more than forty-eight hundred companies with offices all over the world; Roberto, a leading architect from Brazil; Takatoshi and the ever-present Shisano from Japan; Rick Fedrizzi, sitting solidly at the end of the table; and a dozen more colleagues who today had joined together with passion to achieve a common goal. I couldn't breathe until I saw all hands raised high in the air. It was a beautiful sight, one that had flourished beyond my wildest dreams.

All countries with councils would sit on the board. "And now," said Maria, "our officers." The slide that I'd prepared projected on the screen and listed several titles, starting with the chair. I stirred uneasily, desperately wanting to remain on the sidelines on this one.

It was no use. "You have no idea what David can do," Rick Fedrizzi said to the group. They looked at me with huge smiles.

"Everyone in favor of David as our chairman, raise your hand," Maria said. Everyone's hand shot into the air—except mine. When they started to clap, I shook my head. "What's wrong?" Maria asked.

"I can't do it." The room went silent; it was as if a cloud had passed beneath the sun. I felt a flush rising on my cheekbones. Their stillness brought the taste of iron into my mouth.

"We'll help you," Che said.

"Yes," Rick chimed in. "We'll do the work."

I felt a strong pull, like a riptide pulling me out to sea. I filled my lungs with oxygen—and said goodbye to my dream of freedom. "OK," I said sheepishly. Everybody cheered, and I tried to smile. But instead of joy, I felt a heaviness in my chest. A short time later I passed on the chairman's role to Che, who had more infrastructure to deal with it. He was the head of a large Australian engineering firm that he later sold to WSP, a large global player.

Two days later we had our first press briefing. I again took a seat in the back while a half dozen reporters in swivel chairs sat reading our newly drafted press release. "Get up there," Rick urged. I didn't know I was supposed to lead the briefing. The heat of the inefficient fluorescent lights beat on my head. On autopilot, I talked about the organization, then turned to my other comrades, letting each country's founder tell their own GBC story. When we'd finished talking, hands shot up.

"What's your political position?" one reported asked me. I froze. We didn't have one.

"We're not a political organization," I replied. I thought of all the wasted energy and time at the failed Earth Summit in Johannesburg that past August, as competing organizations and governments debated whether global warming existed and, if so, what the economic ramifications would be. "While others are debating and stalling, we're designing and building structures that lessen our global footprint. Green buildings can contribute up to a 40 percent reduction in a country's Kyoto Protocol commitment." As some of the other founders jumped in to expand on what I'd said, chills spread through my body. I was no longer alone!

The next morning I went for a run along the river. It reminded me of the Potomac: windy, with rowers streaking by on the water's surface. I waved to several USGBC acquaintances out walking. After a shower, I dressed and strolled over to the convention center. Inside I found myself greeting people on every hand: old friends, acquaintances, newcomers. It took me an hour to make my way to the registration booth to pick up my nametag and meal tickets for the USGBC conference.

The first day was for members only. The council now had more than twenty-five hundred organizational members (within another year membership would stand at thirty-five hundred and then grow at an even faster climb), and while we expected the turnout to be high, we were amazed to sell out the conference with forty-one hundred people in attendance, a number that exceeded our projections by a couple thousand. The trade expo, with two hundred booths, had also sold out. It was the largest green building event ever! Already, we were projecting five thousand attendees and 350 booths at next year's event in Pittsburgh. I noticed the founders of the WorldGBC roaming the halls as a group. It reminded me of the early days of the USGBC, when we "greenies" would clump together at AIA's enormous national conventions. Little did I know that this would pale in size compared to future conferences.

The morning was given over to the council staff and committee heads briefing the members on our LEED program, with images projected on an enormous screen that hung from the ceiling. (The auditorium was so huge that, from the rear and even with my glasses on, I could barely make out the tiny figures onstage.)

They announced the rollout of LEED-NC version 2.1, a rating system for new construction and major renovations that would simplify the certification documentation paperwork. Loud applause welcomed the change. The speakers briefed us on the pilot programs for LEED-EB (Existing Building Operations) and LEED-CI (Commercial Interior Projects), and introduced us to new rating systems being developed for LEED-R (Retail) and LEED-CS (Core and Shell), as well as new initiatives just starting for LEED Homes and LEED-ND (Neighborhood Development).

The LEED statistics at the time were phenomenal: six hundred LEED projects (up to one thousand in September 2003), totaling more than eighty million square feet of space (Nigel estimated this to account for about 4 percent of new construction in the United States, 130 million square feet by September 2003), in nine countries and forty-nine states. We now had thousands of LEED Accredited Professionals (forty-seven hundred by September 2003). LEED had been adopted as the official building performance standard in dozens of cities and at a dozen federal agencies. Interest in LEED was picking up in the private sector as well, as evidenced by the registration of dozens of projects on our website—though for every project that had paid us a registration fee, I guessed that five or more were using LEED as a free design tool. I knew that trend was a mixed blessing. On one hand, we knew that LEED's influence in the marketplace was even larger than we measured; on the other hand, these projects weren't taking advantage of the benefits from third-party certification, which would, in turn, propel the market ahead. The head of LEED-Retail was Ben Packard, the environmental affairs director at Starbucks whom I'd done some consulting for, leading to his formation and chairing of the committee that ultimately led to LEED's volume-build program, opening the door to thousands of future certifications. He had formed a strong committee of retailers that included Home Depot, Williams-Sonoma, Timberland, and L. L. Bean.

Back then, the council had eighteen chapters; in addition, about two dozen provisional chapters were being organized, sometimes bursting beyond geopolitical boundaries—such as the Cascadia chapter, which encompassed Portland, Seattle, and Vancouver, British Columbia. After the members' lunch, representatives from each chapter displayed their official banners. I ran over to help hold the sign for the Northern California chapter. We already had a mailing list of about five hundred participants.

Then I ventured onto that enormous stage to introduce the world green building councils as our reach went global. My new friends stood on their chairs and cheered loudly in their native tongues.

I took my seat, and Bob Berkebile came to the podium. He was there during that tense first meeting in 1993 with the AIA leadership in D.C., and we had worked together on the Montana State University project. He had recently joined the board of USGBC and became our guiding light of wisdom.

"We'd like to present leadership awards to our founders, chairman, and officers," he announced. I was the first to be called up. Bob introduced me by saying, "I met this young man who had a vision of greening the US building industry. I didn't know what to make of him and his promise, but he had a lot of passion and was good at recruiting us." After me came Mike. (He'd missed the conference due to work back in D.C. with his company, the Sustainable Products Corporation. Several years ago Mike had left his law firm and founded his own leading-edge green products consulting and training company.) Next was Rick Fedrizzi, then Steven Winter, Kath Williams, and Keith Winn, with Herman Miller furniture. Keith had become his company's lead council representative several years earlier, and was now our treasurer. I felt extremely honored as Bob presented me with a beautiful glass sculpture that spelled out USGBC, our round logo on its base and a green glass replica of our logo's oak leaf set off to the right. "For extraordinary and sustained service" was engraved on mine, along with my name and the title "Founder."

A hundred educational sessions in a dozen tracks filled the next two days. It was the world's most extensive green building university. We'd had trouble selecting all the sessions, there were so many submissions—more than six hundred. I facilitated two of the sessions. The rest of the time I mingled, saying hello to hundreds of friends, my head swimming with names and affiliations.

The last night of the Austin conference, I would be giving out green leadership awards, so I wore my dark green textured suit, gold tie, and a dark-green textured shirt I'd bought in Melbourne earlier that year. My USGBC member pin shined from the lapel. Sara Szal, my new girlfriend, had joined me. Finally it seemed as though I'd found the woman of my dreams. We'd first connected online on Match.com and then again on JDate.com, and since our first date, we'd never been apart. "I loved your essays," she said. "I could feel your heart." I'd been looking for a woman who could understand me and had fire and passion of her own. Sara was Harvard Medical School, MIT, and UCSF trained as an OBGYN, ultimately becoming one of the world's foremost hormone experts and a *New York Times* best-selling author. She looked beautiful in a long black dress, white pearls, and her "up-do" hair. It was our coming out: she'd never attended a council event, and I'd never brought a date before. We strolled hand in hand from the hotel to the ballroom at the convention center.

Inside, we were swamped: Everyone wanted to meet Sara. She handled herself as if this was an everyday occurrence. Finally, we took our seats at the head table. There was a roar of voices, like waves on the shore, as people at the two hundred or so tables talked and laughed.

My mouth was dry and I was fiddling with the silverware, nervous and revved up, as always, before giving a speech. I sipped my wine to calm my nerves. Sara, who was chatting away with Rick Fedrizzi, reached over and squeezed my hand. They were meeting for the first time. At one point I looked over and he mouthed the words, "I love her. She's wonderful." Later he told me Sara was exactly the type of woman he always knew I'd end up with: attractive, smart, passionate, committed to making the world a better place, and her own person. And he added: "Don't screw it up."

"Now I'd like to call up our founder, David Gottfried," the emcee, John Bevilaqua, announced. I climbed up the stairs to the stage. Once there, for a minute all I could see was the bright lights. When my eyes adjusted, I had the shock of seeing my face projected on the huge hanging video screen. I could even see the bags under my eyes.

Then my autopilot feature took over as I grabbed both sides of the lectern and looked out at our congregation of "greenies." I felt like the rabbi my mother had always wanted me to be. I began my sermon. "A decade ago, green building was considered the arcane interest of a few environmental organizations and architects. Today, we have become our own industry," I said. The room was silent. I felt Sara's presence and glanced over at our table. She was gazing at me, smiling, her eyes shining. I gave her a little hand wave to the side of the podium. She waved back, and my heart sang.

After my remarks, I introduced the first annual green building leadership awards. The USGBC Lifetime Leadership Award went to our chair of the LEED rating system, Rob Watson. LEED had enabled the US building industry to begin its transformation from conventional to green, and it was the tool that put the council on the global map. Rob and I hugged as I handed him his award. He felt like a brother. When he spoke to those assembled, he broke out in tears. I shared his joy.

Pliny Fisk won our Green Public Service Award for nongovernmental organizations for his thirty years of pioneering work in green building. Our Green Public Service Government Award (accepted in absentia) went to New York Governor George Pataki for his leadership in passing the nation's first green building tax credit. Ray Anderson won the Green Business Award for greening Interface company-wide and for the company's environmental carpet offerings.

After the event, Sara and I walked in the moonlight with Rick back to the hotel. "Do you know what you've done?" Rick asked. I looked at him.

"You've changed the world," he said. Sara squeezed my hand. "You've done what people only dream of doing in a lifetime."

My heart rose in my throat. "I couldn't have done it without you," I managed to get out.

The founders of the WorldGBC were sitting together in the lobby of the hotel. When they asked us to join them for a drink, Sara nudged me. I got the message. I said my goodbyes and pushed the elevator button.

17
THE GREENEST LITTLE HOME IN AMERICA

Since the days at Stanford in Gil Masters' class when I'd designed and built my solar balsa-wood house, I'd dreamed of building my own green home. I love technological innovations and was eager to try out the new LEED for Homes rating system. Sara and I had married in 2003 in a "green" rooftop wedding in San Francisco. She had previously been married and had a daughter, making me a stepfather. In 2005 we had our own daughter, fulfilling another dream.

Two years later we bought the bungalow. On my first visit, before we'd purchased the house, the sun-faded pale yellow exterior of the 1915 bungalow looked tired, as if it was ready for a rest home. The original porch had been enclosed with lots of windows. Thousands of small gray rocks cluttered the front yard, which gave it a dead feeling (although it could have qualified as ultra-eco since it didn't require any water and diverted rainwater from the street sewer). The cracked red concrete walkway added to the forlorn impression, as did the termite-infested front stairs and brownish old-lady faded lace curtains.

Both front doors were propped open, with the yellowed outer one leading to the enclosed porch and a beautiful period craftsman style inner door with a large domed glass panel. This door opened into the living room. As I stepped into the porch, I detected petroleum fumes, probably emitted from tar paper below the faded blue vinyl tile.

I passed into the living room and nearly choked on the smell of the smoke-infested mustard-colored walls. I wondered if we'd ever be able to remove the toxic fumes from the house, but recalled that there were methods to remove the smell from a house fire. Indoor air quality is an important component of a green building and the most important for health.

I held my breath and reflexively shut my eyes: Sara and I are both allergic to smoke. When I opened my eyes I saw a snug living room with original oak floors inlaid with an intricate walnut pattern, and a period fireplace surrounded by charming built-in wood cabinets with leaded glass panels. Above the crusty walls was the wonder of original ceiling beams and moldings. Below the front windows was solid wood paneling. It was rare to find wood like that, never painted and in pristine condition. I felt the heat of the sunlight pouring through the south-facing windows. That was good — unobstructed solar access.

Many of the owner's years of accumulated knick-knacks were still there, including hundreds of small knitted dolls arranged on an upper shelf in the living room. Out the front window, two young girls rode their scooters along the sidewalk. They were about our older kid's age.

I walked into the dining room. To the left, below a large craftsman window, was a lovely built-in wall cabinet, with numerous glass cabinets and a huge stained wood mantel. It looked like a set from an old movie. The dining room had three windows facing the neighbor's house, and a pair of wood-stained French doors that led to the enclosed porch. The walls and ceiling were clad with wood trim, creating a warm, cozy feeling. The faded and peeling wall covering could not conceal the beauty of the preserved décor. With growing excitement, I went through a small wood door that led from the living room into a small dark hallway that connected the dining room to the first bedroom, and from there, into a preposterously tiny and dated kitchen. It had an original Wedgewood stove like the one my Grandma Frieda had in her first kitchen, with a drawer that appeared to be intended to hold coal. To the right were paper-thin cheap cabinets and a tiny, ancient refrigerator that would hardly suffice to hold our younger daughter's containers of milk. It was awful, but I closed my eyes and tried to imagine what the kitchen would look like if we knocked down the wall to the living room and got rid of the hallway. The kitchen could expand to provide room for an island and to allow light from the front of the house to pour into the kitchen and the rear of the house. LEED has a credit for day lighting and, as humans, we crave natural light and our connection to the outdoors.

Next, I walked into the front bedroom. It, too, had oak floors and crown molding, with a small closet. I imagined a bunk bed placed in the rear corner, so our older daughter could invite a friend to sleep over. The room faced west, but was shaded by the neighbor's two-story house. That would provide for comfort by minimizing the heat gain during the warm Oakland summers. In the house we were renting, the west-facing rooms heated up to fifteen degrees hotter than the rest of the house, making it tough for us to sleep during the summer months. Climate control was an important part of green building, including natural shading.

I walked down the hall to inspect what turned out to be the only bathroom. We'd need another one—especially with the three females in the family preferring long bathing routines; and our younger daughter viewed the tub as her swimming pool and playground for dozens of floating and squirting plastic colored toys. The room's faded pink and blue tile, vintage child-size tub, and old-lady smell reminded me again of Grandma Frieda's garden apartment thirty years ago, when she'd lived there with Grandpa Izzy before they both passed away. The decrepit bathroom also had a tiny toilet and enclosed shower apparently sized for a dwarf. Everything would need to be replaced.

In the west rear corner of the bungalow was another bedroom, with three windows, one of them overlooking a desolate yard. The room was dark, but I imagined breaking through the wall separating it from the garden with a new French door that would lead to a new deck made from sustainably harvested redwood.

To the right, six steps led to what looked to be an added-on upper room, on its own mezzanine level. The walls and ceiling were covered with hideous floral wallpaper. The wallboard was buckling in several places. I wondered how much height we could add if we removed the wallboard from the ceiling. Daylight streamed into the room from four large windows overlooking the rear yard, providing the best natural light in the house.

Beneath that space was a ground-level utility room. It had a low ceiling and two doors, one of which swung out to the yard. I could convert it into a family room that would double as a guest room. It had a dated utility sink and an old water heater, which could be moved elsewhere.

The rear landscaping, if you could call it that, included dead grass, weeds, and two overgrown shrubs: one was the biggest bird of paradise that I'd ever seen, its branches reaching in a thousand directions as if it had landed from Mars and declared war on the desolate site. The grounds were about two times the size of the house—a rare find for such an urban location. Sara and I loved to garden, and the lack of anything worth preserving out here would allow us to create a fabulous backyard haven from scratch, perhaps even including an organic vegetable garden fed from a compost and worm bin. The last time I'd grown anything edible (tomatoes) was almost twenty years before, back in D.C.

If the yard was spacious, the house was anything but. At under fifteen hundred square feet, it was 40 percent smaller than the Berkeley Hills house we had sold a year before. We could add space by going up with a second story, or expanding into the large yard—but either option would add expense and delay to the project.

On the way back to the car, I was almost run over by two Harleys with bareheaded riders racing by on the two-lane road. One was doing a wheelie. I noticed several other similar looking old craftsman bungalows across the street.

Apparently the house was a Sears-type kit home that was popular in the early 1900s. Each kit contained ten thousand to thirty thousand pieces. Sears, Roebuck and Company had stated: "A man of average abilities could assemble a Sears kit home in about ninety days." A contractor would charge $450 to build the kid, the company estimated. It was an early model of prefab manufacturing: a kit of parts made efficiently in the plant—a beautiful and highly cost-effective solution we could learn from.

Farther down the block from College were much larger and newly renovated homes. Families were moving into the trendy area, once populated largely by retirees. The newcomers not only improved the appearance and size of their homes, but brought vitality and kids to the neighborhood as well. I hoped that this trend would accelerate.

On the corner was Cole Coffee, our favorite coffee house. It was packed with customers eating pastries and poached eggs and drinking its freshly ground drip coffees. We had strolled over to this local hot spot several times a week from Sara's cottage five years before. I'd taken our older daughter here often as I rode her on the back of my bike to Hearts Leap Preschool in Berkeley. She always ordered a sugar-frosted morning bun and a hot chocolate with whipped cream: without Sara there to raise her eyebrows at me, I acquiesced to the carb/sugar fest. I'd eat a bran muffin, or two poached eggs with a large cup of coffee. Each cup was individually brewed with fresh-ground beans and the slow-drip process. The smell and taste were intoxicating and addictive. Regular coffee hurt my sensitive stomach and the caffeine made me crazy, but I loved the heightened creativity from the adrenaline rush.

Across the street were several benches where two homeless people slept at night. One wore an old cowboy hat and always had a book in hand. During the day, the area was the smoking and tattoo zone, sort of a "Left Bank." I guess that was the trade-off for "urban" and a Walk Score of 92, with the area described as a "walker's paradise." It also was rated high for its Bike Score (82) and not bad for its Transit Score (60).

College Avenue has a wonderful bustle that reminds me of Paris, with small shops for everything: organic produce, fresh meat and seafood, flowers, a corner grocery market, gourmet wine shop, a tea shop, gelato and chocolates, pizza, a popular local bistro, and gift shops. The Rockridge BART station is a seven-minute walk down College, and the train arrives at the San Francisco Embarcadero in twenty minutes. Reasonable walking distance to the BART was a prerequisite for me. Not only do I despise sitting in traffic on the choked Bay Bridge, but I also didn't want to contribute to the environmental impact of driving, cars being second to buildings as the biggest carbon dioxide emitter.

The day after touring the old bungalow, I dragged Sara out to see it. The kids were still in school. The house was hosting an estate sale of all of the previous owner's things. About a half dozen people were poking among the old sweaters, crocheted dolls, dark-brown leather period couch and antique cooking utensils. I bought an old Royal vintage typewriter, thinking that the kids would enjoy learning to type on it, and that it was in any case a symbolic relic for an aspiring writer.

Sara raced excitedly through the house—god knows a tour didn't take long—while I looked out the front windows in the living room, trying not to inhale any smoke fumes. What if she hated it? I turned around to face her when she touched my arm. A huge smile graced her face, and her eyes sparkled. "Honey, buy it," she said. "I don't care what it takes. It's time." We'd been renting for the past eighteen months, moving from one place to another in three rentals while looking for the perfect house.

Once again, we were competing with others for the house we wanted. However, I had reason to hope that the cumbersome Alameda County public auction process would discourage other buyers and allow us to get a deal. A few months later, I was elated to be the last man standing at the auction of the house. I'd stood quietly next to the other five bidders as they bid against each other. And then when there were just two of us standing, I'd lifted my hand. My bid was $10,000 more than that of the gray-haired man in a striped shirt who had just sat down.

When the judge announced me as the winner, I turned around to see Sara doing a victory dance from her seat, her arms pumping and hips gyrating. Our broker, Anne, was next to her. She too, was all smiles in her black Armani suit, with red lipstick and black designer glasses. When I rushed over to hug Sara, Anne said, "That was fantastic." I'm sure she'd never had a client come to an auction with a spreadsheet of possible bid amounts and nine cashiers' checks in his pocket, in increments from $1,000 to $5,000. I'd read that the winning bidder was required to hand over 10 percent of the bid amount immediately, and I wanted to ensure I had the right amount. Afterward, I was pleased that I still had $5,000 left in my pocket, indicating that we'd not hit our maximum price of

$50,000 more than we'd spent. As it was, our winning bid was much higher than we'd anticipated. And the house still needed extensive renovation before we considered it livable.

Little did we know that a few months later the subprime mortgage-backed securities debacle would yank the world into a massive recession. And to think that a few of the houses we'd bid on earlier had been almost double the price and still required work! Losing out on those bids began to seem like a stroke of luck.

A month later, as the two of us were celebrating Sara's fortieth birthday at Kona Village Resort in Hawaii, the same place we had gone on our honeymoon, escrow closed. We were homeowners again.

However, it would be another sixteen months before we slept there.

The next month we rented our new bungalow to two neighbors for a nine-month lease, hoping that would give us enough time to design the renovation, get building permits, and start construction. Our new tenants, interestingly enough, were also renovating a house in the neighborhood.

I was amazed that anybody would want to live in the substandard hovel that our dark little bungalow was before renovation. Our new tenants volunteered to wash the walls with a toxic chemical concoction called TSP (trisodium phosphate) to kill the lingering smell of cigarettes. This was against my green beliefs, but I looked the other way since they were paying the rent and we wouldn't be moving in for another year.

Shortly after we bought the house, my folks flew up from L.A. in my father's Beechcraft airplane to visit us. I wanted to give them a tour of the house, but was nervous. We hadn't even begun drawing up the plans and the house showed poorly in its dilapidated condition. At a deeper level, a part of me thought that maybe I'd made a mistake by buying an expensive house that not only was very small but would require extensive work. It wasn't clear what we'd end up with upon completion. It would take a lot of creativity to help my folks envision what the house would look like later. I guess I wanted my dad's approval, but suspected that in this case, it wouldn't be forthcoming.

Still, I'd always shared what I was up to with my parents, even when I knew they'd have different opinions. So I picked them up from the airport and took them straight to the tired-looking bungalow. Our tenants had moved in and kindly allowed us a peek. I parked in the rear of the large driveway and then raced around the car to help my father out of the front and my mother out of the back. I noticed that with each visit, it took longer for them to get out of the car; both were aging and had ongoing problems with their respective hip replacements.

Beneath a Reno Air Races dark blue hat, Dad's gray hair was as electric as Albert Einstein's. He had a few days' stubble on his face and tired bags beneath slightly red eyes. His breathing was loud, even from the slight exertion of getting out of the car. He'd never fully recovered his stamina following lung cancer surgery fifteen years earlier. Mom was also a cancer survivor. She'd beaten breast cancer a decade before, exhibiting a strength I hadn't known she had. She underwent her treatments without complaining, while continuing to show love and concern for her family, as she'd always done. Both my parents had undergone chemotherapy, which had aged them.

My dad had retired twenty years before, when he was still a few years shy of sixty. He'd sold his management consulting practice to Coopers & Lybrand, which later became PWC (Price Waterhouse Coopers). He'd wanted his sons to join him in the business, but we'd all opted out. I found his work interesting, but I wanted to find my own way. Like many a son, I imagined that I was unable to hear my own voice with my father nearby.

My mother taught grade school in New York until my oldest brother, Rick, was born. Thereafter she stayed home to take care of her three sons and her elderly parents, and then later, of her older sister, Muriel. She and Muriel had a sisterly bond that is uncommon today—one born out of my grandparents' struggle to survive coming out of the shtetls of Poland, to Ellis Island and into the streets of the Lower East Side of Manhattan.

My parents were older, and frailer, but in other ways undiminished. Dad glanced at the front of the house before attacking the stairs. "You paid how much?" I heard him say in my head, though he remained silent. He grabbed my mother's hand and helped her up the five stairs. "We're best friends," my mother had declared on the ride over. "Not bad after fifty-five years," my father added with a proud grin. It was heartening to witness the camaraderie they'd achieved after supporting each other through their respective cancer fights and living together almost six decades.

"This rail is loose," my dad observed now as we walked up the creaking front stairs. I glanced down at the rusting handrail, my eyes following it to the dirt below. We went through the outer door into the enclosed porch and into the living room. "What's that smell?" my father said, sniffing the air. The TSP had failed to erase the smell of smoke from the walls. Mom hurriedly commented on the nice living and dining room wood trim and built-ins. "What wonderful wood everywhere!" she exclaimed, running her hand over the fireplace. "It reminds me of Grandma's old apartment."

The three of us barely fit through the small door leading into the hallway, and then the adjacent one into the tiny kitchen. "This is one of the smallest kitchens I've ever seen," my father said breathlessly. He was scarcely looking at it—though, granted, there wasn't much to see.

"Is this the only bathroom?" My mother eyed the small tub. "How are you going to fit in that?" On the other side was the dwarf shower that was on my demolition list. They didn't comment on that, but there wasn't much to say, except how substandard it was.

When I turned on the hot water in the tiny, yellowed sink, the knob came off in my hand. "We're thinking that we'll gut the bathroom and add a half bath somewhere," I said lamely as I jammed the knob back on. My dad glanced around, scratching his scalp as if a big bug had landed on his head.

I showed them the other two bedrooms and the downstairs utility room, nervously chattering about my renovation plans for the house all the while. At one point my father touched an exposed wood beam in the unfinished ceiling. "Where are we going to sleep when we visit?" he asked. I didn't have an answer.

I'm not sure I breathed during the entire tour, as I waited and hoped for some form of encouragement. But my father kept silent as I babbled on. My stomach was tight. His expressionless face led me to believe I'd made an ass of myself and bought a worthless piece of junk. At least that's what my mind concluded.

We returned to the car. My parents didn't say anything. I put the key in the ignition. "Well?" I finally said, expecting an explosion. "Interesting, very creative," my father managed to get out. I backed out and headed for our rental house a few blocks away. "How much did you pay for it?" my father went on after a pause.

"Only ten grand more than the last bidder," I hedged.

"The wood is beautiful," my mother chimed in again.

My father interrupted her. "I assume you know what you're doing."

Mom said, "Are you sure you're up for so much work? You travel so much. I hate to see you look so tired." She squeezed my arm. I took one of those deep breaths I'd learned in yoga.

Truthfully, having looked at the house through my father's eyes (as interpreted by my brain), I was convinced that we'd made a mistake. But what could I do? We owned it. I felt a surge of regret, but then remembered my dream of creating the greenest home. This house was a perfect candidate for a complete green makeover. "Small is green" became my new mantra, but truly accepting that sentiment felt like trying to eat the piles of green kale that Sara put on my plate—I knew it was healthful and good for my poops, as she told us, but none of us liked it.

That was the way it was with the bungalow renovation. I didn't want just to renovate the house in the ordinary way; I'd been waiting twenty-five years to pour everything I knew about green building into a project like this. I envisioned it as a showcase for green building with all of its facets, including energy and water efficiency, solar energy, and materials reuse and salvaging (waste minimization). I dreamed that the house would also demonstrate green landscaping, including growing organic food, among other healthy features.

Sara and I spent months talking about our visions for the house. We scoured magazines and renovation books. It became clear that we'd need to make every inch count.

Building or renovating my own green home had been my dream ever since I designed and built that model green home for Gil's class at Stanford. With each move, I'd also been carting along several years' worth of green building product brochures and manufacturers' business cards from green conferences. I'd spent hours walking up and down the conference aisles, keeping a lookout for green products that could possibly go into that future dream green home. "Why don't you just throw that out?" Sara would say during one of our frequent purges of unnecessary possessions. But I held onto the bags as if they held the map to a secret treasure.

And now was my time.

First I needed a team. I wanted a contractor and architect who were passionate about green building. A few months after the tenants moved in, I called Chris Avant, a friend of mine who was president of Canyon Construction. I'd met him at various green building events over the years. He'd even undertaken a LEED Platinum renovation of an old barn in Moraga for his firm's new headquarters. Chris' eyes sparkled as he described the eco-restoration: solar electric panels, solar hot water, radiant heating in the floor, and the highest insulating windows — from Germany.

We met at Cole Coffee to talk about my renovation. I ordered a personal drip coffee, and he a latte. I watched as he patiently waited more than ten minutes for them to deliver his drink. By then I'd already ordered another and asked them about the status of his order. "Thanks so much," he'd said with a smile to the woman finally delivering the frothy concoction. You would have thought they'd given it to him for free. Unlike other builders I'd known during my years working in D.C., he was patient and soft-spoken: a type B personality. He also had a reputation for being trustworthy, and ran a seventy-person home building firm known for its green passion. Chris had worked his way up from carpenter to president. I was pretty sure I had the right contractor.

Chris recommended that we hire Berkeley architect Dan Smith. Dan had more than thirty years' experience, much of it in the greening of homes, including solar and straw-bale construction.

The next week, Dan and I toured the house. He had wavy gray hair and round bookish glasses, and wore a heavy brown knit sweater with elbow patches, khaki pants, and thick-soled sturdy walking shoes, like my own. He carried a black bound sketchbook and looked more like a scholar than an architect.

As we went through the house, Dan rapidly drew the existing layout with changes that included opening up the kitchen by removing the hallway and the wall separating it from the dining room — creating a great-room effect (exactly what Sara had told me she wanted). Next to the first bedroom, we'd squeeze in a half-bath. We discussed ways to cantilever a second-floor master suite into the yard or expand by purchasing a prefab building and connecting it to the house. We agreed that a modern kitchen and new master suite would create an interesting contrast to the historic craftsman details in the rest of the house. Dan understood the higher efficiency of solar hot water to solar photovoltaics, and had a good idea for a combined solar hot water/radiant heating system, called a Phoenix. I hadn't heard of that option.

"I'd like the home to exceed LEED Platinum and be net-zero," I told him at the end of our session. "I've always dreamed of showcasing what can be done to green an existing house." He smiled. "Count me in."

I'd found my team.

A few weeks later, Dan sent me the first sketches for the master suite — a big steel box perched over the yard, complete with high sloping ceilings, lots of nonglare windows for north-facing daylight, and its own bathroom. We'd had this setup in our Berkeley Hills home, and I'd missed the quiet and privacy away from the kids.

Privacy came at a price. The new upstairs bedroom, along with Dan's other ideas, came out to double our budget. "A renovation is often more expensive than new construction," Chris explained (a statement I would often have occasion to remember). And our plans called for the overhaul of all of the home's tired systems (heating, plumbing, electrical, structural), as well as for two brand-new bathrooms; a new kitchen with cabinets, appliances, flooring, and tile; new energy-efficient windows; insulation in the walls, attic, and crawl space; a new front entry; and side porous paver driveway. Oh, and retrofits for the entry mudroom, the conversion of the downstairs laundry room into a playroom, a new deck with French doors, and the upgrading of the three existing bedrooms.

It would take three months for design review and comments from the neighbors, and several months to build the addition.

Given our succession of rentals, Sara and I weren't excited about the prospect of extending the construction period from six months to a year.

So there went the master suite addition.

Over the next year, I spent half my days making our dream a reality. And at night I expanded the dream.

I printed out the new LEED for Homes pilot rating system and also Build It Green's Green Point Rated certification guideline, working late into the night to set my individual credit rating goals and overall scores.

Next to the worksheets I made endless lists in a large Excel spreadsheet on my computer, conducting my own minibrainstorm (or eco-charrette as we greenies call it). Achieving a LEED Platinum rating, the highest offered by USGBC, seemed possible. That meant that we'd exceed the eighty points required for a small home through achieving a high level of energy and water efficiency, solar energy generation, water capture and recycling, green materials, and significant waste diversion from the landfill. We'd also achieve a high level of indoor environmental quality through low-emitting products (like paints and glues), exhaust fans in the bathrooms and kitchen, and lots of daylighting.

At midnight I emailed my team the lengthy list of measures that would allow me to achieve the highest rating level. In time, I'd add to the list, after poring over dozens of home renovation magazines and books on green homes. It took more than a week to refine my targeted list of green products and write down the names of the manufacturers.

At my historic downtown Oakland office overlooking City Hall, I finally spread out all of the green product brochures and business cards I'd collected, arranging them into piles according to product type. Soon, a green plan and green partners emerged. My thought was that maybe these leading firms would agree to provide their products for free, or a substantial discount, in return for media exposure and the opportunity to say that they were part of this visionary project.

After three months, I signed around fifteen deals that helped a lot with the renovation costs. In the process, I discovered many leading-edge green products that I hadn't known about and made a number of useful new business acquaintances. I loved the process of researching technologies and then negotiating deals, as each transaction boosted the performance and green sex appeal of our home.

I wanted to vet each product and company for its relative ecological footprint, but I didn't have that time. In any case, I knew from my green building consulting work and years of tracking green product innovation that we had a highly credible package: solar PVs and hot water, tile with 70 percent recycled glass, all ENERGY STAR-rated appliances, FSC-certified hickory wood floors, a recycled steel bathtub, LEDs, and salvaged redwood decks. It doesn't take the most cutting-edge products to achieve a LEED Platinum rating; rather, it takes well thought-out and integrative design and systems.

I became a man obsessed. "It'll only take a few minutes," I'd promise Sara and the kids on Saturday afternoon. I'd force them into the car to visit the next eco-home improvement store, lighting outlet, Expo product center, or appliance showcase. My pockets bulged with lists of items we needed. Each night, I'd flip through more renovation books and magazines, adding to my list. Sometimes I'd even wake up in the middle of the night to jot down a new entry.

Sara was soon over the thrill of being hauled up and down endless store aisles, but she had a better sense of aesthetics than I did, and I needed her along when I went shopping. The kids I bribed with nightly visits to the local chocolate and gelato shop.

I reveled in the sweets as well; they helped calm my nerves from the magnitude of pending product decisions as well the occasional panic at the ever-escalating costs. Dark chocolate bars or covered almonds were the most soothing, preceded, of course, by a glass of hearty Napa Valley cabernet.

Sara cracked, though. "I've had it!" she declared one Saturday when I turned the wheel toward a third building supply store. The kids fought over a small slimy green rubber creature in the back seat. "Can't we just go to a movie or a park like a normal family?"

God knows I didn't blame her. I look back and see a man possessed. Renovating a house of my own on green principles was like inhaling 200 percent fresh oxygen. I'd waited years to pour everything I knew about green building into a project like this. I envisioned it as a showcase for green building with all of its facets, including energy and water efficiency, solar energy, and materials reuse and salvaging (waste minimization). I dreamed that the house would also demonstrate green landscaping, including growing organic food, among other healthy features.

So of course I went overboard.

It wasn't just the weekend shopping trips. Once the construction began and the tenants moved out, I had to be at the house every day, whether anyone needed me there or not. The girls came with me after dinner enough times to have learned a pretty good impersonation of a construction superintendent. They balanced on the wood framing that was all there was left of the kitchen floor to watch their playroom take shape. I thought it was a great time for the children to learn about green building, despite their youth. And by the time construction was done, they were ready to become green tour guides for the home, as our older daughter did years later for the sixth-grade green club.

I learned a lot myself. Despite having worked in the building industry for years, I'd never watched the construction process on a daily basis. When Dan Smith finished the plans, I marked them up with a red pen, as if I were preparing for a trial where my life depended on the outcome. I reviewed the plans over and over—finding more things to comment on with each pass. I must have driven Dan crazy.

And it was the same with each tour of the house during construction. If Sara or the kids were along, they'd be moaning for me to leave—"Da-a-ad!" or "David, we'll be late ..."—but there was always something more to inspect. So I took up going to the house twice a day—once alone, and then returning with whoever would agree to join me that evening. I can only imagine what a pain in the neck I must have been for the workmen, as they heard my big feet coming up the front steps once again.

I'd always dreamed of creating a home that would be net-zero electricity. But as I learned, that isn't easy. It requires a combination of measures and iterative steps. The first is making the home's outside envelope as tight as possible. The house was built in 1915 and, like all houses of that era, had no insulation. So the first step was insulating the walls with blown-in cellulose (fire-treated shredded newspaper), the attic rafters with sprayed-on Icynene foam, and the crawl space under the house with batting. We replaced the drafty old single-pane windows with dual-pane, energy-efficient windows and stained the unfinished Douglas fir wood cladding they came with to match the house's original wood trim. Since some of our windows were of craftsman designs with lots of small glass panels separated by wood trim comprising each window, we were lucky when the manufacturer agreed to provide one large dual-pane glass window for each opening, and a craftsman grid glued on top to match our original design. They also had a casement window package that fit within our original windowsill—greatly lowering the cost by excluding any exterior demolition and stucco patching.

We tested the home's airtightness with an air blower test, and then filled gaps with weather stripping, caulking, and foam. This measure provided the highest return on investment: for $600 and in one day of work, we were able to halve the home's energy loss. We'd retain the home's heated air in the winter for much longer, and stay cooler in the summer by keeping the outside heat out. Finally, we added a damper and glass doors to the fireplace—a prerequisite for the LEED rating.

A goal of net-zero energy also dictated the need for new highly efficient systems and appliances to cut the energy load. Thus we installed a new hydronic (hot water) wall-mounted radiator heating system, superefficient solar hot water heater, high-level ENERGY STAR-rated appliances (refrigerator, stove, microwave, dishwasher, washer and dryer) and energy-efficient lighting (compact fluorescent and LED). We also added energy-efficient overhead fans to each of the bedrooms for the occasional sweltering East Bay summer days. The integrated compact fluorescent overhead lights would also prove helpful, as would the fans' capability to run in reverse during the winter to distribute rising hot air. We didn't need air conditioning at all, given our moderate climate and the bedroom fans.

According to an energy model run by Dan Smith, our design of a superefficient building envelope, combined with highly rated and controlled appliances and systems, would lower our home energy load by about 75 percent from what the house used before, and around 35 percent below that of a comparably sized new California house.

We were pleased with the outcome, which also contributed many LEED points. To supply the house's vastly reduced energy requirements, we installed sixteen solar-electric panels, which took up most of our roof space while leaving room for three solar hot water panels to cut down on natural gas use. This earned us all ten of the LEED points for renewable power. The panels would supply approximately 60 percent of the electricity for the house. Of course I wanted to produce more electricity than that, but it was a good start, and so I let go of my net-zero energy goal for the time being. I thought it was prudent not to install more solar than practical at the outset. The three panels would preheat our radiant (hot water) heating system, an installation that included individual clean-cut metal radiator panels on one wall in each room. I loved that we'd be able to adjust each panel with its own control—allowing me to tune the supply of heat according to how much we needed in a particular room on a daily basis. The solar hot water system used natural gas as a boost to the preheated solar water. Gas is more environmentally benign than electricity, emitting 43 percent fewer carbon dioxide emissions per equivalent unit of energy.

To a systems engineer and a green building enthusiast like me, "beautiful" means optimal performance and ratings such as LEED Platinum and even beyond: net-zero energy, water, and waste.

For Sara, "beautiful" means aesthetically satisfying. Paints that were healthy and didn't off-gas toxic fumes were necessary, but she wanted vibrant and soothing colors. When it came time to pick our paint brand and colors, I'd focused on reading the environmental performance data for various paint brands. The type we ultimately selected was highly rated and contained zero VOCs (volatile organic compounds). I told our construction project manager that five colors would be sufficient. Even that seemed like a lot since I'd lived in my Marina bachelor apartment for ten years with every room painted landlord white.

Sara hired a colorist. I'd never worked with one before. One night after she and the expert met over at the house, Sara came home with a huge grin and sparkling eyes, like a little girl who'd just had her first pony ride. For a change, she was the one who encouraged all of us to walk over to the house before the sun went down. The house still had no lights during that phase of the construction. As we approached the faded yellow façade of the old bungalow, I saw six different color patches painted on the outside. It looked as if our younger kid had painted the swatches instead of the colorist. The palette included a deep green color for the main façade, and various brown and yellow accent colors. "That looks good to me," I told Sara, as we made our way into the entry mudroom and through each room of the house. I kept silent for the rest of the tour, taking it all in. But my pulse raced faster and faster as we entered each successive room. Thirty different colors for a 1,500-square-foot house! Three or four different colors per room. When we got to our bedroom, I found myself looking at dark brown walls, with two lighter accent colors. "Well?" Sara asked after I'd been silent for more than a minute, breathless. I hesitated further.

"It looks dead," I finally blurted out. "Why would I want to sleep in a brown room?" She flashed me her wounded look, as if I'd slapped her, and left the room. I remembered that I'd balked at a bold deep yellow in our Berkeley Hills house. A month after we'd moved into the house, though, that room had become my favorite. I'd do my thirty-minute yoga practice in it each morning before work. The combination of the sun's morning rays glistening off the yellow created a feeling of warmth and comfort that I soon associated with deep breathing and healing. No surprise, then, that I eventually fell for the warmth and calming energy of the brown Sara chose (she says it's cocoa).

Over the years, I've had a similar impulsive reaction to hundreds of her suggestions, from vegan organic food to dozens of diets, wildly colored shirts she'd bought me, and independent films. "You know you love it," she'd often insist as I rebelled. And in the end, more often than not, she was right. Come to think of it, I fought her about the timing and speed of when we'd get married, buy a house, have a baby, take long vacations, and eat superhealthy food—even to abandon gluten, sugar, caffeine, and alcohol. Even though I love green building and the concept of a green life, my basic nature is that of a hunter-caveman. But by coming out of my cave of habits, I discovered that I craved what Sara offered. Many of the changes she introduced to my life helped elevate my green life score, enhance my life, and bring great joy.

Money was a worry. Many nights I woke up in a sweat wondering how we'd afford our ambitious plans. Our timing couldn't have been worse. The economy was plummeting—the worst crash since the Great Depression. Our 401(k)s were now 201(k)s. Was this the best time to be pumping money into a diminutive, aging craftsman bungalow in a declining house market? I fretted that the house could never be worth what we were putting into it—kind of like a new car that loses so much of its value the day you drive it off the lot. And I'd heard the horror stories about construction costing twice as much as the estimate. I wanted to create a visionary green house, but I also slept better with more cash in the bank, a trait I'd learned from my father.

My business wasn't flourishing because of the amount of time I was putting into the house—it was almost a full-time job (at least the way I was managing the dream renovation)—and Sara's new integrative medical practice was still just getting going. But I wanted to do this house project and wouldn't have replaced the opportunity for a million-dollar contract.

One of my last change orders was to construct a small structure in the backyard to serve as my home office. The plan was that I'd pay for this new building out of my business, and close my downtown Oakland office, saving monthly rent and parking fees. I was on the advisory board for a company that had invented a 120-square-foot structure (called a Lifepod) that could be converted into a home office. They agreed to donate the metal frame, roof, solar PV panels, and an inverter (needed to convert the solar power generated from DC to AC). All I needed to do was make the open-framed metal shed into a habitable home office. Dan Smith figured it out and sketched plans that called for a concrete pad (with 50 percent fly ash), exterior galvanized metal façade, energy-efficient windows, entry door, drywall, cellulose wall insulation, compact fluorescent lights, and a reclaimed (vertical-grain) redwood entry deck.

I was excited about the idea of working at home. A 30-foot commute to the rear yard was definitely green. It's amazing how many of us go to work each day, leaving behind a vacant house — at a financial and environmental cost. Work typically provides social and collaborative space, but much time is spent doing isolated tasks that could be done at home: computer, telephone, reading, and writing.

Six months after the start of the renovation, I moved my one-person office into the rear structure office. The main house wouldn't be done for a few more weeks. Despite the cacophony of saws, drills, vacuums, and hammers, I enjoyed being in the middle of our construction zone.

The opportunity allowed me to get an education on how cruelly expensive and time-consuming custom remodeling is. One day they delivered the "green" cabinets and island for the kitchen. It took them five days to level the island and build out its custom base, and another five days to custom cut and glue the 70 percent recycled-glass tile trim. Carson, our carpenter, a tall, solid, Nordic-looking man with blond hair and bright blue eyes, patiently measured, cut, and installed hundreds of one-inch square tiles. At the intersection of the tile to the cabinets, there was only room for one-half an inch of tile. It took two days for Carson to hand cut each tile to fit. I asked him why he didn't just skip this task and paint the half-inch section under the cabinet. It was impossible to see that the small gap was untiled, unless you stuck your head under the cabinet and looked up. To me, achieving that level of detail was too costly, as was the week spent on getting the bottom of our custom island trim perfectly balanced. If the item had been ordered from IKEA, it would have self-leveling feet, but since it was custom, it required an additional week of work. On the other hand, our cheap IKEA desks were still off-gassing (that new car smell) after more than six months, and the file cabinet lock never worked.

Still, did we really need such a high level of customization for our renovation? Obviously we didn't. I wouldn't do it that way again. After all, how many of us hire an architect to develop customized blueprints for our cars? From what I can tell, most of us are content with the multitude of model options available at the dealer, along with choices of color, stereo system, GPS, sunroof, upholstery, and such. But when it comes to our residences, many of us insist on custom construction. To a great extent, it makes sense for renovation. In a remodel, standardization is difficult.

Nevertheless, IKEA will tailor its standard kitchen cabinets, islands, and countertops to your kitchen's dimensions. The savings in money, time, and hassle are significant—and the quality is acceptable for most of us. In terms of green, Home Depot (Eco Options line of products) and Truitt & White, a local store, are becoming more aware of sustainable solutions. And the same is true for contractors and subcontractors such as electricians and painters. Our painting contractor describes his business as a green company, avoids toxics, and patiently works with customers on eco-paint choices (even when there are thirty colors).

But with new construction, customization isn't always necessary. Many options in prefabricated new houses and small additions are now available. *Dwell* magazine and West Coast Green, in the Bay Area, display many options at conferences and exhibitions through various vendors and showcase models. When we were just starting the design process, we considered deconstructing (and recycling) the bungalow and buying a new prefabricated home. Michelle Kaufmann even did several layouts for us, using a few of her different prefabricated home models. Green building performance was a major consideration in her design. She also said the cost would be around $250 per square foot, plus the construction of the foundation that the prefabricated home would sit on once it was craned off the delivery truck. Our cost ended up about double that price, and our construction period was seven months instead of a few days.

How much is enough? The question comes up constantly during home design and construction. For each family, the answer is different. Placing a green filter on the answer provides useful guidance: less square footage earns more LEED points, as do more efficiency, less waste, healthier components, locally sourced, recycled, reused, and reclaimed materials. Ultimately, the goal is to achieve a lower ecological footprint, both in building a house and while living in it. Still, when we finished, I wished we'd built that luxurious master bedroom suite. At the time I didn't think we needed it, and we could do with less. But I'd forgotten my Brentwood roots and the ingrained preference for flying first class and staying at luxurious hotel suites. As the frog said, it's not always easy being green. Sometimes we just want more, even if it isn't warranted.

Since the 1950s, the average home size had gone up 155 percent, from 983 square feet to 2,505 (and from 268 square feet to 982 per person—up 266 percent). In 1950, only 1 percent of homes had four bedrooms or more; by 2003, 39 percent of new homes had four or more bedrooms. This growth occurred while the average number of occupants per home was decreasing (from 3.67 down to 2.55)—and their girth was increasing. My parents' first few homes were small. I shared a bedroom with my brother

Glenn for my first eight years—I thought that was normal, even when he'd draw an imaginary line down the middle and punch me if I crossed over. That made it hard to get dressed, since the closet was on his side. On the other hand, I had the door on my side, which made it hard for him to exit. But he was bigger.

Giving up a separate master bedroom suite was painful, but replacing the rear bedroom window with a French door that led out to a new, recycled redwood deck, complete with an outdoor shower, helped ease the pain. Dan Smith helped us figure out how to gut and expand the room's closet (incorporating the old dwarf shower in the bathroom) so that it would be big enough for Sara's and my clothing and shoes. We put a replacement shower in the new tub, as well as a second one outside, since we couldn't fit it in the new powder room.

I was subsequently amazed at people's enthusiasm for the outdoor shower. It's a thrill to shower outside, breathing the fresh air and enjoying the view of the tall neighboring trees. (Of course, we created an enclosure to shield us from the neighbors' view.) We also connected the drain to the gray-water system so that the mostly clean water would be filtered and then used for irrigating our plants.

The renovation resulted in new everything, except for the basic shell and walls of the house and wood trim. The bathrooms had new recycled content steel sinks, dual-flush toilets from Australia, a new steel tub and vanity in the main bathroom, and high-recycled-content tile and wainscot. The blue-green marine tile had abalone in it, which sparkled in the light. The powder room sported a solar automatic faucet that limits the kids' excessive water usage and even turns on in the dark.

During construction, I had times of real panic: one night I visited the house after they'd finished installing the recycled-glass tile on the bathroom floors. I noticed that the hundreds of individual glass pieces were not level. My pulse raced as I ripped off my shoes and socks and walked on the uneven glass tiles, dragging my feet to see if the edges would cut my skin. Later that night I took Sara and the kids to the house so that Sara could render an opinion. She agreed that the workmanship was inferior and that the two floors had to be replaced. Thankfully, the tile company, one of our home partners, agreed that the material had been installed incorrectly and provided new goods for free. Our contractor had its best carpenter install the tile, and the problem disappeared.

Another panic came when the bright white radiator panels were installed in each room. By then, the thirty paint colors had been applied, blending together as if in a Monet. I'd seen the mistake when I made my evening tour on the way home from work: beautifully curated three- and four-color palette blended rooms bombarded by stark white metal Martian-looking radiators placed right in the middle of the wall.

After dinner, I brought Sara and the kids back to the house. I held my breath as Sara made her way through the house and spotted the glaring radiators. Finally, after what seemed like an eternity, she turned to me. "You ruined my house."

By the end of the next day I'd found the solution, having searched the Internet and called the manufacturer on the East Coast well before our sunrise that next morning. We'd paint each metal radiator to match or accent the given wall by powder-coating them, a process used by auto body shops, and one that would hold up under relatively high water temperatures. Astutely, I had Sara pick each color—keeping silent even if I disagreed with her selections.

Sara wanted a large bathtub to soak in. I shuddered at the idea of my eco-friends catching sight of such a water hog. I might as well buy a Hummer and park it in the driveway. My solution was the gray-water capture system. Our contractor introduced us to Kevin, who looked more like a wild-eyed scientist than a water-capture designer, with his disheveled long hair, thick glasses, and Mexican vest over an untucked shirt. He carried a 15-inch Apple laptop around the way other people carry cell phones. His two workers added to the grunge image, so that collectively they looked like a rock band. I never understood Kevin's design, but I wanted to be state-of-the-art in water capture and reuse. The global focus has been on climate change (and well it should be, with the decade from 2000 to 2009 being the warmest on record), but the data suggests that water is the next major crisis. As water tables drop around the globe, we're running out of potable water. One recent study suggested that in the next few decades, at least one-sixth of the global population might be short of water as a result of climate change. In addition, rising sea levels—as much as twenty-three inches in the next one hundred years—could reduce fresh water supplies by up to 50 percent in coastal communities—where 40 percent of people on the Earth live.

With Kevin's design, we would capture about half of the roof's rainwater in exterior wall-mounted rain storage bins, each a fifty-gallon recycled plastic vat. The Bay Area has ample rain to harvest, and we planned to feed one of our toilets with that rainwater for about nine months a year. Two or more baths, plus my shower each day, as well as numerous sinkfuls of daily water use, were more than enough water to provide for our low-water landscaping. The extra gray water would then be filtered and dumped into a rock pit to trickle down to replenish the depleted aquifer below our property. We installed porous brick pavers for our driveway and the house's entry walkway. Nine inches of rock beneath the bricks served as a giant water-capture and filtration bin. From what I can tell, no rainwater that hits our property makes its way to the city sewers, where energy is expended to treat, pump, and dispose of the valuable water in the Bay.

Recycling was an important aspect of our renovation. I asked the contractor to reuse and recycle all construction and demolition debris, and in fact almost none of it ended up in the landfill. We also donated the old appliances to a local product-recycling warehouse: vintage Wedgewood stove, the dated refrigerator, yellow-stained tub, and tiny square sink. The contractor also took back the old doors we couldn't reuse, as well as extra lumber and spare parts to use in other projects.

We used hundred-year-old, vertical-grain reclaimed redwood for the two decks, front entry stairs, and outdoor shower, and that cut down on having to buy virgin wood and kept the old timber from the landfill. By fixing up the front mudroom, lower-level utility room, and attic, we were able to effectively use space that wasn't being used before. This also increased our living space, and in turn meant fewer materials and a lower environmental impact than adding new space.

"I want a fabulous kitchen," Sara had insisted from the beginning, and in fact the kitchen became the heart and soul of the house. An island with drawers on all sides and an expansive rounded eco-countertop in the middle was designed into the heart of the kitchen. We installed custom-designed "green" cabinets manufactured by a local shop. All appliances were energy efficient (ENERGY STAR rated), including: refrigerator, induction cook top, downdraft vent, dishwasher, oven, and convection microwave that could serve as a second oven.

Green materials were a must. We specified an FSC-certified (Forest Stewardship Council) hickory wood for the new playroom, mudroom floors, and redwood fences. We chose an oak floor that matched the original wood in the adjoining bedroom and dining room. I tried to find FSC-certified oak, but found it too difficult to match the existing floor's narrow depth. After a week of effort, I gave up and ordered the non-FSC replacement and moved on. I hate to admit that it's sometimes easier (and less stressful) to select material that's readily available. We installed pull-down stairs to the attic, making the space available for storage. This required cutting out an opening large enough for a sturdy folding wood stairway, and reinforcing the wood joists and ceiling to be able to handle the added weight.

After the main house was finished and we'd moved in, I turned my attention to the desolate front and rear yards. We hired David Thorne, a local landscape architect, for the job. Both Sara and I liked David when we met him at the property, and we hired him the next week. Dressed in worn jeans, tennis shoes, and a work shirt worn out like a teenager, he looked like a park ranger. We liked his interest in our green project and openness to design the site work to complement the house's high performance level. He usually did landscaping for much larger houses than ours, but he liked our green imperative.

David's plan called for low-water plants and trees (vine and Japanese maples, arbutus marina and a luma apiculata), a large Stonehenge-type gathering circle of Napa basalt boulders in the rear, just behind the reclaimed wood deck, and an organic vegetable garden behind the rear office structure.

The landscape contractor planted the bigger trees and shrubs on the property, but happily left most of the grounds for Sara and me to plant. This was a goal of ours—to improve the site with the labor of our own hands. Sara turned out to have a keen sense of landscape design and plant selection. I too liked getting my hands dirty and watching things grow. In addition to selecting and planting a variety of low-water wild grasses, I planted a multitude of vegetables for the garden (artichokes, lettuce, onions, tomatoes, and strawberries). The artichokes grew as if bent on taking over the entire vegetable plot and monopolizing the sunlight. Sara liked the physical work and was even happy to pull weeds in the rain. I have been amazed at how fast plants grow. Our array included many California natives, such as California poppy, arroyo lupine, wild mint, seaside daisy, mugwort, yerba buena, yarrow, and salvia. Sara also planted an herb and dye garden: lemon balm, ashwagandha, toyon, lemon verbena, basil, yarrow/milfoil, echinacea, and rosemary. She and our younger daughter had taken classes to learn how to make natural dyes to create bioregionally dyed clothing.

The plan was to water all of the plants, ultimately amounting to more than a hundred, with our captured gray water. However, it didn't take much time for the drip system emitters to clog up. It seems that the contractor didn't install the larger orifice version that Kevin specified. For the first six months, many of the plants didn't get watered, as each contractor pointed the finger at the other.

We ended up the one-year project with about sixty change orders. Granted, many of the changes we'd asked for. However, I still battled with the project manager over the budget and many of the other change orders. Renovation is really a process. Once a wall is opened up or a window removed, the scope naturally grows. It could be discovery of unforeseen conditions, or the owners (us) coming up with new ideas and additions to the plans. At some point, though, it's imperative to set a maximum budget and stick with it. We increased the maximum about twenty times.

Once we finished the project and moved into the house, I began beating myself up about the cost of the renovation. In fact, I was embarrassed to add it all up, much less disclose the total to anyone. The smallness of the house and nonritzy neighborhood didn't really support the cost, and as a person whose career has been in real estate, I should have known better. Late at night when I couldn't sleep, my mind went through all of the details and sequences of events. What could I have done better? We bought the house in a public auction, managed the project intensely, hired a friend's construction company, and saved significant product costs through my green industry partners program. I guess we could have bought a much larger home—one that would appreciate more rapidly in tandem with such a high renovation cost. But its value likely would have fallen more with the crash. I could have drastically cut the scale of the renovation—but how? Much of the house was unlivable to us. At one point, before we began the construction work, we did bid on another, much larger and grander house. However, I was relieved when we were substantially outbid. If we'd won that one, the starting price would have equaled our ending price for a fully remodeled green home.

We were fortunate to receive a lot of media coverage on the house. When we erected the rear office structure's metal framing and roof in one day, Discovery Channel's *Renovation Nation* show came out to film. It was exciting to spend the day with the host, Steve Thomas, who'd been the star of *This Old House*. It was exhilarating to see the small building's framing, roof, and solar panels go up in a few hours, especially given the slow custom work we'd witnessed with every aspect of the renovation project in the main house. Steve was filmed climbing up onto the roof with drill blazing. He looked more like a gun-slinging outlaw than a TV celebrity. We later became friends.

The LEED process was fairly involved, including submittal of an extensive binder that documented each credit we were claiming. USGBC sent out a home rater who inspected the house on several occasions and signed off on our application. My team worked well together in completing the requisite paperwork, as well as ensuring that our plans and the actual construction work complied with our LEED credit goals. I was elated when our LEED for Homes provider called to tell us that we had not only achieved the highest rating of Platinum, but we'd also received the highest score ever—106.5 points (26.5 points over our platinum threshold).

However, as the leader, we became the target to beat, and several homes have now exceeded our rating, to my great joy.

Receiving the acknowledgment for what we'd achieved felt great and helped to mitigate my misgivings about the cost and the small size of the house. Our small footprint had lowered our platinum threshold by ten points, from a base level of 90. A large home is penalized for its size, raising the platinum minimum to 100 points. This helped further my justification for buying such a small home.

The LEED for Homes rating system is primarily used with new homes and wasn't really designed for existing home renovations like ours. As such, we didn't receive any extra credit for saving more than 95 percent of the existing home, versus building all new. We also rated the house with Build It Green's GreenPoint Rated system, using their existing home renovation version. We were excited to earn their highest certification score at the time that we applied, and a year later we were given two of their annual awards: Judges Choice-Commitment to Sustainability, and Achievement in Remodeling.

Later on, after USGBC issued a press release on our achievement, the media coverage increased. The main spread was in *Metropolitan Home's* May issue—featuring six pages and a half dozen photos. Other articles, blogs, and shows appeared, including six minutes on NPR's *Living On Earth* radio show and an eight-part video series on Planet Green's website. The coverage helped get out the green building message, and the renovation of an existing small bungalow gave many homeowners new ideas. The opportunity to showcase, teach, and hopefully inspire is part of my reason for being, and a critical part of a green life. It also fuels me.

18
REGENERATIVE VENTURES

In 2008 I rebranded my consulting company, which I'd called WorldBuild for the past decade, as Regenerative Ventures. I was fond of the word "regenerative," as it indicated the highest level of "green"—beyond sustainable and net-zero. For example, a "regenerative" building could be defined as one that produces more energy than it consumes (energy positive), and recharges the water aquifer by allowing rainwater and captured, treated bathroom water to go directly down through the soil and not be diverted by nonporous pavement to the city sewer system. Not easy to achieve, but I'd never been one to aim low.

In addition to continuing to serve as a strategic consultant to firms such as UTC's Carrier Corporation and Thomas Properties Group, I began serving on the advisory boards of companies that use innovative technology to create products and services that compete favorably on price and performance, while reducing mankind's impact on the environment. These companies raised venture capital investment for their building-related start-ups, such as software and materials-based products and services.

For years I'd wanted to become a venture capitalist, but had never had the opportunity to go work for one of the dozens located nearby in the Peninsula, south of San Francisco. And I'd been advised that it is *deathly* to try to raise the capital for your own fund, especially having never served as a venture capitalist. Limited partners who invest in new funds like to review the principals' investment track records. And I had none.

By joining numerous advisory boards of venture-backed start-ups in the building industry, I found a small innovative way to become a venture capitalist of sorts. When you join an advisory board for small private start-ups, you're typically given stock options in the given company that vest over a period of time, usually around three years. And if the company is purchased or happens to have the luck to go public, you can exercise those options at your stock "strike" price that was set when the advisory stock deal was signed. And if the luck holds out, the option stock price will be much less than the market price for the stock. Well, that's the idea, at least in theory. In some way, tracking down and receiving stock in start-ups was my antidote to founding and funding USGBC and the WorldGBC. In those cases, I'd carried the start-up risk without receiving any stock. In nonprofits, no one owns the stock. Even though I was thrilled at our outcome, I often couldn't help but imagine the millions Mike, Rick, and I would have earned if USGBC had gone public. Ownership of LEED and its Greenbuild conference alone was worth a pretty penny.

Having now been involved in more a dozen start-ups, I've found that the CEOs of these firms are passionate and driven. In contrast to traditional building industry firms, many of them came from the high-tech industry, transferring their fast-paced work ethic and tactics to the more static and laggard building industry. The historic research investment rate in the building industry was about one-tenth that of high-tech. But these new firms operated more like Silicon Valley tech firms; they invested heavily in research and development, setting up state-of-the-art labs and hiring the best university and industry PhDs to provide quantum technology breakthroughs. This is just the shot in the arm the building industry and the world need if we are going to make an impact on global warming and water depletion, while reducing waste and our dependence on limited resource materials.

One of my advisory board companies was Calera, funded by Vinod Khosla, the billionaire cofounder of Sun Microsystems and a former partner at Kleiner Perkins, a powerhouse venture firm—the one that works with Al Gore. Brent Constantz was the founding CEO of Calera: a Stanford professor and passionate visionary who founded three other successful companies, two of which made cement for bone fractures. When I met him the first time at his office in Los Altos, I encountered a tall man dressed in shorts and flip-flops. A mountain bike leaned against a wall. We had lunch and I became enthralled. His company was inventing a new cement and an aggregate product from carbon dioxide directly from a coal or cement plant. The resulting material could then be placed into concrete as a replacement for the cement or the aggregate, or both, making it carbon neutral and even negative. Carbon sequestration was an amazing accomplishment that to date was only being achieved by trees, plants, and the ocean.

Calera said its product was the first to sequester CO^2 from industrial emitting sources (such as a coal plant), and convert the CO^2 into a unique calcium carbonate cement system that can be used to make a variety of building materials. The firm's researchers learned how to create their products by studying the formation of corals. As I learned on my first tour of the plant, Calera had hired more than a dozen PhDs and installed scientific equipment that was state of the art. I felt as if I was at NASA and was thrilled to be part of bringing this transformative innovation to market.

Another Khosla-seeded company whose advisory board I joined is called View, formerly known as Soladigm. It makes dynamic (electrochromic) glass. In short, the glass can switch from clear to almost dark by user or sensor control—especially helpful when the direct afternoon sun hits the glass. This transformation prevents solar heat gain and unwanted glare from entering the space. It is so effective that window blinds aren't needed. I recall first meeting View's CEO, Rao Mulpuri, who was armed with a PhD in materials engineering and business training at Harvard. His eyes were so bright and he talked so fast that I thought I must be meeting a modern-day Henry Ford. Mulpuri's thoughts on products, the company, and the industry spark out of him. In his presence I feel like I need to be fully caffeinated and ramp up my brain synapses. The firm has raised venture capital five times, totaling $184 million, and its new manufacturing plant in Olive Branch, Mississippi, is shipping products—a revolution in window technology.

I also joined numerous other advisory boards over the ensuing years, as venture capitalists actively moved green building into their cleantech investments. At the time, this included Serious Materials (later named Serious Energy), Scientific Conservation (later called SCIEnergy), Hara, Integrity Block, Project Frog, Envision Solar, and Sustainability Roundtable. A few of these companies have drastically changed their management teams, and one has gone out of business. It's not clear to me which of my advisory board start-up companies will strike it big, but I hope that a few will have an "exit" via an IPO (initial public offering) or a profitable acquisition. I'm still waiting hopefully while I continue to nurture and root for the firms' continued prosperity.

If you dig new green technologies, go to www.regenbuild.com and sign up for our list. I'll be providing more information on cool products and interviewing CEOs.

One day it dawned on me that it would be beneficial, not to mention a new business opportunity, if I brought all of the firms in my consulting and advisory board portfolio together into my own network—especially since they were all noncompetitive. Venture capitalists often gathered their portfolio companies that they'd invested in together. My idea was that the companies could share best practices in greening their companies and product offerings, talk over common goals and challenges, and even more importantly, share business development opportunities. Many of my advisory board companies had been asking me for introductions to some of the same parties, such as Walmart, Starbucks, Apple, Google, Gensler, Hines, and WSP. My friend at Walmart helped advance the idea when he challenged me to gather all my firms in one location for him to visit.

Of course I had to expand the challenge further and make the network into a larger business opportunity. I did this by setting the goal of recruiting other leading green product manufacturers and service providers spanning all parts of a building. They would come from approximately fifty or more different building industry product and service categories, including areas such as drywall, windows, carpeting, mechanical systems, lighting, and elevators. I'd select only one company from each category—so that all members were noncompetitive. And that became the business plan for the Regenerative Network, born in 2010. As a network, the idea was that we'd effectively experience a "network effect" every time we added a new member to the group. In theory, members would (partially) contribute their contact base of clients and corporate and product knowledge that was not confidential or trademarked in the rapidly growing green building marketplace.

As I'd learn, however, I knew little about running a network, including how to recruit and keep members happy over a number of years. This was always a problem we'd faced at USGBC, especially in the five-year down economy—when membership highs dropped.

In our first year, we'd performed an extensive analysis of prospective members, using our own sustainability screen (called the Regenerative Balance Sheet, "RBS"), which included a weighted amalgamation of what we viewed as the most important criteria for green companies and products. I rehired Huston Eubank, a former employee back in 2000, who since had worked with Bill Browning and Amory Lovins at the Rocky Mountain Institute, to help me develop the RBS and serve as my Chief Knowledge Officer. We both fell in love with the RBS tool, even though a few of the highest-ranking industry companies weren't interested in joining our Network and we found it impossible to rate the cleantech start-ups who didn't report much environmental information for us to rate.

The RBS was a 100-point rating system. It contained four main categories for use in evaluating the sustainable company performance of prospective members of the Network: corporate culture, environmental impact, social performance, and transparent data reporting. Within these four areas, we came up with a survey questionnaire that contained about 250 questions. The idea was that my staffers would review the prospective Network members' websites and other public information, and rate them using our RBS survey. We performed around eighty RBS reviews on established industry companies, and got scores ranging from a low of 2 to a high of 63 (out of 100). The results made us think that the questionnaire was sufficiently rigorous. We thought it would be useful not only as an initial green company screen, but also as an ongoing environmental management system tool to identify areas of improvement and to measure yearly progress.

In April 2010, we barricaded ourselves in Berkeley's LEED Platinum David Brower Center for our first RegenForum: two full days, including five-star catered meals and California wine tasting. Nineteen founding Regenerative Network members attended.

Most of the first day was highly collaborative, with members going around sharing not only who they were and what they made, but highlighting how the Network could best help each member individually and as a group. As I looked around the full room of active participants in the Tamalpais room, across from our new office, I couldn't help but feel that we'd reinvented the early days of forming USGBC back in 1993. However, USGBC had grown big, and our last Greenbuild (in Phoenix) had almost twenty-five thousand attendees. Long gone were the days when we could all share and build one-on-one relationships with all of the conference attendees. And unlike the council, the Regenerative Network's mission was boosting the business of our members through green building. We also planned to boost member value through our "network effect" of sharing business leads and strategic knowledge that could create a competitive edge in the green building marketplace. I hoped to help develop a brand for the companies as well, given that I'd handpicked exclusive industry leaders.

As I looked around the room I saw many familiar faces and corporate names from those early days of building USGBC, including John Bradford from Interface; Jim Allen, president of Sloan; John Mandyck from Carrier; and Anita Snader from Armstrong. And sitting beside them were passionate representatives from my new advisory board company start-ups—bringing new ideas and high-tech methods to our slower-moving industry. And in turn, our established Network members could teach them how to scale and distribute to the green and traditional building industries across the globe.

Sitting in the room next to my old and new green building colleagues were our seven RegenExperts. Standing tallest was Malcolm Lewis, CEO of CTG Energetics, which he later sold to The Cadmus Group before he passed away about six months later. Malcolm and I had worked closely together for the past twenty years. His sudden death in 2012 struck me hard, and it was also a big loss for the industry. He exemplified the spirit of our movement—always eager to help find a new path up the mountain and to use his scientific mind to create effective solutions. In 2013, USGBC established the Malcolm Lewis IMPACT! Award. Recipients are recognized for their high-impact, volunteer-driven work that supports a USGBC initiative.

Also there and sharing mind-expanding ideas with our members were Dan Slone (USGBC and WorldGBC General Counsel and green attorney extraordinaire), Bill Browning (previously with the Rocky Mountain Institute and now with his own firm, called Terrapin Bright Green), Anthony Bernheim of Sustainable Built Environments, Ted van der Linden of DPR Construction, and Rahul Young, a former employee and now managing director of ICF's Bay area consulting practice. Bob Fox of Cookfox Architects was another RegenExpert, and later we added Nadav Malin with BuildingGreen and Zorana Bosnic, Sustainable Design Director with HOK.

Our second day of the RegenForum was Marketplace Day. It was amazing to watch our nineteen founding members, each sitting at a separate table for speed dating. A Buddhist prayer bell was hit every fifteen minutes for the next rotation to start. We'd recruited about seventy green architects, building owners, engineers, contractors, and brand-name tenants (like Apple, Google, Walmart) to "date" our members. Midway I began placing mounds of chocolate candy on each table to help participants make it to the grueling finish line. Not surprisingly, they all made it through the nineteen rounds. "That was more fun than I anticipated," John Mandyck, my longtime client from Carrier said to me. "I had no idea what to expect," he added as he looked down at the stack of business cards he'd collected.

Over cocktails I toasted another client, Randy Scott, from Thomas Properties Group, over a cold glass of Calera chardonnay that I'd selected. "Speed dating was my favorite part," he remarked with a sparkle in his eye. We learned about a lot of new technologies that we can take home with us, he said. "I knew you'd pull it off."

I glanced around the large art gallery room on the first floor of the Brower Center and thought I heard David Brower talking to me: "Thanks for turning the lights on," he'd said to me after we last had lunch before he died. I'd met him at that event hosted by Ray Anderson—I was glad that his firm Interface was one of our Network founding members. Before he died in 2011, Ray had helped me recruit Interface. He often said, "Fellow astronauts on Spaceship Earth, we are all in this together." His legacy was huge, setting a bold path for CEOs to follow as they endeavor to green their companies so passionately, as Ray had done. I can still hear his Georgian accent and feel the warmth and transforming effect of his radiating smile.

Later during the cocktail party, I felt someone pinch my rear end. I turned around to see Sara with a glass of our Napa cabernet and reaching over to kiss me. "Great job, honey," she said as we toasted to another start-up victory.

Over the years we tried more speed dating in Berkeley, and then in New York and San Francisco. Later came RegenSalons, RegenCharrettes, RegenBids and RegenProjects as I tried to keep the energy fresh and add value for my members.

In July 2013, we gathered at Interface's showroom in downtown San Francisco. On the second day of our RegenForum, I felt goose bumps and was almost moved to tears as Tony Gale and Gina Klem from Starbucks joined our group of fifty-plus attendees for our third RegenCharrette in two days. This was after brainstorming as a group at the million-square-foot new tech campus for NVIDIA with its design and development team and at a new downtown office building, owned by Kilroy Realty Corporation and designed by Bill McDonough's firm.

"Our canvas is white, and I'd like you to follow the innovation of Renzo Piano," Starbucks Corporate Architect Tony Gale said in his opening reports. "And we love to partner with industry." It had been more than ten years since I'd last worked with Starbucks, back when we came up with the idea for the company to chair LEED Retail with USGBC. And Tony and I had met more years back than that, when he served as the Chief Architect for the City of Seattle and sat on USGBC's national board.

When Tony and Gina finished their opening remarks, I stood up next to them. Into the mic I said, "Our charge today is to invent a 3,500-square-foot free-standing Starbucks in Northern California." I paused to take in the engagement of the sixty-plus quiet members, guests and experts of our Network. Huston flashed me a thumbs-up while taking notes on his Mac—typing in rapid-fire strokes like he didn't want to miss a beat. "It's your opportunity to not only help envision the state of the art RegenStore, but to help define and specify it. Now's your time to let your technologies and innovations fly." I then walked the microphone over to our first participant, with the intention of making my way through the entire room in the three hours allotted to the Starbucks® RegenCharrette.

After we'd finished from front to back, with frequent encouragement and enthusiasm from Tony and Gina, I looked at our Starbucks guests and asked, "Well, what do you think? Did we hit the ball over the fence?"

"That was a first in the world," Tony said. "Wow, I've never experienced anything like it. So many fantastic ideas."

In his opening remarks, Tony had said that Starbucks has 18,500 stores and that they'd certified about 185 of them in seventeen countries as part of the LEED volume program that they helped invent after LEED Retail. It was hard for me to grasp that with such exposure, our three-hour session was a first.

Gina later wrote to me: "I want to thank you for inviting Tony and me to participate in the recent RegenForum charrette. I was blown away by the experience of being able to present our idea and receiving such informed, thoughtful, and relevant feedback. I was amazed by the brainpower, passion, and experience in the room—and now believe that we can really execute this project!"

As I made my way home, I began thinking that I'd like to develop their store of the future. At least I hoped I could be involved. Of course I immediately started thinking about a plan.

A few weeks later, I flew to Sydney to meet up with Che Wall, Maria Atkinson, and Suzie Barnett, the team that developed the Green Building Council of Australia and its Green Star rating system. The purpose of the trip was to explore their licensing of my first global Regenerative Network outside the United States, called RegenX. If this takes hold, the concept could expand to Vietnam, South Korea, and Japan, then beyond further into Asia Pacific. I'm wondering if the Network would be a good model to expand to many of the hundred or so countries that now have green building councils. Perhaps other council founders are also looking for ways to capitalize on their country and regional network of contacts, name recognition and business savvy. And it would again be wonderful to share global best practices—this time in the building of a private network that each of us has ownership in.

19
SHADES OF GREEN

Most of us greenies say that if you want to be green, buy a Prius, put solar on your home, LEED-certify your building, and turn vegetarian. And yet greening is much deeper and more complicated than that. Taking on more debt for my house helped it achieve more points over Platinum in the LEED for Homes green rating system, but it also meant that we had to make more money. Private schools provide a better education and smaller class sizes for the kids, but we have to drive them there and back home, instead of walking to the local elementary school. It also costs more than $20,000 after-tax per child. Which is greener? It's an endless debate of trade-offs and priorities—many that even flip-flop over time.

My experience has taught me that there's a limit to what you can do to green your house, green your business, and green your life, and there are many trade-offs. At what point does an eco-guru call it quits and give up on implementing the higher green level product or measure for an inferior one that has a lower level of ecological performance, but actually works or is just much easier?

On the other hand, what is a reasonable level of inconvenience if it serves the greater good? (I recall one of our USGBC board members wiping his hands on his pants during a bathroom break at one of our board meetings so he could avoid using a paper towel.) Do you eat only homegrown vegetables? If Sara and I tried to, we'd probably starve. Do you ride your bike to work in the rain, or haul your kids to school in a Burley bike chariot even if you are pressed for time? I did make it one year without a car when we first moved into our LEED Platinum home. However, the extra time and inconvenience added to my stress, which lowered my green health score, even as my eco-footprint points increased—in my Life Balance Sheet™ Rating System.

Striving for eco-perfection isn't always the greenest method when one has a busy life and two kids. For me, 90 percent is often enough. Lower stress is also *green*.

The issue of trade-offs and compromises became clear to me with the remodel of the bungalow and our sale of it three years later to take advantage of the down economy and move into a gorgeous, much larger Mediterranean up in the Berkeley Hills. It came with a vacant, buildable lot, which already has me thinking of a net-zero prefab or passive home. I recall more than a year after moving into the bungalow, Sara and I were awakened at 3 a.m. by a strange garbage disposal noise under our bed. It was the night after the workmen had hooked up the gray-water drip irrigation system under the house. "What's that?" I shouted out in the darkness to Sara. I leaped out of bed, grabbed a flashlight and ran into the early morning rain to get into the crawl space under the house. The noise was coming from the large pump beneath our bedroom floorboards that pulled gray water out of the two partially submerged fifty-gallon storage hogs and sent it to a drip system that irrigated the backyard. I unplugged about six electric cords until I isolated the pump's power and put an end to the grinding noise. But sleep was over for that night.

That was the first incident in a year of problems with the gray and rainwater systems, including the powder room toilet tank constantly running out of rainwater and, even more charmingly, spewing out brown rainwater. My contractor swore the water was discolored from decomposing leaves. The sand filter for the gray water clogged up twice, making the house smell like a sewer (two days before I hosted a house tour for Build It Green).

We had removed most of the interior walls of the house to expand the living space and let the daylight penetrate. Our bedroom was right off the new kitchen and the smallest of footfalls woke me. Sharing a bathroom and a half with two little girls and my wife proved hard, even though I fell in love with my outside shower. Our folks had to stay nearby at The Claremont Hotel when they came to visit, which squashed my vision of close family gatherings with late-night conversations.

I'd gone far in my commitment to sustainability, but at what cost? I'd spent a hundred thousand dollars more than the "market" value and green had contributed to that increase, as had the overall high cost of custom renovation. From a financial standpoint, it would have been better to spend the dough expanding the house's square footage by adding two more bedrooms and bathrooms, and skipping the greening and some of the custom improvements. I'd expected our ambitious water recycling systems to work, at least after a few months of testing and retooling, but after a year, I felt that I'd hit my limit. "Do those men live under the house," my younger daughter asked one day when two men emerged from the basement yet again. I smiled ruefully, realizing that I'd allowed my enthusiasm for water efficiency to go too far. When I sold the house, I unplugged the gray-water system, not wanting to warrant it as fully functioning. I'm sure its day will come, but more likely when it's more off-the-shelf and not custom technology.

It's not green, after all, if it doesn't work. But thankfully, most of our innovations did work.

When I first started USGBC, some members felt that we shouldn't allow in "toxic" product manufacturers—those with

Superfund sites and no eco-consciousness. I believed then, and still do, that we need to work to green all walks of life, including large polluting manufacturers and big footprint houses. If we opt only for perfection and moral rectitude, we'll lose. Some of our existing buildings and homes are energy and water inefficient, and will never achieve a performance level of net-zero (energy, water, waste). But even they can improve by small steps every year. The LEED green building rating system only certifies buildings that are determined to be at the leadership level (the "L" in LEED). To date, if a building operates below the "L" level, USGBC is silent. Initially, USGBC decided that the minimum bar for the "L" level for LEED certification would begin with the top 25 percent of buildings (LEED Certified-level), and then go up from there to higher levels of sustainable performance (Silver, Gold and Platinum).

My friends in the Cascadia Chapter of the USGBC have introduced a living building rating system (the Living Building Challenge) intended to go beyond LEED Platinum, with prerequisites that the structure be net-zero in energy, water, and waste. The rating system also requires that the project "contain design features intended solely for human delight and the celebration of culture, spirit, and place." The high standard has had so much interest that there's now an organization to incubate it: the International Living Building Institute.

At the end of the day, we strive to live our lives comfortably and healthfully, but this doesn't need to be at war with a high level of green performance. In fact, sustainability needs to be part of all that we do, even embedded into its fabric, so that a nongreen option does not exist. But we're still in transition and in the transition period there's compromise and some things that don't yet work. Nevertheless, it's still important to be conscious of the green path and adopt its approach when possible and realistic. Public education and consumer demand will lead industry to provide more solutions, including ones that work flawlessly and come at an equal or cheaper cost while providing a solid return on investment.

PART THREE: REFLECTIONS

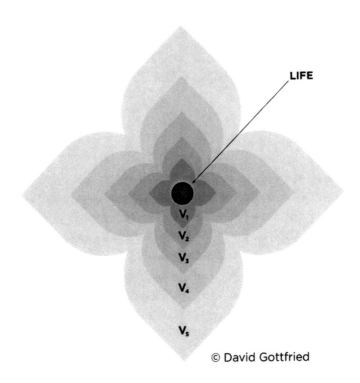

LIFE

V_1
V_2
V_3
V_4
V_5

© David Gottfried

VALUE RINGS™

$V_1 > V_2 > V_3 > V_4 > V_5$

V1: Life
V2: Life Sustaining: water, air, food, soil, shelter, security
V3: Economy, Government, Utilities
V4: Essential Products & Services
V5: Life Enhancers

20
THE GBC MOVEMENT
AT TWENTY

Two decades ago, when Mike, Rick, and I launched USGBC, never in our dreams did I think we were creating a global movement across one hundred countries. As of October 2013, there were 56,000 LEED Commercial and Neighborhood Development projects (totaling just over eleven billion square feet) and another 119,615 residential units using LEED. USGBC also had about 190,000 LEED Accredited and Green Associate professionals.

There are now Green Building Councils in approximately one hundred countries, with about two dozen green building rating systems. Some 63 percent of global new construction starts are planning green projects for 2015. Green building now consists of about 10 percent of GDP. We celebrate World Green Building week the third week of September each year, followed by an annual Congress. The 2013 WorldGBC Congress, in Capetown, South Africa, focused on GBC staff development for the world's seven hundred GBC staff. One of the WorldGBC's recent partnerships is with the World Bank's IFC (International Finance Corporation), with the goal of providing more incentives and decision-making tools for green development in developing nations (about half of the WorldGBC member countries).

Paul Hawken said that we created the world's greatest "sand-box" for ecological transformation. As I assess the last twenty years of GBC history, I believe it's important to reflect upon how we changed the world and the ingredients that helped build our unprecedented engine for transformation of the world's largest industry.

1. DREAMED BIG

When Mike and I first started USGBC we had an extravagant goal: to transform how the entire US building industry designed, built, and operated buildings—commercial, industrial and residential. The work picked up on that earlier green building standard we'd first sketched out at ASTM.

We chose the name "Green Building" instead of "sustainable." We felt that the word "sustainable" had been tarnished by environmental organizations that were then actively engaged in suing product manufacturers. The word "green" gave us more scope, and it had connotations of both the environment and money—and we wanted to play in both of these fields. The word "Council" fit the kind of industry coalition we hoped to form. We wanted all types of professionals at our table—in fact, pretty much everyone was encouraged to join us in our open model.

Our dream also addressed the full spectrum of environmental transformation, including energy efficiency, clean energy generation, water efficiency, transportation, purchasing, health and productivity for building occupants, materials production, and site issues. Each of these areas had separate organizations. However, we were likely the first organization in the world to unite them under the umbrella of green and bring them together in one membership coalition.

And we made our logo round, like a seal. That had the advantage of making us look like an official governmental agency

231

or certification body. In fact we became one when LEED was introduced to the market in 1998.

2. MODEL

Coming up with the right model for our organization contributed greatly to our success. As Mike and I surveyed the landscape, we saw mostly sector-oriented organizations. We were the first US horizontal entity to welcome all sectors and parties to the table. Deciding on open membership was a good call as well. This made us noncompetitive with all of the individual sectors and professional societies. Instead of recreating their areas of expertise, we simply invited them in, and benefited from their body of knowledge and professional best practices. We didn't want to learn and represent architecture or mechanical engineering, for example; rather, we wanted to recruit the pioneers and leaders from each field with the most sustainable building knowledge to bring to our holistic coalition.

It's hard to advance quickly in a closed structure, one that limits active engagement from fresh and expansive minds. The more open and collaborative and democratic the organizational structure, the more innovations and growth. Ego and pride of ownership must be shooed out of the way. That was hard for me, to move aside and let newcomers contribute and take ownership. I learned it, though. USGBC and WorldGBC were never about Rick, Mike, and myself, but rather about the contributions and shared vision of thousands of others, all coming together to transform the building industry. Rick calls this our "*human* capital."

From the beginning, we'd agreed that USGBC would be a nonprofit. The nascent green building field required up-front nonprofit mission activities such as standards definition, education on the totality and individual facets, research and technical work, and a high degree of public good that would come about through conferences, white papers, and sharing of information.

We decided to make USGBC a membership organization, initially founding it as a 501(c)(6) entity that is often used for membership-based entities. We targeted organizational members as opposed to individuals, believing this approach would lead to faster transformation and broader representation. Not all members could afford to pay the same dues, and we wanted them all to participate and help us build the council. So we decided to tier our dues levels. For example, a large manufacturer member would pay $10,000 a year, whereas a small manufacturer would pay $500, and our nonprofit environmental groups would pay $300. Nevertheless, each dues-paying member would get one vote, even if the member paid much less than a large member. I was surprised that our first members all agreed to this, and pleased that the larger members seldom used the influence that one might associate with paying more money to the organization.

A green building marketplace did not exist when we set out. But we always understood that we were building one. First we had to build our coalition, then define green building collaboratively, providing education on the subject and demonstrating the multitude of environmental, monetary, and social benefits it brings. Then products and services would follow, creating new jobs and economic opportunity.

As an entrepreneurial-led nonprofit, we wanted to encourage our members to help us innovate and grow quickly. And like a business, we wanted to be first to market and "own" our market. We'd let the members lead and then bring them into our fold via consensus. I'd learned about consensus from Mike at ASTM. But unlike ASTM, we still wanted to move quickly and exhibit the highest end of the leadership curve. There's sometimes a conflict between consensus and transformation, which requires putting the highest level of points on the board towards regeneration.

The future of Earth cannot always depend on compromise, but mandates the utmost performance improvements.

Becoming an open and integrated membership organization across all sectors of the building industry made us more powerful as an entity, allowing us to represent green building and speak with credibility. We built committees to speak for the industry, but deferred to the expertise of professionals to help guide us and get the work done. In effect, we built the first green building orchestra in the United States, if not the world—a collection of individual players and their respective organizations that contribute to the whole.

Before USGBC, the only organized national green building effort in the United States came from the American Institute of Architects (AIA). These efforts included the pioneering work of its Committee of the Environment and some visionary lectures at national conventions. The AIA's work touched mostly their constituents—architects, and to a certain extent some product manufacturers and the corporate architects for other building industry segments, such as building users and even governments. However, predominantly, sustainability discussions were conducted in industry silos. The same was true at other national professional societies at the time. We invited them all in. Instead of trying to learn sustainable architecture or engineering, we asked them to represent their specialties. This approach made them our friends instead of competition, although a few of the societies initially did stay away from joining us, waiting on the sidelines as they gathered more data on our motives and approach. Ultimately, most of them joined us and helped expand our mission within their fields and helped give us great credibility, including the ability to speak for the breadth of the industry.

It became a personal agenda for me not only to recruit the societies, but also to find their sustainability leaders, those who would help green their industries. I expanded this goal to all sectors of our membership. Many of our initial recruits went on to became the "fathers" of green building for their sectors, such as Steve Ashkin for green cleaning, Jerry Yudelson for green marketing, and Ray Anderson for green carpeting and manufacturing. Over the 20 years, it has been exciting to see who would seize and capture the green building reins for a given field. The greening story has expanded way beyond buildings into fields such as green product labeling, sustainable food and agriculture, wood and forestry, concrete and cement, and cars.

To balance out having manufacturer members, Mike and I worked hard to recruit nonprofit environmental organizations. We especially wanted those that had the highest credibility and contacts with government as well as technical expertise. Our first recruit was Bill Browning, with the Rocky Mountain Institute. Beyond RMI, we recruited NRDC, National Audubon Society, and later on dozens of other important environmental organizations that not only were performing the world's best work in their given fields, such as health, but also brought balance to our coalition.

Right up front, Mike and I decided that we wouldn't initially allow federal governmental agencies to become members of the council. Rather, we invited them to become liaison and strategic partners. This role made it much easier for the agencies to work with us, since they didn't pay dues or vote. Instead, we partnered in sponsoring conferences, such as our conference with NIST in 1994 and 1995 and the federal government green summit (with about 30 agencies); and the US DOE generously supported our LEED pilot. In 1993, we also were thrilled to support the greening of the White House and Executive Office Building, an effort that has led to about $300,000 in annual savings. It was not only pioneering work, but also a blast for us to participate. That was during the tenure of Bill Clinton and Al Gore, both of whom were keynote speakers at our Greenbuild conferences after they'd left office.

It wasn't just that the governmental agencies helped us. We helped them, too. We provided a convenient and easy method for them to meet progressive building product manufacturers and other enlightened members representing the full spectrum of the industry. This led to many strategic partnerships, research projects, and grants that helped propel government into the field of green building and, accordingly, better serve the public by boosting energy efficiency, clean power generation, water and materials efficiency, and waste reduction, and even by improving transportation impacts. Years later, we opened up membership to federal agencies.

From the start, we did actively recruit local and state governments as members. We found that their representatives became active and industrious participants in our programs, especially LEED. In 2000, when the City of Seattle announced that all civic buildings would be designed at a minimum level of LEED Silver, that move kicked off a competition among local and state agencies to get into the LEED game with their own buildings. And later, many governmental agencies offered incentives to private developers and owner-occupied buildings to also adopt LEED. Those incentives helped accelerate the adoption of green building into the private sector. They included dozens of creative initiatives. The ones proven to work best include: real estate and income tax credits, building permit issuance acceleration, extra bonus density for the project, grants, and design assistance.

So many cities have embraced and expanded our mission that USGBC developed a large document listing more than one hundred pioneering initiatives. Local governments' leadership and zest for transformation continue to inspire me, as the trend accelerates globally. I have personally enjoyed helping advance the green building programs for the following cities: San Diego, Los Angeles, San Francisco, San Jose, Berkeley, Oakland, Orinda, Pleasanton, and Santa Monica. I also enjoyed consulting with state government agencies of California and Montana. I've enjoyed my overseas collaborations with several countries: China, Australia, Mexico, Canada, Israel, and Abu Dhabi, not to mention helping personally form GBCs in more than a dozen countries. My GBC colleagues can greatly expand this listing as we've trotted around the globe since first coming together.

Sure, there was some friction. Our early board meetings were like the Wild West, with shouting matches, table-pounding and occasionally the slam of a door as someone stalked out, never to return. We made some enemies with our missionary zeal and aggressive recruitment and growth methods. I can remember many nights staying up late in a bar or hotel lobby somewhere worrying about our strategy and the many problems that threatened to derail us. When I felt that my flame was getting low or I wanted to attack someone for hurting our mission, Mike would recite passages from *The Art of War*, such as: "The supreme *art of war* is to subdue the enemy without fighting." And, "Opportunities multiply as they are seized."

How our coalition model held together was sometimes a mystery to me. Looking back, I credit our belief in leadership, transparency, professionalism, a strong and balanced board of directors, and a growing base of dedicated volunteer members across all industry sectors.

3. LEADERSHIP

Without leadership we'd never have gotten anywhere. At first it was Mike and myself, and then Rick joined our core founding group as our chairman.

Mike liked to push and move fast. He also brought his decades of environmental knowledge and ASTM leadership experience. As a litigator, he understood conflict and controversy and even relished it. Rick brought with him the global corporate mentality that he'd learned at Carrier. Rick was less confrontational than Mike and I were. We tried to learn that skill from him, but he remained the master, keeping USGBC members from leaving even when the heat became overwhelming.

A decade later, as our third staff CEO and President, Rick built up our staff to more than 260 passionate and dedicated professionals and grew our membership to a high of twenty thousand organizations. He had a knack for selecting and mentoring staff. Whenever I'm in the USGBC D.C. office (a large LEED-CI Platinum space on L Street), I get to witness how enthusiastic Rick is with everyone, asking them not only about their work, but also about their spouse's and kid's birthdays, and how they were feeling. It's fair to say we became like brothers, each with our unique personalities and strengths. The three of us together made a great start-up team.

Having Rick as our founding chairman was huge. When we set out to recruit a chairman, we wanted someone from a prestigious global building industry company, but even more important, someone presidential in stature and passionate about our mission. In Rick, we got everything we wanted.

At the end of 2011, the WorldGBC also benefited by Rick's solid leadership, electing him its chairman, following the tenure of Tony Arnel, Victoria's Building Commissioner in Australia.

Mike, Rick, and I built an eclectic and vibrant founding board of directors. Generally it included the first members we'd found and liked from each of the thirteen sectors of our membership. We wanted board members who came from a credible organization and who had years of leadership in the given industry sector, but more important, shared our mission and bold dream. We wanted transformation agents who were on fire to find a great purpose for their lives. And we found them. When I'd tell a prospective board member about our vision, instead of grilling me on our budget and asking dismissively for a brochure, he or she said, "Cool! Count me in." And then they'd get to work adding their unique talents, networks, and knowledge to the general effort.

Beyond great staff and a solid board, we also built great committees to develop our products, beginning with the LEED committee led by Rob Watson from NRDC (a global environmental advocacy organization). I first met Rob around 1992. He was working on energy issues in Russia and had been involved in greening NRDC's headquarters in New York. He immediately got what we wanted to create and understood how to immediately add value and take us higher than we could envision on our own. Other significant leaders included Board Chairs Steven Winter, Jim Hartzfeld, Kevin Hydes, and Mark MacCracken. Committee Chairs included Alan Traugott, who started our chapter committee, and Kath Williams, who shepherded our education committee and served years as Vice Chair.

The same can be said for the leadership of the WorldGBC. A few of the USGBC leaders, such as Rick Fedrizzi and Kevin Hydes, went on to chair that organization. GBC officers in other countries did the same. What an honor to serve on the WorldGBC board with such a diverse geographical representative, but to witness similar passion, vision, and understanding. I often wonder if we all were getting the same messages from a higher spirit.

4. VOLUNTEERS

Thousands of member volunteers contributed a staggering amount of valuable and effective hours. Without our volunteers, LEED wouldn't have come to be, and neither would our Greenbuild conference, Center for Green Schools, and dozens of our other committee creations.

The volunteers push themselves to the limit, often working through many evenings and weekends while doing their day jobs during business hours. Some of our members come to Greenbuild and participate in committees even though their employers don't support the effort, taking vacation time to attend the annual conference and paying for the costs personally. I'd never seen this level of dedication in my career and am still often surprised at its vigor. It gives me hope for our future. The crowd that I love most are the younger members and volunteers—our Emerging Professionals group. We also established USGBC Students as another tier of up-and-comers who can actively contribute during their forthcoming careers. USGBC has a vibrant Green Schools program under its Center for Green Schools started in 2010, which awards its own fellows designation for exemplary credentials and service. I've been fortunate to address the Emerging Professionals a few times and am awestruck at their earnestness and their willingness to put themselves out there, even against great odds—sometimes within their organizations. Their gusto often propels them to start their own green building companies and nonprofits and contribute to best practices. And at a deeper level, they kindle my spirit and help recharge my internal flame, so that it can become renewable.

5. BUSINESS SAVVY

One critical decision from the first was to run USGBC as a business, even though it was a nonprofit. Mike, Rick, and I each came from the private sector and understood the need to create revenue, have clients to bill and budgets to meet. Our board of directors also understood this approach.

Many start-up nonprofits fail to understand that they are businesses. When a nonprofit runs out of money it is still broke, just like a for-profit business. Although it was difficult to measure, it was often said that we had become the world's fastest-growing nonprofit.

USGBC adopted other modalities often seen in private entrepreneurial start-ups. This included an ability to develop and trademark LEED and create a global brand. Unlike many nonprofits that rely mostly on charitable foundations for monetary support, we launched numerous LEED-related products and the highly profitable, world's largest green building event, Greenbuild, that created multiple sources of revenue. At the height of the economy in 2007, USGBC's annual budget grew to about $100 million.

USGBC and the WorldGBC created an unprecedented entrepreneurship opportunity for its members and those that embraced the new field. This spawned what likely amounted to about a thousand global green consultancies and other related start-ups across the spectrum, from education to software and green building products.

One key part of venture investment and start-ups is to not only quickly scale the business, but to either take the private company public through an IPO (initial public offering) or have a successful "exit" through a merger into a larger entity. We're still awaiting more IPOs and mergers and acquisitions in the green building space, following the early successes in solar and wind. What many of the well-funded start-ups and the venture capitalists have learned, however, is that the building industry takes much more capital and time to scale a company than a pure information technology (IT) start-up.

Nevertheless, our Greenbuild conference became a shining example of financial success. Since 2002, Greenbuild had grown its annual conferences to draw about twenty-five thousand attendees. The conference's trade expo would sell out annually with more than a thousand exhibitors, many signing up for the next year's show within days of the last one in order to obtain a good location on the exhibit floor. Selling Greenbuild in 2013 to Hanley Wood without losing control of its content was a coup for USGBC. It showed Rick Fedrizzi's business acumen and marketing prowess, along with that of the talented executive team, board of directors, and GreenBuild staff. The transaction also helped solidly endow USGBC for the future.

Like the USGBC in the United States, the WorldGBC was the first to market globally—to create a UN (United Nations) of green building councils. In 1998, when I started working on the WorldGBC, there were other global groups within the green building fields, but they had different missions. The underlying engine of the WorldGBC is strong country green building councils, armed with a credible and effective green building rating system. USGBC remains the anchor organization, with the largest staff and budget by several times. However, many other GBCs have also grown greatly since their founding, including the GBCs in Canada, Australia, United Kingdom, India, Germany, Singapore, Taiwan, and France—along with dozens of others that now have from hundreds to thousands of members in their green building councils. On a recent trip to Sydney, I learned that the Green Building Council of Australia has more than sixty employees and manages its Green Star rating system, which has about fifteen hundred registered and certified buildings totaling seventy million square feet of space. The CEOs of many of the GBCs come from the private sector and nonprofit management, and exhibit not only leadership skills, but shrewd marketing, product creation, strategic partnering, and strategic planning as well.

6. LEED

LEED's success and global adoption in about 140 countries has been astonishing. LEED was to USGBC as DOS was to Microsoft (and Mac OS to Apple): it became our operating system and growth engine.

The green building rating system served a dual purpose: first, as a green building guideline and secondly, as a third-party certification system. With LEED's launch in 1998, USGBC's membership took off, going from several hundred to more than twenty thousand in about seven years. LEED expanded into a full program and suite of products, including the initial LEED-NC (New Construction) system, and then other LEED products: retail (LEED-R), commercial interiors (LEED-CI), existing buildings (LEED-EB), homes (LEED-H), and neighborhood developments (LEED-ND).

Each of these LEED rating systems had a corresponding LEED Reference Guide and later on, a LEED accredited professional exam. USGBC offered thousands of LEED workshops. LEED got its own logo and of course, the prestigious and valuable LEED building certification plaque awarded for buildings that met the criteria. Opting to offer LEED certification only via a third-party validation process was pivotal. If we'd offered LEED only as a self-certification guideline, it wouldn't have had the market adoption it has had. Also, most governmental financial incentive programs require third-party verification to make sure the given building actually met the LEED requirements. The certification's extensive documentation requirements have spawned an enormous green building consulting industry—to help facilitate the green design and submittal process.

LEED was brilliantly designed under the leadership of Rob Watson and later on, Scot Horst and Joel Ann Todd, as well as that of Peter Templeton, Malcolm Lewis, and Nigel Howard. Its credit system in five main green building categories (site, water, energy and atmosphere, materials and resources, and indoor environmental quality) was comprehensive in hitting the main environmental building categories. And adding an innovation category opened up the door for new advances and things we'd forgotten. The award levels — from Certified to Silver, Gold, and the high of Platinum — made the LEED game fun and challenging, like its own Olympics to see who could claim the highest scores within all building sectors, as I'd done with my own home.

Other people were pivotal in designing and managing initiatives to develop the various other LEED product offerings, including reference guides, trainings, continuing education, and Accredited Professional exams. These folks worked long hours to develop the standards in committee and take it through the membership balloting process. The task seemed to me like scaling Mount Everest. I know that they were proud when the standards launched and gained market traction. With each board meeting of USGBC from the year 2000 on, we'd be updated by the capable LEED staff on the metrics of each system: number of buildings registered for LEED, number of buildings registered and certified, and the associated aggregate square footages. Even today, I memorize and recite these statistics like the birth dates of my two kids.

Inventing the LEED Accredited Professional exam was another stroke of genius. After studying and passing the rigorous test, professionals (and some college students) can put LEED-AP on their resumes and business cards. Employers inquire about this professional accreditation when interviewing, and USGBC members would compete to see who had the most LEED-APs on staff. As of 2013, we had five separate LEED AP exams for each of the various LEED rating systems, and a total of about 157,000 LEED Accredited Professionals

A few years ago USGBC introduced a lower-tier professional designation: Green Associate. This brings less experienced industry professionals into the LEED system, as well as encourages them to learn about green building. As of 2013, there were 33,000 Green Associates. Later on, LEED expanded its requirements by requiring annual professional course credits, similar to that required by professional societies, such as the AIA. And then a LEED Fellow program was launched that honored those who not only had the most LEED and project experience, but who also had been leaders at their USGBC local chapters and at the national level.

Many of our WorldGBC country members either designed their own national green building rating systems, or licensed one from more established green building councils, such as LEED from the USGBC, or BREEAM from the United Kingdom, or Green Star from Australia. LEED can also be used without licensing, as long as certification occurs in the United States. (Canada and India certify their own LEED buildings and all other countries' LEED projects are certified in the United States.) A few years ago, USGBC created its LEED international program. As of this writing, there are thirty countries on the LEED International Roundtable, which has worked very well. And we have ten more countries that want to sign up with us. We have completed the LEED EU Alternative Compliance Paths for LEED EB (existing building) to comply with EU directives.

I've been surprised at the fantastic global uptake of LEED, as it uses US-based standards for energy efficiency and other US-based codes and performance standards. Noteworthy projects outside of the United States want to attach themselves to the world's largest standard and to affiliate with the United States through LEED certification, even though it means extra design costs to translate foreign standards and codes to those referenced in LEED. Some large US-based global corporations, such as Google, Apple, and Intel, mandate its use in their facilities around the world.

McGraw Hill's *Green Outlook 2011* report has shown that in the US marketplace, a LEED building is worth about 11 percent more by obtaining higher rents, lower expenses, and higher building occupancy. LEED buildings are also designed to be healthier to building occupants, and contribute to improved productivity (associated with more daylight, better air quality, and more individual comfort control).

7. PURPOSE

Aside from solid economics and performance-based efficiency and health, one of the most important ingredients of the success of USGBC, WorldGBC, and individual country GBCs is purpose. This was essential to attract and hold our "*human* capital." Without giving our hundreds of staff and thousands of volunteers and participants a broader sense of purpose, I don't think we would have prevailed in our early years. When we didn't have fancy color brochures, LEED, and the peer-reviewed data of the financial benefits of green building, it took something more to recruit and retain GBC participants. The magic of USGBC and the one hundred other country GBCs is that we're playing in the Earth's most important game: continued growth and prosperity in the face of increased risk of environmental catastrophe.

Participating in building USGBC, using LEED, and attending Greenbuild and local chapter events gave thousands a deeper feeling for the movement. They met others who were inspired to make a difference, who were asking deeper questions and dedicating their careers to doing better. They also discovered that green building was good business and could provide them with long and vibrant careers.

You can make great lifelong friends when you give of yourself and come together to embrace a shared mission. I believe we even went further, becoming comrades in building the world's greatest marketplace for ecological transformation.

8. DATA

Numbers and data matter, including numbers of members, LEED projects, and aggregate square footage, as well as ROI on projects and increased building value. It's important to collect credible data, such as energy and water savings and health and productivity gains, and then verify it with third-party validators. When green makes more money and is more valuable, the market turns — and that's a turning that we've been seeing during our twenty-year history. Gathering the statistics to prove the business case has been another focus of the GBCs since LEED was launched. Thankfully, the numbers do prove the business case, despite some ill-informed media stories to the contrary.

There are so many areas to expand our data collection and analysis. The business case tops all priorities, as the economy is the best driver for transformation, especially when green is good business. It is vital that we continue to understand how many green jobs we're creating, and how much ecological impact we're reducing. McGraw Hill projects approximately nine hundred thousand new nonresidential green jobs will be created by 2015 as the share of green projects grows to 45 percent.

Art Gensler, founder of Gensler architectural firm and one of my few mentors, always told me that we should pay attention to Pareto's Principle of 80-20, which states that for many events, roughly 80 percent of the effects come from 20 percent of the causes. We often didn't pay enough attention, but Art and Pareto were sages. It's important not to err on the side of purism, as we often did in our early days, but instead to focus on the elements that matter and discard or disregard the items that just don't make much of a difference.

9. LESSONS LEARNED

I learned that if we'd strived for perfection, we'd never have succeeded. When we steered towards perfection (100 percent), we ran into obstacles. I never forgot Richard Denison's message about how he'd turned a potential legal wrangle with McDonalds into a partnership that became a win-win, instead of going for a solo victory. I recall when we started that some of our members wanted to exclude some "toxic" building product manufacturers. Fortunately, we prevailed, believing that it was important to invite everyone to our table—the bigger and more toxic, the more critical their presence. We could then work on them inside our tent and eventually replace their "toxic" methods for more environmentally and ultimately more economically beneficial products. We learned that without the world's largest manufacturers at the table, we couldn't move towards transformation and that change was greatly magnified with them in the game.

It was hard for me to see that if someone was an obstacle to change and growth, we needed to sidestep that person. Emotionally I don't like to hurt people. However, our mission was bigger than any individual's feelings. I still feel this way. Passionate volunteers who were nonetheless keeping us from hitting the market effectively and with a product that was consistent with our mission had to be worked around. We invariably had a few leaders who were trying to make a splash through their leadership. But we had to remember that USGBC and the WorldGBC are about our collective mission, not about individuals.

Mike taught us that speed is quality. We pushed forward as fast and as hard as we could, despite being an entrepreneurial-based nonprofit. After always pushing hard to launch new products, USGBC learned in time to balance its inventions with quality and speed. The LEED standards development and balloting process, for example, created its own timeline, which sometimes became rather lengthy.

We could have done a better job paying attention to our customers and what they wanted, instead of pushing out what we thought the market needed. Our dedicated and passionate USGBC staff sometimes failed to perform enough market research and listen to the customer. In later years, I believe that under Rick's corporate leadership we learned to pace ourselves and do market research. During our earlier years, we were driven by youthful passion and were listening more to ourselves than to anything else. It took me decades to learn what I did and did not know.

When I wrote my white paper on how to improve LEED, at first I was insular in my thinking. While I was out running one day during this time, it dawned on me that I'd forgotten to reach outside of my own head. I went back to my office and lined up about sixty expert calls to solicit outside feedback on LEED's effectiveness and areas for improvement. I asked for suggestions on how we could simplify the certification process without losing our quality and credibility.

I recall that meeting with Art Gensler when he reemphasized the 80-20 rule. "We can streamline the process and still achieve most of the results we want," he said. He felt that we'd gone way too far toward demanding perfection in our documentation and review certification process. If someone really wanted to cheat that badly, we should do our best to catch them with simple flags and screens, just as the IRS did with taxpayers. And he had another good point: why did we require so much documentation as part of the LEED paperwork submission? It made me think of my dad's motto: do not confuse effort with results. Often the documentation had little to do with the ultimate and actual results.

On the WorldGBC front, we made some mistakes—I made some mistakes—in agreeing to work with several weak country

GBCs. I went too fast and failed to perform better due diligence on the founders and their founding boards. Since our formal founding in 2002, the WorldGBC has had to kick out two or three founding member country green building councils. In one case, the founder kept stealing our intellectual property and rebranding it as his own. His memory and ours never seemed to sync up. And in another country, the founder employed the GBC as a tool to get consulting business, holding back the country from the benefits of an open, nonprofit approach. The WorldGBC, however, has had to learn how to work with a hundred countries, each with its own laws and ways of doing things. Both the USGBC and the WorldGBC have been learning how to operate globally, as they better learn about other cultures and different methods to accomplish things. There are also other values and priorities in terms of environmental measures, such as water over energy efficiency, and use of waste streams, air quality, and transportation. In terms of social performance measures, some of the countries with GBCs have higher priorities before green building: potable water, HIV prevention and treatment, literacy, housing, and safety for their citizens.

When I'd written the Five Commandments for the planet Earth and given them to David Brower in 1999, he'd added a sixth one that became the most important one: "What Have We Forgotten?" (See Appendix). As the years go by, I'm finally learning to continually ask this question. In relation to the GBCs, I'd say that we've forgotten to involve all buildings in the green building game, instead focusing mostly on those that can qualify for certification at the minimum bar level (for USGBC, LEED Certified). Well, what about the millions of other buildings, most of them small? We need them to be part of the green building improvement game. When I accompanied a friend to a Weight Watchers meeting, I noticed that they welcomed all people of all weights, not only those who were already fit or who could run a 10K or finish a triathlon. If we apply this analogy to buildings, then we must encourage all the couch potato buildings to put on a pair of tennis shoes and go out the front door and break a sweat.

The United States has about 4.5 million commercial buildings, and we're greening maybe about two hundred thousand at best with LEED. The government's ENERGY STAR program has 22,000 certified buildings, with an average score of 85 out of a total of 100. There are other building and home-rating programs in the United States as well. This work is significant in terms of energy savings, but still we have a long way to go to hit the majority of buildings.

About five years ago, Mike, Rick, and I resigned our lifetime USGBC board slots. As CEO, Rick still serves on the board. At the time we'd already each served fifteen years on the board. We were also on the Executive Committee, accounting for half of the votes. We tried to steer the organization as stewards, but felt we had too much influence and ran the risk of burnout. It's hard for founders to step aside and let new blood take the reins of leadership. (Apparently this is known as "founder's syndrome.") My role on the board of the WorldGBC also termed out about two years ago.

It took years for me to make the transition from parent to grandparent of the USGBC and WorldGBC. I now watch from that front-row seat, enjoying a deep inner feeling of contentment. However, it's still hard at times for my ego to accept a passive role—one that's more mentoring and message based, as opposed to operational. A transition at the top is normal and typically healthy for organizations. Founders need to know when it's time to hand over the baton. In some cases, though, an organization can lose its vision and veer away from its mission, requiring an adjustment—as we'd found in 1996 when I had to come back and steer USGBC for another three years, until we were solid enough to recruit Christine Ervin as CEO.

I wish the WorldGBC's hundred country members would find better ways to share their knowledge and practices with one another. I think the time for massive collaboration is coming with the help of social media tools, websites, Internet WebEx meetings, and virtual community applications. It also requires a deeper commitment to share and not sit on important lessons learned and products that aren't vital intellectual property. And then there's having the time to share. As I learned in my Regenerative Network, if we provide items of value to each other, then we can in turn receive. This is the essence of building a network effect among the GBCs where the collective is much stronger the individual. I believe this state already exists for the WorldGBC, but could be enhanced through new measures of collaboration.

I'm still amazed at the early adoption of green building by local and state governments that led to change. They can set standards, as we saw, for their own buildings and operations. Yes, they have procurement laws, but they can also employ high-performance standards in their own building specifications and beyond to the private sector. We watched this occur with more than a hundred cities and dozens of states and federal agencies and thank those leaders for sticking their necks out for change, despite often creating more work for themselves.

I keep coming back to the same conclusion: that it's the individual (inside an organization, or acting independently) who creates transformation. We must instill, nurture, and sustain passion and spirit in our employees, colleagues, students and kids. This is the engine of change.

21
WHAT'S NEXT?

Our work to date has been impressive—far greater than we could ever have envisioned two decades ago. There is much to celebrate, with GBCs in one hundred countries and green building becoming an industry itself, already hitting several hundred billion dollars around the globe. Who would have thought that USGBC's Greenbuild conference would have keynote speeches given by the likes of President Bill Clinton, Secretary of State Hillary Clinton, Vice President Al Gore, and Archbishop Desmond Tutu while rocking in baseball stadiums to bands like Maroon 5, Train, and Bon Jovi?

LEED and the dozens of other green building rating systems in the world have had a huge impact, with more than eleven billion square feet, representing 175,000 projects, being greened worldwide. Nevertheless, the percentage change in the world's overall use of energy, water, and materials is minor. We still have far to go. Below are a few thoughts about what we are doing, and what more we can do, to cut down our use of energy and conserve our dwindling water resources.

1. GREEN PRODUCT INNOVATIONS
I love the advent of new technologies, especially those that are disruptive and can provide quantum leaps in performance. These

products come from both established industry billion-dollar global leaders as well as tiny start-ups operating on sweat equity and a big dream.

Why are the lights on when nobody's home? What can we power down when energy is at peak-demand charges during the hot summer? Intelligent sensors can wirelessly communicate information to a hub and save energy in all kinds of ways. They can collect data on many different inputs: amount of light, movement, temperature, and all types of VOCs such as formaldehyde, CO_2, and CO. The hub can process the data and combine it with its programming and other data, such as time of day, day of week, and real-time utility rates. Building equipment can then be adjusted to provide for optimal conditions and also energy (and water) efficiency and improved occupant health and productivity. Too much formaldehyde? A sensor will alert a mechanical system to send more air into the room. External energy sources, including solar, wind, thermal storage, and cogeneration can be used to reduce utility demand, especially during peak periods.

Intelligent sensors can be incorporated into just about every building component. Every utility outlet can be intelligent, as well as every light switch, appliance and lighting fixture, thermostats, and water and energy meters. A company called Nest makes a great smart thermostat that learns your heating and cooling behavioral patterns and uses artificial intelligence to efficiently heat and cool your house. It communicates wirelessly over your home Internet network. Like a faithful unseen servant, it learns to automatically control your real-time temperature according to your historic pattern of use. It also has an occupancy sensor inside, detecting when you enter a given space. A cool app allows you to control the temperature. I once lowered the temperature on my family from Beijing. (How happy they were about that is another story).

Lights that are on where no one needs them, as well as lights that kick out heat, are a waste of energy. Armstrong makes an electrified ceiling grid powered with low-voltage DC power. You can just plug in an LED light wherever desired and readily move it around. No electrician needed. Solar energy is generated as DC current; it's a great match to power the lighting system directly.

Plug load is an area of energy usage that has long been in the dark ages in terms of our understanding the energy draw, as well as in controlling ongoing usage. Enmetric Systems solves this with an intelligent outlet surge strip that reads the power draw of each plugged-in device. Each outlet can then be individually controlled from the software cloud. This can be especially useful in some high-end tuned green buildings, where the plug loads have emerged as the highest energy draw, beating out even building HVAC and lighting.

Windows that turn from clear to dark greatly reduce building heat gain from southern and western sun. The electrochromic glass works so well that window blinds aren't needed and HVAC loads can be reduced—additional first-cost savings.

One way to eliminate the waste that accompanies any construction job is a house made of pre-manufactured parts. Project Frog makes buildings from a kit. Many configurations are available through the company's catalog—a fast and cost-effective way to create beautiful and energy-efficient buildings. Project Frog's motto is "better, faster, greener, cheaper." In 2013, the company received its largest order ever, for 250,000 square feet of new Frog education buildings to be installed for the South San Francisco Unified School District.

Cypress Envirosystems' products make a dumb building smart very quickly and without invasiveness. Using a wireless pneumatic thermostat, the company retrofitted a 300,000-square-foot building in California in eight days with no disruption. The conventional solution would have taken six months, caused a lot of disruption, and cost five times more. The utility paid for everything, so the investment had an instant return, but on average, the payback is under eighteen months, even without utility incentives.

2. ENERGY EFFICIENCY IN EXISTING BUILDINGS

New commercial and residential construction projects are increasingly being greened, and can take advantage of the new green products emerging daily.

But we're still using too much energy in the hundreds of thousands of existing buildings and homes with leaky windows, uninsulated walls and roofs, and wasteful water use as well. This problem will take creative solutions to solve. Owners can't afford to spend $15,000 making necessary alterations even if they eventually get the money back in smaller energy and water bills. It's also hard for most building owners and homeowners to figure out which energy and water efficiency improvements are cost effective.

The average annual return on a portfolio of ten effective energy-saving measures for your home is 16 percent, and some measures provide greater than a 100 percent return on investment. Thus energy efficiency can provide a higher annual return than most of us receive in the stock market, and at lower risk.

Many of us invest in retirement and college education funds. Why not invest instead in funds that help pay for the massive green (energy and water) transformation we need—now and for future generations?

One idea is that each city would create an energy-efficiency investment fund. The funds could come from city residents, who would invest a portion of their retirement savings. In a way, they'd be creating a green-distributed utility that would help retrofit their homes and community buildings. The investors would also benefit from annual returns provided by the energy savings at the meter. Given the high return on investment and the low risk, financial institutions may also want to invest as well. If the cities guaranteed the return of funds, a green bond could be issued at a low interest rate.

The annual return would be even higher if utilities provided rebates on efficient measures installed in buildings and homes. Tax credits could then be added to the mix by state and federal governments.

We could study solar PPAs (Power Purchase Agreements) for a sample contract and business terms. Building owners and homeowners would enter into a contract that would be recorded with the deed of the property and stay with the structure upon sale. We could study both positive and negative lessons from the PACE (Property Assessed Clean Energy) programs to implement this new initiative.

When utilities install smart meters and more efficient power generation, they just do the work, and pass through the costs to ratepayers. They can assist in doing the same with ensuring the credibility and relative ease of specifying and installing high-performance energy-efficiency improvements. Perhaps utilities should just fund the work, and figure out the savings and amortization from the monthly utility bills. This system could serve as the "power plant" of the future—one that avoids the requirement to build new power capacity through energy efficiency.

Imagine the number of jobs we could create in the process of installing weather stripping and caulking, insulation, new furnaces, air conditioners, water heaters and appliances, LED lighting, new window film and even new dual-pane windows where appropriate, and wireless controls with demand-side management capabilities!

3. WATER EFFICIENCY

Water efficiency could follow the same business plan. Like those for energy, water conservation measures should be funded on a first-cost basis by government, local utilities, and private investment funds. Rebates and investment tax credits can help accelerate adoption by boosting financial returns. Water efficiency can have a good return on investment. The investment returns would be higher if we valued our increasingly scarce water supply based on our vital need for it, and the true market economics of supply and demand. A huge portion of the Earth, estimated as high as 40 percent, is deprived of clean water. This impacts about 1.6 billion people. Even our primary lakes, rivers, and underground water aquifers are drying up, including Lake Mead, the Colorado River and Ogallala Aquifer.

Lower monthly water bills should pay back the up-front loans for the more efficient technologies that are installed in buildings and homes.

Our homes and buildings consume at least 14 percent of our potable water supply. Thus a good place to start is by installing more efficient fixtures and flow devices. Water-efficient appliances exist for dishwashers and washing machines. Next, it's important to capture and reuse rainwater for landscaping and toilets. Gray water can be captured from sinks, tubs, and showers, then filtered on-site and used for landscaping and toilets. Some jurisdictions don't allow these uses yet, but I believe water codes should be re-written globally.

Installing porous paving will allow the underground aquifers to refill. Composting toilets and waterless urinals work. One waterless urinal can save about forty thousand gallons of water per year. They do require maintenance, but many have demonstrated impressive water savings and practicality even in high-use areas such as stadiums. Composting toilets treat waste via an aerobic processing system that treats excreta, typically with no water. The byproducts of this process (humanure nutrients) can be used as soil treatment for plants.

Australians have adopted a process called "sewer mining," or, literally, reclaiming sewer water for nonpotable purposes through microfiltration and reverse osmosis treatment. The Pennant Hills Golf Club in Sydney, Australia, has cut its potable water use by 92 percent by mining a sewer that runs through the course.

Native plants thrive without extra watering. In our bungalow, we ripped out the old lawn and installed decomposed granite in between the planting areas and as a walkway. Several large boulders served as seating and brought more of nature into our yard.

The employment opportunities to be created by a water efficiency revolution could add up to hundreds of thousands of additional jobs in the United States alone, and the same or greater overseas.

I really don't know what we're waiting for. By 2030 it's projected that we'll be at a 140 percent carrying capacity for water on Earth. (The carrying capacity is the maximum population the environment can support.)

4. GOVERNMENTAL CARROTS AND STICKS

Government can offer more incentives to help accelerate the market transformation to green building. Take solar thermal. Most green building advocates and many mechanical engineers love solar hot-water heating, preferring it as an effective system in terms of performance to solar photovoltaics that generate electricity. However, the tax credits for solar hot water aren't that great, when they exist at all. And the systems can be expensive to install, so without better tax breaks people will continue to shy away from them.

Tax credits are beneficial, as we've seen in the solar industry and previously in encouraging historic preservation. The states of New York and Nevada offered tax credits for green building, which persuaded some projects, such as MGM Resorts International's CityCenter, a massive $8.5 billion hotel, condo, and shopping center development in Las Vegas, to go green. Hitting a certification level of LEED Gold was worth millions of dollars of savings in annual real estate taxes. New York's tax credit, passed in 2000, provided $25 million in income-tax credits, including up to $10.50 per square foot for a high-performance base building and half that much for tenant improvements. Government can help in other ways. The US General Services Administration requires a minimum of LEED Gold certification for all new federal buildings and renovations; the Army, Navy, and Air Force have similar requirements.

During the economic downturn, President Obama funded dozens of green companies that were developing new technologies through grants and low-interest loans. Many companies were able to accelerate their product innovations and hire hundreds of workers.

This is an appropriate role for government to play, one with attractive precedents as well as current examples. For example, historically the US government played a crucial role in developing computer chip technology. Its missile programs led the development of the technology, and then forced it into mass production. Government programs accounted for the entire $4 million integrated circuit market in 1962, when the average price per circuit was $50. Government demand supported the nascent integrated circuit market until costs fell enough to allow firms to sell to businesses and individuals.

Government can set standards for green products. In order to make informed purchases, we need information on products, including environmental performance data, health and toxicity ingredients, and social criteria. The performance data requires its own "nutrition label" of reporting, such as energy (carbon), water, waste, and other life-cycle assessment indicator figures.

There has been some progress on this front: new reporting methods are emerging, such as EPDs (Environmental Product Declarations) and HPDs (Health Product Declarations). EPDs summarize the environmental characteristics of a product in a way that is accessible, consistent, and comparable, based on a life-cycle assessment (LCA) and an ISO standard.

While EPDs provide a lot of information, they don't deal well with human or environmental health. As a result, and due to demands for this information from many fronts, a joint initiative of Healthy Building Network (HBN), BuildingGreen (publisher of the highly respected *Environmental Building News*), and twelve major manufacturers recently formed an Open Standard Working Group that has developed the new HPD standard format for reporting product content and associated health information. HPDs are currently in a pilot phase with thirty major manufacturers participating.

Government can also pass tougher regulation and building codes. California's Title 24 code is the highest standard in the country for efficient use of energy and water, mandating that all new construction projects reduce energy use by 15 percent, water use by 20 percent, and water for landscaping by 50 percent. The energy law has kept per-capita energy use just about flat in California for nearly four decades, whereas use in the United States has gone up approximately 50 percent. Are the other states noticing this? Cities can help as well as states. Many localities now require higher levels of energy efficiency, some going so far as to require "net-zero" buildings by 2030. (A net-zero building generates as much power as it uses during the course of the year.) Many cities require a minimum of LEED Silver or even Gold for their own buildings. Arlington County, Virginia, was one of the first to offer real estate developers extra square footage for going LEED certified. Other cities have offered green incentives that include parking requirement reductions, accelerated building permits, grants, fees for green professional consulting, and approvals for planned unit developments.

According to Vancouver City Councillor Andrea Reimer, under the leadership of Mayor Gregor Robertson, Vancouver wants to be the greenest city on the planet—an initiative that has resulted in $100 million of new funding and about one thousand new jobs. To me, this type of visionary planning and action explains why Vancouver has the strongest economy in Canada. From what I could tell during Andrea's recent talk, city officials in Vancouver are specific, bold, focused, aggressive, innovative, and collaborative—all traits we need for our shared future prosperity.

5. OPEN SHARING AND TRANSPARENCY

I've always believed that the key asset (and human intellectual property) of the world's one hundred GBCs is not just that they offer green building rating tools and annual conferences, but also that they bring together the individual and collective experience and knowledge of the thirty thousand organizational members representing millions of passionate and visionary leaders across all sectors of the building industry.

Sharing opening and transparently is vital to our future. We've always offered the LEED green building rating system for free public downloads. Our new standard balloting is open to all members to comment and vote on. My best organizational creations (USGBC and WorldGBC) were handed off to the public sector as nonprofit organizations so that the industry could take ownership and accordingly advance the early innovations.

Reporting and associated transparency will continue to increase in importance and requirements. Consumers (and the public) want to know (or to be able to decide for themselves) what they are buying and which companies, products, and brands to purchase. In the building field, some of the leading architects and engineers need a slew of product performance data in all of these areas to make informed decisions; this requirement may originate in-house, but it is increasingly driven by their clients. LEED and other global rating systems have credits associated with relative performance that can only be determined by collecting and evaluating the respective data for all products in the new or renovated buildings. Many believe that there are LEED-approved products, but that's not true. There are only products and systems that contribute to LEED certification.

When we are strong, we are not afraid to share, although sharing does not come naturally in a business context. And yet we all win when best practices are highlighted and methods to improve revealed.

I'm glad to say that transparency is growing all over the globe. The open-sharing ethic has even penetrated previously competitive companies ("coopetition"). Of course they're not sharing the secret sauces (intellectual properties and patents) that are pivotal to their business, but they have found many areas where they can swap knowledge to everyone's advantage. Our Regenerative Network facilitates sharing of knowledge among leading industry manufacturers.

We also saw this happen with our many LEED committees and at Greenbuild's one hundred-plus educational sessions. The WorldGBC has an annual GBC Congress and promotes best-practice sharing of GBC and green building knowledge. It's an important part of its mission.

How can we best harness and share that body of wisdom for transformation? One way is to use software tools that help unlock the massive amount of useful data and create an engaging and vibrantly continuous flowing stream of knowledge value.

When USGBC was small, we used to be able to go around the room of members in three hours, and each would share for one minute. I taped, transcribed, and published the excellent information that was exchanged, calling it our annual *State of Green*

Building. But now we're too large and the movement is global. LinkedIn Groups, Facebook, Twitter, and many more social media tools are already helping connect us. But we can do so much more.

Transparency requires providing detailed information that is public and readily accessible. Websites arguably have become the best method for communicating. Software reporting tools and services are popping up. One cool app is GoodGuide, recently purchased by UL Environment. Its mission is to help guide safe, healthy, green, and ethical product purchasing. Goodguide has a team of scientists who rate products from a score of zero to ten. GreenWizard offers a software service that connects building projects to green product manufacturer information on twelve hundred manufacturers. It also helps synthesize the data into a project's LEED documentation. According to the website, the software tool makes it easier to gain access to manufacturer environmental reports, such as: Environmental Product Declarations (EPDs), Health Product Declarations (HPDs), Life-Cycle Assessments (LCA), and various certifications (such as SCS, GreenCircle, Cradle to Cradle).

6. ONE GLOBAL GREEN BUILDING RATING SYSTEM?

Since the WorldGBC was founded, we've learned a lot from the development of rating systems in various cultures and climates. Japan's CASBEE was the first to embed building information modeling (BIM), and Australia's Green Star system has three separate award modules (design, build, and operate green) and also bioclimatic adaption. In the United States, the Living Building Challenge, a rating system that calls for net-zero energy, water, and waste as well as other high threshold performance levels, is gaining traction. Its organizing body hosts an annual conference in the Pacific Northwest that brings in more than one thousand enthusiastic attendees. Google is the system's largest supporter.

Transparency by itself doesn't solve the confusion that can result from all these different rating systems. Multinational firms that support green building practices are finding it difficult to navigate the world's dozens of rating systems, each tailored to the codes and standards and bioclimatic conditions of the given country, as well as their cultures and market.

Obviously one universally recognized rating system would help.

One idea that's been put forward is creating equivalencies among the various global rating systems in terms of energy, water, waste, etc. This would help us understand the difference, say, between LEED Platinum and Three Stars (China) or Six Green Stars (Australia). Since climate changes (and then water) are our biggest issues, performing an equivalency study based on carbon dioxide and liters of water consumed would be a good starting point. The United Nations Environment Programme (UNEP) Sustainable Building & Climate Initiative (SBCI) has done some preliminary work in this area for measuring energy use and reporting greenhouse gas emissions from building operations.)

Adopting one of the existing systems is another option. But getting everyone to agree to work together could be tough (think of how the global carbon treaty summits go). But that may not be as big a difficulty as it seems. I would have thought this about LEED, but it's being used in about 140 countries even though it references many US standards, such as ASHRAE and ENERGY STAR. Projects outside the United States now make up about 20 percent of all LEED projects, and in 2012 and through October 2013 the floor area of newly registered LEED projects outside of the United States has exceeded fifty percent, growing as an overall percentage each year. To address this trend, USGBC, through its LEED International Roundtable, is working to create alternative compliance paths for projects outside the United States, providing flexibility to ensure a common language for all green buildings.

The paths address geographic and regional issues. Another global trend is dual certification, where projects outside the United States obtain both a LEED certification and also that of the local country. I witnessed this when meeting recently with Intel in Israel.

But there's a precedent. In the last century, there were three different codes of building regulations in the United States: one on the East Coast and Midwest, another in the Southeast, and still another that covered the West Coast and parts of the Midwest. By the early 1990s, though, as business became increasingly borderless, the need for a national model building code had become pressing. In response, the three code organizations agreed to combine their efforts, unify their codes, and follow an orderly process of rationalizing and then publishing the new combined International Building Code.

We can learn from this example as we work toward unifying our green building rating systems around the world. In 2010 the International Code Council released its own International Green Construction Code (IGCC), based on the state of California's green building code and developed in partnership with the AIA, ASTM, ASHRAE, and the USGBC.

We can also simplify our rating systems and the back-end certification. Most green building certification processes are costly and laborious, and often require the hiring of an outside consultant, which can be expensive. Using intelligent review and filtering systems can result in building certification applications that are comprehensive, yet relatively few pages, containing only the most vital green categories of information. Energy and water bills are the true data we need, not models and projections. At some point, I envision that the operational building rating systems will incorporate some type of real-time certification that adjusts with the building's monthly utility bills.

7. EDUCATION

All college and university educational programs should include courses in sustainability as part of their mandatory curricula. I'd go even further and require students to undertake a sustainability-benchmarking project in order to graduate. The project should incorporate base casing, goal setting, implementation of improvement opportunities, and measurement. It could entail review of a local company, a specific product, or even the student's own home or the school facilities. This initiative could be enhanced by an annual awards competition. Schools could also advance sustainability education at their institutions by hosting an annual US and global sustainability product or business plan competition. The winning teams could get venture-backed seed funding and business incubation coaching.

8. GREENING BUSINESS

"(T)he game has changed. (Milton) Friedman's argument that businesses have 'one and only one social responsibility'—to maximise profit for shareholders—now seems not so much wrong as built for another time. Today, businesses that pursue commercial interests without giving due consideration to the communities they're involved with are not competitively advantaged; they're embroiled in controversy, exposed to supplychain shocks, caught out by regulatory changes, and are well on their way to becoming socially irrelevant to customers. ... The power of net positive is the clarity and boldness of the vision. ..."—Phil Drew, *Guardian Professional*

When private companies go public on the stock market, we call this an IPO, or initial public offering. We could invent a GPO (green public offering), for companies that have a high green score. I'd like to see venture capitalists, investment banks, and stock markets encourage more GPOs and track GPO companies against non-GPOs to see who has a higher success rate in terms of income, profitability, and market stock price to earnings ratios (P/Es). Governments and consumers should work to reward companies that are "green" and increasingly value their offerings.

Environmental nonprofits, governments, and educational institutions should be educating financial institutions, companies, and the public on the benefits of green companies and their products and services.

Many companies are prospering in the green economy, and more of their stories need to be told in a vocabulary and language that executives in the C-suite can understand: dollars and cents, competitive edge, market growth, and higher profitability.

The rise of corporate CSOs (Chief Sustainability Officers) in the C-Suite is an encouraging trend. Their green activities place a high priority on (in declining order): waste reduction, employee engagement, renewable energy, green building, NGO engagement, and annual sustainability reporting. McGraw Hill's *2012 Greening of Corporate America* report states that by 2015, 47 percent of the 203 large companies surveyed will embrace green initiatives. Of those firms, 37 percent replied that company sustainability activities are tied to revenue generation and boosted profitability.

As a result, recently we're hearing more about companies with net-positive goals in terms of energy efficiency, water, and waste. Some of the benchmark companies in this area include Marks & Spenser, Kingfisher, and BT Group.

Marks & Spencer (M&S) has a vision to make sustainability "the business we do." Its Plan A (there is no Plan B) sets out one hundred five-year commitments. Plan A was a cost in its first year and cost-neutral in its second, but by 2011 to 2012 it started delivering a net benefit. The company has reinvested £185 million in net benefits back into the business during the last five years. Customers have embraced the M&S program, including one that gives them a chance to give back: the company's "shwopping" initiative netted eleven million used garments that were donated to Oxfam's second-hand clothing stores.

Kingfisher is Europe's largest home improvement retailer with more than 1,060 stores in nine countries. The vision of its "Net Positive" program is to go beyond zero impact to create positive change. "It's a much more effective way to drive change than the incremental approach of 'cut 20 percent by 2020,'" the company says.

BT has been measuring its carbon impact and putting sustainability at the core of its business strategy for twenty years. Its new "Net Good" program's 2020 goal is to help customers reduce carbon emissions by at least three times the carbon impact of BT's business. The methodology behind the plan is open source. The company says, "We want to share it because we want other people to be able to adopt and improve it or perhaps come up with something better."

9. REPORTING

Many companies now prepare detailed annual sustainability reports on their operations. Progressive firms set and report on their progress in meeting aggressive goals for their LEED building rating level, greenhouse gas (GHG) emission thresholds, energy and water consumption, suppliers, transportation, governance, waste going to the landfill, and dozens of other goals, including social and corporate citizenship.

There are also some green company annual surveys, such as the Dow Jones Sustainability Index of 2500 companies, and various rating systems and guidelines. One of the most widely recognized and accepted reporting methods is GRI (the Global Reporting Initiative), which provides common, accepted standards for organizations to measure and report their economic, environmental, social, and ethical behavior.

Other rapidly growing programs in this area include the International Integrated Reporting Council, Carbon Disclosure Project (CDP)—used by many of our Regenerative Network members—and Extractive Industries Transparency Initiative (EITI). An integrated report is a concise communication that shows how an organization's strategy, governance, performance, and prospects lead to the creation of value over the short, medium, and long term.

Reporting and rating systems started with buildings and products, and some are now looking more holistically at the full spectrum of environmental and social performance of a company. Green Seal is piloting a Sustainability Standard for Product Manufacturers that takes a holistic look at company operations, while UL Environment published its enterprise-level sustainability standard, ULE 880: Sustainability for Manufacturing Organizations. It tries to promote verifiable Global Reporting Initiative reporting standards through quantifiable measures where there are clear protocols for reporting.

One common name for ideas such as these is the Steady State Economy. In their typical lively way, Australians call it the "Nega economy"—meaning that the only growth we can afford is nega-growth, where every footprint needs to be minus-two footprints, and the smaller your eco footprint, the more money you'll make!

I've been professing the same concept for a decade, expanding upon Amory Lovins' 1989 invention, negawatt power, to negafootprint. A negawatt of power means that a watt of energy conserved is equivalent to a watt of power generated. In a negawatt market, we can trade negawatt credits and create an exchange. I believe we can do the same by inventing a negafootprint exchange. Eco-footprint is much harder to calculate than negawatt, of course, but science is working to make these calculations easier, as we look beyond just energy and take into consideration the full life-cycle assessment of products, including buildings.

We all live under the same blue sky and breathe the same air on this beautiful planet. I encourage you to assess your own green progress, goals, and future activities and redouble your efforts—individually and through organizations—so that our children and our children's children will look back and say, "It wasn't easy to do, but they all pulled together: individuals, businesses, and governments all over the globe, and preserved it for us." It is our moral mandate (and smart business) to work toward leaving a planet that can sustain life for generations to come.

EPILOGUE

I pedaled the indestructible green rental bike along Tel Aviv's bicycle path along the historic waterfront headed to Jaffa. The late summer heat and humidity dripped down my back as I felt the cooling effect of the slight wind. Ahead were the ancient walls of Jaffa. Coasting down the moderately sloping path, it was almost impossible to fathom that Jaffa's history dates back to 7500 BCE and included a litany of biblical conquests: King David and his son King Solomon during their building of the first temple, the Babylonians, Phoenicians, Alexander the Great, Maccabean rebels, Romans, Arabs, King Richard the Lionheart, Ottomans, Napoleon I of France, British, and the Haganah, as Jaffa ultimately became part of the State of Israel.

To my right the gorgeous warm waters of the Mediterranean offered up nicely forming waves to about thirty surfers, including two standing up on paddle boards. Long gone was the blood of the thousands of dead who fought to maintain ownership of this militarily strategic Port, providing access to the Promised Land. As I pedaled rhythmically with vigor, I felt a freedom and inner peace I hadn't felt in a long time. First, I had returned as a grown family man to Israel after twenty-seven years, and thirty-two years since studying Hebrew at the University of Haifa's Ulpan and a month of attempting to study industrial engineering and management in

Hebrew at Technion (Israel's Institute of Technology). And more importantly, I was here on a mission to expand green building within the country: working on *Tikkun Olam*, a Hebrew term that dates back to Isaac Luria, a sixteenth-century Kabbalist. It means helping God and society to restore our broken Earth. And through this transformational work, I was strengthening my soul and working to rekindle my inner light.

After five minutes of hard cycling, I passed a slew of small Israeli flags decorating a brick archway alongside a stone building adjacent to Jaffa's Port. Next door was an outdoor coffee shop facing the ocean with about a dozen people sipping away in between heated conversations. I wondered if they were discussing politics, as Israelis often do, especially given the heated-up tension in Syria's civil war. My wife, Sara, and eight-year-old daughter were supposed to join me on the trip, but they stayed home as the United States and England decided if they'd bomb Syria in retaliation for Syria gassing its people. The day we were to fly out, USA Today's front cover featured a photo of a mother in Jerusalem donning her newly issued gas mask. As a result, I went alone, determined not to abandon my comrades at the Israel Green Building Council, now in its fifth year.

"And now I'd like to introduce David Gottfried, founder of the US and World GBCs," Galit Cohen, Deputy Director General for Planning and Sustainable Development for Israel's Ministry of Environmental Protection, said in Hebrew. I walked out onto the stage at Tel Aviv University. It was September 2013. Behind me, a slide with the logo of the Israel GBC read: The Explosion of Green Building, the title of my talk.

I walked with spring in my step to the podium and looked out across the large sloped auditorium full of about 750 Israeli green building professionals. I wore my black Armani blazer, even though no one else had a jacket, and an olive green Prada dress shirt that

Sara had bought me, tucked in to my stretchy black Lululemon slacks, the same size that I'd worn in Israel three decades ago. My platinum wedding band that had adorned my wedding finger for ten years flashed in the light.

"It's wonderful to be here and to speak to Israel about green building," I said loudly in my simple broken Hebrew. I'd dusted off my brain wiring to the Hebrew database, often crossing over to my Spanish one.

"Over thirty years ago I studied here and dreamed of making a difference, as our biblical forefathers had done. What a dream to be here as a participant in the Israel Green Building Council's fifth annual green building conference. We're proud to have the ILGBC as an active participant of the WorldGBC's one hundred countries." I breathed deeply, taking in the reality of what we'd created over the past twenty years.

I then shared the statistics I'd gathered showing the amazing growth of the green building marketplace around the world and particularly in the United States. Already it was almost $100 billion in size and estimated to double again to $200 billion by 2016. When the US economy collapsed during the past five years, green building held its own and continued to grow by about 30 percent a year. Design and construction firms that had integrated green building into their corporate strategies had grown greatly and profited accordingly. Real estate owners also benefited with higher rents, faster leasing, higher occupancy rates, and lower energy, water, and waste expenses and as a result, higher net income. This meant an overall increase in profitability, return on investment and an associated higher building value, numbers that we'd only dreamed of obtaining just a decade before.

"As Jews, our life journey is not only about making more money, but also performing *Tikkun Olam*," I said at the end of my talk. "We're now speaking out and taking bold action for sustainability and performance efficiency as we green our buildings," I added. I thought of the Holocaust, when our ancestors walked to their deaths in silent hope that they'd be saved.

After my talk on the economic explosion of green building, I walked off the stage standing taller. A tanned, fit gentlemen slightly older than me extended his hand. "Your talk was excellent," said David Leffler, Israel's brand new Director General of the Ministry of Environmental Protection said to me, shaking my hand enthusiastically as I returned to my seat. We'd met an hour before my keynote to discuss what the country's new environmental leadership could do to accelerate green building within the small country. Apparently my words struck a chord, as David asked to meet me later the next day to continue our discussion. During the conversation, I learned that he had served in the Director General role for many governmental agencies and had also been the Parliamentary Assistant to Yitzhak Rabin. At the end of an hour and a half meeting at my hotel's café overlooking Tel Aviv's vibrant waterfront, I asked him to consider me his green building coach. He smiled and shook his head affirmatively.

The next day when I got on the plane to fly home, the guy in the next seat asked me what I was doing in Israel. I told him I'd given a lecture at a green conference and had some meetings. He put down the newspaper he was reading, *The Jerusalem Post*, and told me he'd just read an article that a building in Haifa had certified with the LEED system. I replied that it was likely Intel. I knew this from meeting with them and the Israel GBC the day before. He handed me the paper saying that he was done with it.

I looked at the article heading on Page 7 and it said: "Green building is an economic necessity." I began to read the full-page article and quickly broke out into a full-face smile: it was mostly about my talk at the conference two days before. It also discussed the talk by the Minster of Environmental Protection, Amir Peretz.

"This isn't because we want to hug the trees and do the right thing," it quoted me as saying. "This is the future of the economy," it ended.

I'd written a brief for *Haaritz* newspaper and the financial newspaper *Globes*, which also sent a photographer to my hotel to take my picture, but was shocked that my talk and message had made its way to a full page in the Jerusalem paper. Economics is the key to capitalism, and I'd finally honed the message that green building is a global business opportunity.

It's amazing to think that we're building the bridge leading capitalism from a consumption-based modality to one that embraces resource efficiency, health, and productivity. Through the incentive of improved economics, we're learning from the rules of nature and mirroring them with economic equations and valuation methods that provide hope for our continued survival. Waste is the archenemy of value and wealth, and it depletes economic profitability. Buildings historically have been among the largest polluters, even though they are generally highly profitable. But as green building continues to expand globally and GBCs and their green rating systems proliferate, the profit calculation is for green is growing strongly. We're moving step by step toward my dream that the billionaires of the future will make their fortunes by embracing green; hopefully those who negligently look the other way will eventually lose money and perhaps even go bankrupt.

A book in a box shipped on the Internet highway is cool, but the small fuel cell that I just got in Australia that efficiently powers my laptop is brilliant, as is the iPod-inspired Nest robotic thermostat that learns our home's heating and cooling patterns and can be controlled by an app on my iPhone. We're at a critical turning point for the Earth, having crossed the seven-billion mark in population at the same time that we're hitting a concentration of nearly 400 (395 as of August 2013) particles per million of CO_2. The world's leading scientists say that 350 is the threshold of safety, and that we're hitting levels that may cause irreversible climate change resulting in increasing natural disasters, each potentially costing billions of dollars. Scientists further report that the need for immediate drastic action is now, as our seas warm, icebergs melt, and the oceans become more acidic.

I believe that the Earth will ultimately take care of itself as it heats up. However, it remains to be seen if we'll have the continued long-term privilege of living in this haven. Global green building initiatives in our one hundred GBCs give me hope. Their inventiveness, passion, and accelerating success are extraordinary. Even still, we're just playing in the realm of doing "less bad," what I call Stage 1. As we progress in our performance efficiencies, we advance towards a state of doing no harm, or what we call "net-zero" (Stage 2). But the Earth requires even more, the later phases of restoration (Stage 3) and then regeneration (Stage 4).

We can't easily control the actions of others. Governments can regulate change and transformation, which is essential. Voluntary rating systems such as LEED and Green Star can lead behavior if the benefits are strong, as we've witnessed. I believe we need more. Questions of where, when, and how the change we need will come plague my mind. I don't have many of the answers and don't like to walk in the mud, which can start to feel like quicksand. My dad taught me many invaluable lessons and I thank him for that. His paperweight motto, "Do Not Confuse Effort with Results," helps direct me to focus on moving the needle in a way that actually helps the Earth and its people sustain. On a personal level, it has led me to carefully define results that matter in my life (defining a green life): health, love, family, meaningful work, lots of nature, growing and learning, charitable giving, stewardship, and contentment.

When I felt overwhelmed at a given task, or a multitude of them all competing for my time, Dad often said: "How do you climb a mountain?" And the answer: "One step at a time."

I'm here because my grandparents fled to the United States to escape being killed during World War II. They gave my parents the gift of life. But that opportunity requires that we use our limited time here productively, embracing *Tikkun Olam*.

My relatives who perished in Europe weren't able to fight back with effective action and instead went to their deaths quietly. Now there's a different kind of silent holocaust, and it's threatening to kill the future for our children, or grandchildren, or great-great-great-grandchildren some unknown generations to come long after we're gone. We weren't given a map and compass to guide our lives. Our parents, sages, and religion try to provide guidance. Green building has given me a path to seeing divine light and to healing my leaky vessel as I deepen my soul. It has led me to travel the world, seeking out and banding with thousands, if not millions, of other green building searchers. And in the process, we have not only discovered kindred spirits, but through our work we have found purpose as well. As I continue placing one foot in front of the other, climbing what Ray Anderson called Mount Sustainability, I try to remember David Brower's words that became our Sixth Commandment for the planet Earth, "What Have We Forgotten?"

Green building is indeed exploding, but will it be in time and in step with the greening of all other systems, such as our cars and the products we consume? It's up to each of us to redouble our efforts and keep pursuing results in the metrics of the Earth, as these efforts become the basis of value and wealth.

I end with heartfelt appreciation for your work in helping steer our ship and for rekindling my hope and spirit.

AFTERWORD: THE ART OF BEING A SERIAL FOUNDER

By Dan Slone
General Counsel: USGBC, WorldGBC and Regenerative Network

There are serial entrepreneurs, who have founded multiple, successful companies, and serial change agents, who have guided change in multiple institutions, but David Gottfried is the exceptionally rare individual who has been, and will continue to be, a serial founder of change movements. As most of us struggle to simply meet our daily commitments, why has David been able to do so much? Embedded in the stories he tells in *Explosion Green* is David's secret formula for his success — his five critical skills.

First, David leads an enthusiastic life. He is passionate about green buildings and about the creation of green building councils as change agents. This enthusiasm led to his founding the U.S. Green Building Council and the World Green Building Council. These passions take place, however, in a context of many others. He is enthusiastic about the success of green companies, which has led to years of consulting with some of the best companies in the world, as well as David's creation of the Regenerative Network so that those companies could help one another. But as you read in *Explosion Green*, David is also enthusiastic about his family, the design of his house, his office, his writing, and his painting, among other things.

The breadth of David's passions makes his second skill important—he has the ability to focus. He commits to an endeavor and makes it happen. Most of us have long lists of the things that we want to do. David is developing a long list of what he has done.

David's biggest accomplishments spring from his third skill—the ability to harness and leverage the enthusiasm of others. The creation of the USGBC and the WorldGBC is not a story of a single individual. It is a story of many dedicated people who were inspired to contribute huge amounts of time and effort, as well as to go to their companies and their friends for the capital necessary for these entities to be successfully born.

David's fourth skill is that, as soon as an undertaking begins to come together, at a time when most founders would insist on establishing repeatable protocols, David questions everything, causing rapid changes and adjustments. This culture of rapid beta-testing and adjustment has been central to the success of the USGBC, the WorldGBC, and Regenerative Network.

Besides questioning, this culture requires a commitment to goals, not process, as well as a willingness to put up with the messiness of constant creation, and active listening to complaints, concerns, and feedback.

Finally, one of the most important skills enabling David's serial success is the ability to set his foundlings free and move on to the next passion. Once they are stabilized and their culture established, David steps back, giving other incredible people the chance to shape and grow the entities.

Explosion Green provides the sense of the purposefulness with which David has applied this set of skills to changing the building industry. He helped create the USGBC, an engine for greening the industry. This engine uses a mix of green building standards created by a cross section of stakeholders (LEED); a powerful annual conference (Greenbuild); a process for creating a knowledgeable army of practitioners; and a broad base for education and advocacy. He then created the WorldGBC, an organization to rapidly spread that nonprofit business model throughout the world. Then David focused on helping to create world-class businesses in the green building industry. David's next undertaking will be to address the lives of the people who occupy the green buildings, helping them to build their own green lives full of the same enthusiasm that drives his. May his enthusiasm continue to benefit us all

THE EARTH COMMANDMENTS

1. We shall live in harmony with all life that flies through the air, swims in the waters, walks on the land, and that which remains rooted.

2. We shall protect and preserve the Earth and all living systems for all generations.

3. We shall restore that which has been damaged, especially the air, water, and soil.

4. We shall not multiply beyond the capacity of Earth to sustain itself and all of life.

5. We shall embrace and cherish the Planet Earth, as we were born to it; and together we shall become stewards of its future.

6. What have we forgotten?*

* This 6th Commandment was added by David Brower when I presented him with the first 5 commandments.

© David Gottfried

BOOK SPONSORS

A very special thank you to the following organizations for helping make this book a reality.

Adobe

Adobe Systems Incorporated
http://www.Adobe.com

CALMAC

CALMAC Manufacturing
Corporation
http://www.calmac.com

Lutron Electronics, Inc.
http://www.lutron.com

Office DEPOT.

Office Depot, Inc.
http://www.officedepot.com

SLOAN.

Sloan Valve Company
http://www.sloanvalve.com

U.S. Green Building Council
http://www.usgbc.org

ACKNOWLEDGEMENTS

I want to thank my wife, Sara, for her eleven years of support in helping me reach to higher levels and pursue all that I can be. And for bringing health and relationship to the green life equation.

I'd like to thank my kids, for their love and support for all of my crazy and continual inventions and agreeing to undertake the journey of green.

To my parents, Ira and Judith, who instilled in me a spirit of innovation, curiosity, tenacity, drive, and love for the planet. My father, who ran his own business for three decades, was one of the first in computers and then management consulting. Thank you, Dad, for always being there for me and giving me the tools to live and realize this story. And to my two loving and supportive brothers, Rick and Glenn.

This book would not have been possible without the incredible friendship, leadership, and enduring vision and flame of Rick Fedrizzi. He has been the foundation and glue to the USGBC over the past two decades and much of this story. Equally, Rick has helped inspire and lead the WorldGBC as its current chairman and one of the first supporters of the organization and its potential.

To Mike Italiano for being there as a big brother in the beginning and helping to coach us during the pivotal start-up years and through understanding of *The Art of War*. Your spirit and vision are embedded in the GBC story.

Thanks for over a decade of collaboration with Huston Eubank and his great help with "What's Next" in this book. Your heart is gold and your work holistic and spirited.

A special thanks to Adair Lara for her third book project with me and helping me tell my story yet again. Without her I'd still be working on draft documents. And to Elaine Hooker for her awesome and spirited editing. You were a joy to work with. To Jean Orlebeke for your beautiful cover design and layout of the book. And to my publisher, Morgan James. I greatly enjoyed working with Rick Frishman and David Hancock. Thanks to Crystal Patriarche, my PR agent at BookSparksPR.

There are so many others to thank for their support, encouragement, and contributions to the book and to the GBC story, including:

Thanks to: Jeff Davis, Noah Hagey, Donald Simon, Che Wall, Maria Atkinson, Paul Hawken, Art Gensler, Ken Ullman, MD, Jeb Berkeley, Bill Browning, Dorothy Divack, Jane Henley, Judith Webb, Kevin Hydes, Rob Watson, Nils Kok, Alan Traugott, Greg Kats, Harvey Bernstein, Michelle Yates, Dan Slone, Jim Allen, Anthony Bernheim, Nadav Malin, Ted van der Linden, Yalmaz Siddiqui, Qiu Baoxing, Nellie Cheng, my cousins in D.C., Gil Masters, David Brower, Zorana Bosnic, Sim Van der Ryn, Bill McDonough, Jim Thomas, Randy Scott, John Mandyck, Chuck Angyal, Kath Williams, Bob Berkebile, Bob Fox, Leslie Murphy, Lynn Simon, Kristin Douglas, Bill Reed, Dan Geiger, Dan Smith, Anne Van Dyke, Fanny Wilson, Larry Smith, Martin Wood, global GBC Staff, Regen Network members.

ABOUT THE AUTHOR

David Gottfried is the father of the global green building movement, having founded both the World Green Building Council and the U.S. Green Building Council, which have likely done more for carbon mitigation than any other organizations. He has two annual awards in his name, and has published the memoirs *Greed to Green* (2004) and *Greening My Life* (2010). Gottfried has appeared as a guest on KQED's *Forum* with Michael Krasny, Discovery Channel's *HowStuffWorks* and Planet Green's *Renovation Nation*, ABC News, *GreenSource*, Grist, PRI's *Living on Earth*, *The Jerusalem Post*, Australia's *Financial Times*, and dozens of other publications.

Visit David Gottfried's personal website and receive a free digital copy of *Greening My Life* at www.dgottfried.com.

Regenerative Ventures: www.regenv.com

Regenerative Network (Green product consortium): www.regen-net.com

Green Building Online Video Series: www.regenbuild.com

Regen360 (Green Life Academy): www.regen360.net

CPSIA information can be obtained at www.ICGtesting.com
Printed in the USA
LVOW07s1057020714

392699LV00003B/88/P